The Multilateralism of the New Development Bank on the Sustainable Economic Growth in BRICS Nations and Beyond

The Multilateralism of the New Development Bank on the Sustainable Economic Growth in BRICS Nations and Beyond

EDITED BY

NDIVHUHO TSHIKOVHI
Durban University of Technology, South Africa

FULUFHELO NETSWERA
Durban University of Technology, South Africa

JIEJIN ZHU
Fudan University, China

BRUNO DE CONTI
University of Campinas, Brazil

RAJEEV SIJARIYA
Jawaharlal Nehru University, India

AND

MARIA APANOVICH
MGIMO University, Russia

emerald PUBLISHING

United Kingdom – North America – Japan – India – Malaysia – China

Emerald Publishing Limited
Emerald Publishing, Floor 5, Northspring, 21-23 Wellington Street, Leeds LS1 4DL

First edition 2025

British Library Cataloguing in Publication Data
A catalogue record for this book is available from the British Library

ISBN: 978-1-83662-293-2 (Print)
ISBN: 978-1-83662-292-5 (Online)
ISBN: 978-1-83662-294-9 (Epub)

Contents

List of Figures and Tables

Figures

Tables

About the Editors

Ndivhuho Tshikovhi is a Postdoctoral Fellow at the Durban University of Technology (DUT) Faculty of Management Sciences. He holds a doctorate in social and political sciences from the Université Libre de Bruxelles, Belgium. He also studied abroad at various renowned universities, including Fudan University, China, and the University of Mannheim, Germany. He obtained his master's degree in entrepreneurship from the Tshwane University of Technology, South Africa. At the University of Mannheim, he was part of the Mannheim Center for Entrepreneurship and Innovation team and also a guest doctoral student at the Institute for SMEs Research and Entrepreneurship. Parallel to his studies, he worked as a research assistant and an art business incubation coordinator, taught entrepreneurship skills and business management, and was a project leader for Students in Free Enterprise (now ENACTUS TUT). He was also elected to lead the Capital City Junior Business Chamber between 2012 and 2014. In addition to numerous conference presentations, he has published several papers on entrepreneurship, public policy, and corporate social responsibility in emerging economies and specializes in BRICS nations. He has received countable research grants from National Research Foundation (NRF), South Africa to Erasmus Mundus by the European Union, also the German Academic Exchange Service (DAAD), Germany and the National Fund for Scientific Research (NFRS) in Belgium and National Institute for the Humanities and Social Sciences (NIHSS), South Africa, and recently the British Council, UK, individually and some jointly with other researchers.

Fulufhelo Netswera, an Executive Dean Faculty of Management Sciences at Durban University of Technology (DUT), tasked to develop the DUT Business School. Prof Fulu has worked as a Director at North West University Business School, a Deputy Dean Faculty of Management Sciences at Cape Peninsula University of Technology (CPUT), a Director at South African BRICS Think Tank (SABTT), a Director at Turfloop Graduate School of Leadership (TGSL) of the University of Limpopo, a Research Management Director at University of South Africa (UNISA), a Manager Research Grants at National Research Foundation (NRF), a Senior Researcher at Council for Scientific and Industrial Research (CSIR), a Chief Researcher at Human Sciences Research Council (HSRC), a Researcher at Institute for Democracy in Southern Africa (IDASA), an Institutional Researcher at Technikon Southern Africa (TSA), and an Assistant Lecturer at University of the Western Cape (UWC). Prof Fulu was a board member at PIKITUP (City of Johannesburg), a board member at HSRC, a Vice Chairperson at South African Business School Association (SABSA), an Executive Member of Southern Africa Research and Innovation Management Association (SARIMA). Adjudicator for Women in Sciences Awards (WISA) at Department of Science and Technology (DST); adjudicator at National Science and Technology Forum (NSTF) Research Awards. Was an Emerging Philanthropy Fellow at City University (New York), an Erasmus Visiting Fellow at Groningen University (Netherlands), an Adjunct Professor at TUT, an Adjunct Professor at UTAMU (Uganda), and a current Visiting Professor Lincoln International Business School (UK). Holds a DPhil (Stellenbosch), BA Hons in Economics (UWC), PGD (Buckinghamshire Chilterns University College), among others.

Jiejin Zhu is a Professor at the School of International Relations and Public Affairs and the Deputy Director of the Center for UN and International Organizations Studies at Fudan University. His research interests are international organizations, global governance, international political economy, BRICS, and G20, etc. He has published 4 books and over 50 papers in academic journals, including the *Pacific Review*, *Global Policy*, *International Organization Research Journal*, *World Economics and Politics* (in Chinese), *Foreign Affairs Review* (in Chinese), among others. He has done the research project China's Proposal for G20's Institutional Transition which is sponsored by China National Social Science Foundation, China's Path Selection in Global Governance Reform which is sponsored by Shanghai Social Science Foundation, and Institution-Building of the BRICS New Development Bank which is funded by China International Development Research Network. Currently, he is doing the research on China's Rise and International Institutional Change.

Bruno De Conti is an Associated Professor at the Institute of Economics, University of Campinas (Brazil). He holds a PhD in Economics from the University Sorbonne Paris-Nord (France) and the University of Campinas. He is a Nonresident Senior Fellow at the Center for Africa-China Studies (CACS) at the University of Johannesburg (South Africa). He was a Visiting Professor at the University Sorbonne Paris-Nord, Universidad Autónoma de Madrid (Spain), Moscow State Institute of International Relations (MGIMO, Russia), Free University of Berlin (Germany), Universidad Nacional de Colombia and Southwestern University of Finance and Economics (China). At the University of Campinas, he is the Coordinator of the BRICS Network University – Economics – and the Director of the Confucius Institute. His main research is on the International Monetary System, Chinese Economy, and BRICS.

Rajeev Sijariya is currently an Associated with Jawaharlal Nehru University (JNU) as the Chairperson of the Special Centre for E-Learning (SCEL) and as a Professor at Atal Bihari Vajpayee School of Management and Entrepreneurship (ABVSME). He is also the International Students Advisor for the University. He has vast teaching and corporate experience of over 24+ years. He has done MSc (Physics-electronics), MBA, and PhD in Management. Hon'ble President of India in his capacity as the visitor of Banaras Hindu University nominated him to the court of prestigious BHU. He has received various awards and project grants. He has guided many PhD students and has published many research papers. He is an author, Researcher, Academician, thinker, Motivator, orator, Corporate Trainer, a Social Activist.

Maria Apanovich is graduated from MGIMO University (School of Political Sciences) in 2007. In 2009 graduated from the Double-diploma Master program "International Relations" MGIMO, Moscow – Free University Berlin, Humbolt University, and University of Potsdam. Thesis topic "Migration as a Challenge For The European Security in the 21st Century." In 2013, she defended a Candidate of Science dissertation in Political Sciences, topic "Political Aspects of Migration Process" (adaptation of the migrants, case of Germany and Switzerland). Maria Apanovich has been teaching at MGIMO since 2013; she is a Lecturer at the Department of Demography and Migration Policy since 2017. Her research interests include Migration and Integration of the Migrants, High-qualified Migration, and Education.

About the Contributors

Xuwen Cao holds a PhD in Economics from Universiti Malaya and is an Associate Professor of Economics at Changzhou Vocational Institute of Textile and Garment. Her research interests include international economics and trade, industrial upgrading, and energy economics. She explores the intricacies of global trade systems, the mechanisms driving industrial advancements, and the economic impacts of energy policies, aiming to provide insights for both academic and practical policymaking purposes.

Daniel Campos de Carvalho is an Assistant Professor at the Law Department at Federal University of São Paulo (UNIFESP), Brazil. A Graduate Professor of International Relations at Federal University of ABC (UFABC), Brazil. A Graduate Professor of Law at São Paulo State University (UNESP). PhD in International Law (University of São Paulo – USP).

Ana Elisa Saggioro Garcia an Assistant Professor at the Institute of International Relations at PUC-Rio. A General Coordinator of the BRICS Policy Center. A Professor of the Graduate Program in Social Sciences at the Federal Rural University of Rio de Janeiro. PhD in International Relations from IRI/PUC-Rio and Master in Political Science from the Free University of Berlin (Germany).

Murilo Gaspardo is the Deputy Dean (2022–2026), and he has been the Dean of the School of Human and Social Sciences of São Paulo State University (UNESP) (2018–2022), Campus of Franca – São Paulo – Brazil, where he is an Associate Professor of State Theory and Political Science at the Department of Public Law. He is also an honorary fellow of the Global Policy Institute (GPI)/SGIA/University of Durham/UK. He was educated at the University of São Paulo (USP) Law School (under-graduate, master's, and PhD).

Leonid Grigoryev, a Tenured Professor, an Academic Supervisor of Department of World Economy, Higher School of Economics, Moscow; a Member of the National Research Council on BRICS. Former Deputy Minister of Economy and Finance, Chairman of Foreign Investment Committee in 1991–1992; Leading Fellow of IMEMO RAN; Director General, Bureau of Economic Analysis; Advisor to Executive Director of RF, the World Bank, Washington; Deputy Director General – Russian Energy Agency; Chief Adviser of the Head of Analytical Center under the Government of RF; President of Association of Independent Centers of Economic Analysis, RF; Member of ECOSOC, United Nations 1999–2007.

Robert Hanson is an associated researcher at the Center for Ethics, Politics, and Society at the University of Minho. He got his PhD in Philosophy from Durham University, UK, on intercultural ethics and politics before working as a lecturer at Durham (UK), Tübingen (Germany), and Groningen (Netherlands). During this time, he has published on a diverse range of topics ranging from the politics of respecting cultural practices on the dead and, most recently, the ethics of pragmatic approaches to climate justice.

Xiaochen Hou received her PhD in International Politics from School of International Relations and Public Policy, Fudan University. She was a visiting scholar at Georgetown University during 2020–2021. She is a Policy Analyst and a Program Manager of the BRICS Summer Program in the Center for BRICS Studies at Fudan University. Her research interests focus on international development, development finance, BRICS cooperation, and global governance. She has published some papers on development banks and industrialization, BRICS cooperation, and global economic governance.

Eka Khorbaladze is a Policy Analyst specialising in transregional cooperation. Currently, she serves as a Research Coordinator at the Centre on Contemporary China and the World in Hong Kong while pursuing her PhD in Political Science at Lomonosov Moscow State University. Her research focuses on regional integration processes and the dynamics of US–China–Russia relations. Eka's academic portfolio includes contributions to over seven articles and two monographs. To date, she presented at more than 40 international conferences, engaging in collaborative work with think tanks in China and Russia. From 2021 to 2023, Eka conducted research at Yale University. She is a member of four US-based political science associations, a board member of two journals and the founder of the initiative "Expert Views on Global Politics." Eka holds two Master's degrees: the most recent one from Tsinghua University as a Schwarzman Scholar in Global Affairs and the second from the State University of Management in Russia. She completed her undergraduate studies in International Relations.

Ruhi Lal is a highly skilled advertising professional, an Academician, a Researcher, and an author presently working as a Professor at Manav Rachna International Institute of Research and Studies. She is D.Litt. from VBU and holds a PhD in Mass Communication. She is a recipient of Best Media Educator of the year 2021 by MFI, India. Received 5th Gyan Shree National award from Savitri Foundations. She received "Vishist Sewa Samman" from BJP Delhi in Dec 2021. She has 22 years of work experience blend of 8 years of Industry and 17 years of Teaching and Research experience at Amity University. Dr Lal has 148 research contributions including 13 books, 4 patents, 52 research papers published, 148 publications (13 – Scopus, 2 – Web of Science, 35 – UGC Care Listed Journals, 8 peer reviewed journals, 30 case studies, 39 research papers presentation in conferences, 15 book chapters. Six funded Research Projects – three MHRD projects, two MGNCRE, one Radio Amity with DAVP & SMART NGO, one Amity MOOC Project, one corporate project).

Jonnas Esmeraldo Marques de Vasconcelos an Adjunct Professor at the Law School of the Federal University of Bahia (FD-UFBA). A Professor of the Postgraduate Program in International Relations at the Federal University of Bahia (PPGRI-UFBA). A Professor of the Postgraduate Program in Law, Governance, and Policies at the University of Salvador (MDGPP-UNIFACS). PhD in Economic Law and Master's in Human Rights both from the Law School of the University of São Paulo (FD-USP).

Alexandra Morozkina is the Deputy Dean for Research at the Higher School of Economics, a Senior Research Fellow, Financial Research Institute of the Ministry of Finance of the Russian Federation, and the Head of Structural Reforms Division at the Economic Expert Group. Alexandra has been working in the field of international organizations for several years, was a member of BRICS and G20 Expert Councils for Russian Presidency, a current member of the Expert Council at *Rossotrudnichestvo*. Dr Morozkina has a number of publications on development finance, international organizations, and sustainable development. Also Dr Morozkina teaches several disciplines at Higher School of Economics, including author's course "Problems of Economic Development in BRICS Countries."

Zakia Tasmin Rahman is the Head Coordinator (Radio Amity 107.8 MHz) and an Assistant Professor with Amity school Communication, Amity University, Noida. She has a PhD in Mass Communication. She has 22 years of work experience, 5 years of industry experience, and 17 years of Teaching and Research experience. Dr Zakia has 60 Research contributions – 6 books, 32 research papers, case studies developed, 29 research paper presentations, 10 chapters in books published. Guided undergraduate, post graduate, and PhD scholars for research report writing, dissertation, research papers, minor projects, and major projects. Conducted conferences, seminars, workshops, webinars, and guests lectures on mass communication and mass communication–related subjects. She worked on funded projects of SWAYAM, DAVP, and SMART and 50 projects of Radio Amity 107.8 MHz's on Community Outreach.

Rajah Rasiah is a Distinguished Professor of Economics at the Asia Europe Institute, Universiti Malaya. He obtained his doctorate in Economics from Cambridge University in 1992 and was a Rajawali Fellow at Harvard University in 2014. Among his prestigious awards include the Robert McNamara Award by the World Bank in 1993, the Celso Furtado Prize for advancing the frontiers of Social Science thought (Economics) from the World Academy of Sciences in 2015, and the Merdeka Award Outstanding Scholastic Achievement in 2018. He was awarded the Distinguished Professor of Economics Award by the Ministry of Higher Education of Malaysia in 2017.

Ravinder Rena is a profound academician and a distinguished scholar in economics, a writer, an editor, and an adviser with over 32 years of teaching and research experience. Prof Rena is currently working as a Professor of Economics, DUT Business School, Faculty of Management Sciences, Durban University of Technology, South Africa. He serves as a Visiting Professor at the Department of Innovation Management Industries, Academy of Engineering, RUDN University,

Moscow, Russia. He bagged numerous prizes and awards throughout his career. He published over 10 books, 150 articles in refereed journals, and 50 chapters in edited Books. He is the founding Editor-in Chief of an *International Journal of Education Economics and Development*. He currently serves as an Associate Editor, the Bottom Line, published by Emerald. He served as an Editor and an Editorial Board Member for more than 35 reputed journals across the globe. He serves as an Executive Member of the BRICS academic research forum. His areas of research: Economics of Education, International finance, Microfinance and Entrepreneurship, BRICS and African economy.

Rafaela Mello Rodrigues de Sá an Assistant Professor at the Institute for International Relations and Defense at Federal University of Rio de Janeiro. She has a Master's in International Relations from IRI – Institute of International Relations at PUC-Rio. Graduated in International Relations at the Catholic University of Petrópolis (UCP). She is a Project Assistant at the BRICS Research Institute, Durban University of Technology.

Irina Yarygina is the Head of the Working Group Financial and Investment Cooperation, BRICS Expert Council – Russia. Head of the Economics and Banking Business Department at the International Institute of Energy Policy and Diplomacy, Moscow State Institute of International Relations under the Ministry for Foreign Affairs of the Russian Federation (MGIMO-University). Head of Programs, Professor, Financial University under the Government of the Russian Federation.

Foreword

Irina Yarygina

With recent transformations in the International Order signaling trends toward changes in the various dimensions of power, it is important to reflect on the initiatives of the BRICS grouping, with their challenges and potential.

In this context, the functioning of the New Development Bank (NDB), often referred to as the BRICS Bank, needs to be analyzed as one of the central elements of the new trends in multilateralism.

Edited by Ndivhuho Tshikovhi, Fulufhelo Netswera, Jiejin Zhu, Bruno De Conti, Rajeev Sijariya, and Maria Apanovich, the book "The Multilateralism of the New Development Bank on the Sustainable Economic Growth in BRICS Nations and Beyond" presents discussions dedicated to unraveling the complex elements of the NDB.

Introducing a new era in global finance and cooperation, the emergence of this institution signifies a pivotal shift in the dynamics of international development. An insightful exploration about this debate is presented within the pages of this book.

In the following chapters, the authors navigate the intricate landscape of the NDB, weaving together a comprehensive narrative that dives deeper into its origins, mission, and impact on the world stage. The BRICS nations – Brazil, Russia, India, China, and South Africa have come together to establish a financial institution that seeks to improve sustainable infrastructure and increase economic development in BRICS nations and beyond.

What makes this book particularly compelling is the ability to discuss about the complex financial and geopolitical concepts into accessible insights through the history and functioning of the NDB. The readers will gain a profound understanding of its role in fostering sustainable development, infrastructure projects, and innovation across diverse regions.

The publication also makes it possible to understand different perspectives from the five countries that founded the NDB. The chapters bring together varied debates by Brazilian, Russian, Indian, Chinese, and South African professors and researchers.

In this sense, readers will be able to examine the work of the main institution within the BRICS grouping, based on an in-depth analysis of the challenges and opportunities that the NDB presents. Through meticulous research and thoughtful commentary, the author explores how the BRICS Bank has become a catalyst for collaborative initiatives that transcend borders and conventional norms.

Congratulations to editors and authors that contributed to this book for capturing the essence of this groundbreaking institution in these pages. May this book contribute to a broader dialogue on global finance, development, and the collaborative spirit that defines the NDB.

Acknowledgments

This work is based on the research project supported by the NIHSS, South Africa.

NATIONAL INSTITUTE
FOR THE HUMANITIES
AND SOCIAL SCIENCES

Part I

Introduction to Multilateralism and NDB

Chapter 1

Introduction To: The Multilateralism of the New Development Bank on the Sustainable Economic Growth in BRICS Nations and Beyond

Ndivhuho Tshikovhi[a], *Fulufhelo Netswera*[a], *Jiejin Zhu*[b], *Bruno De Conti*[c], *Rajeev Sijariya*[d] *and Maria Apanovich*[e]

[a]Durban University of Technology, South Africa
[b]Fudan University, China
[c]University of Campinas, Brazil
[d]Jawaharlal Nehru University, India
[e]MGIMO University, Russia

The BRICS New Development Bank (NDB), alternative to the World Bank (WB) provides alternative development financial resources thereby filling a massive gap in investment infrastructure and sustainable development in the BRICS and developing countries. NDB's focus is resources development in the emerging and developing economies. Its expenditure is estimated to reach at least US$ 1 trillion annually. It will also give emerging and developing countries a greater voice in the development finance architecture. Emerging and developing countries have significantly increased their weight in terms of global GDP and global economic growth. Perhaps most importantly, some emerging and developing economies have accumulated very large, long-term foreign exchange assets, which they have typically placed in sovereign wealth funds. Many of these resources are invested in developed countries with relatively low yields. The NDB provides a valuable addition to the existing network of multilateral, regional, and national development financiers, which seem to perform far better. NDB's support for productive development infrastructure investment works closely with national development banks, which have far greater local knowledge. The BRICS Multilateral Cooperation and Co-Financing Agreement for Sustainable Development spotlights the low-carbon economy and will include elements such as projects for mitigating and

The Multilateralism of the New Development Bank on the Sustainable Economic Growth in BRICS Nations and Beyond, 3–7

Published under exclusive licence by Emerald Publishing Limited
doi:10.1108/978-1-83662-292-520251003

adapting climate change, infrastructure projects in keeping with the principles of sustainable development. Investments are mainly in renewable energy and energy efficiency or that foster the sustainable use of biodiversity, ecosystems, and the regeneration of natural resources, in addition to efforts aimed at developing, disseminating, and transferring environmentally sustainable technology.

In Chapter 2 "Challenges and feasibility of a democratic global financial governance" by Murilo Gaspardo and Daniel Campos de Carvalho, the challenges and the feasibility of a democratic global financial governance (GFG) are discussed. The authors argue that a democratic GFG will only be feasible if its institutional framework has as reference a concept of democracy which is compatible with the complexity of this field, and a flexible design suitable for facing its multilevel democratic deficit. The BRICS, on the one hand, are key actors for GFG reforms. However, on the other hand, the world faces a very unfavorable political scenario due to thematization of the GFG democratization by the BRICS. The authors seek to fulfill the gap in literature and provide a framework for future specific empirical-normative research.

In Chapter 3 "Finance, Governance, and Sovereignty after COVID-19: A Normative Argument for the Need to Democratize Global Finance," Robert Hanson explores how the COVID-19 pandemic has given us renewed cause to reflect on the nature of national sovereignty and what it means to value it in an era of global crises and certain crediting International Organizations (IOs). The author does so by focusing on the role disproportionate voting power in crediting IOs played during the pandemic in projecting certain Nation States' (NSs') short-term financial interests at the expense of tackling the virus' threat to every NSs' national sovereignty. The pandemic has demonstrated that a commitment to valuing national sovereignty in an era of global crises entails a commitment to democratizing global finance by pooling sovereignty and capital into more democratic crediting IOs.

Chapter 4 "BRICS – A Comprehensive Mechanism Bringing Changes into the World Financial System and International Climate Diplomacy" by Eka Khorbaladze explores BRICS being a "comprehensive coordination mechanism" dealing with a multilateral agenda of cooperation. The short list of shakes, on the one hand, adjusted BRICS's strategy to global crisis, but, on the other hand, BRICS has been facing a variety of modern-day challenges which are far beyond this scope. The paper intends to examine the most important issues for BRICS development and pay special attention to such prominent spheres as finance and climate change. As a result, a coherent picture of BRICS agenda of cooperation, as well as a prospective path of fostering, is presented. The author concludes that the BRICS countries have made outstanding achievements in the field of financial and economic cooperation. Among them are: deepening their economic cooperation, the advancement of the BRICS countries in the reform of international financial institutions which resulted in an increase in the representation of emerging market and developing countries.

Chapter 5 authored by Ndivhuho Tshikovhi, Fulufhelo Netswera and Bruno De Conti "De-dollarization, the New Development Bank, and BRICS Trade Currency changing Multilateralism and Geopolitical Arrangements" delves into the questions and excitement raised about the beginning and end of USD dominance and examines the role of the BRICS banks in the rising power of de-dollarization. The authors suggest that over the long term, the diversifying implications to the BRICS bloc and other nations such as the "so-called BRICS plus/friends" depend on the influence and buy-in from the raw material resources countries. For instance, the Gulf countries, which play a crucial role in supporting the USD (e.g., via oil prices and large USD reserves to maintain the peg), are increasingly looking toward China due to the structural changes in the oil market, which plays into the geopolitics of the multilateralism. As a result, slowing globalization, driven by events like the COVID-19 pandemic and the war in Ukraine, has prompted – among other things – some countries to use non-USD currencies for bilateral trade, which plays a role in the decrease of the share of USD in total reserves globally.

In Chapter 6 "NDB and SDGs: Does the bank fulfill its mandate?" by Leonid Grigoryev and Alexandra Morozkina, the authors discuss the changes to global sustainable development agenda and contribution of NDB to sustainable development goals (SDGs) in member countries, potential instruments and priority sectors in the longer-term and implications for the global financial architecture given the changing global economic environment. They looked at the alignment of NDB projects with the SDGs and concluded that NDB primarily contributes to the SDG 6, SDG 7, SDG 8, and SDG 9 with the lead of SDG 9 (41 projects). This is consistent with the Bank's mandate highlighting infrastructure as a primary sector of investment.

In Chapter 7 "The New Development Bank's Role in the Low Carbon Transition: An Analysis of Institutional Strategies and Projects Financed" by Rafaela Mello Rodrigues de Sá, the role of the NDB in financing the low carbon transition is examined. Considering a new guideline for 2022–2026 where there is a target of directing 40% of total approvals to projects that contribute to climate change mitigation and adaptation, including energy transition, it becomes important to reflect on in which way the BRICS bank has been acting in the sphere of sustainable finance in its first years of operation. Thus, the chapter aims to assess how the NDB contributes to the energy transition process in the BRICS countries toward a low carbon economy, based on the projects financed by the bank and through analysis of institutional strategies (for 2017–2021 and 2022–2026). It is evident that the NDB contributes to the BRICS transition process to a low-carbon economy, but with differences between countries. On the one hand, the NDB favors more the transition in the energy sector in China, South Africa, and Brazil; on the other hand, the institution collaborates more with the decarbonization process in India, China, and Russia. Despite this, there are still limitations and challenges that hinder the NDB from becoming one of the main sources of incentives for its member countries to reach the climate targets.

Jonnas Esmeraldo Marques de Vasconcelos and Ana Elisa Saggioro Garcia in Chapter 8 "Notes on the performance of the New Development Bank" analyze the performance of the Bank. The NDB was intended to be a bank from and for the South, a green bank, and a noninterventionist bank, leading to high expectations for its performance. However, after it started its operation, the analysis shows that NDB has faced limitations on the operational level. The chapter consists of three parts: discussing the creation of and expectations for the NDB, analyzing its funding policies and performance, and presenting challenges for its future. The financial institution created by BRICS was evaluated by considering NDB's Articles of Agreement, NDB's General Strategy (2017–2021), NDB's Annual Reports, and a comparison with the Asian Infrastructure Investment Bank's performance.

Chapter 9 "The role of BRICS Business Council and the New Development Bank in Environmental, Social, and Governance (ESG) agenda" by Rafaela Mello Rodrigues de Sá focuses on which ways the BRICS Business Council (BBC) and NDB expand and strengthen the ESG agenda within the BRICS grouping, particularly with regard to the activities of BRICS companies and the governance of the group's main financial institution. The authors do this by detailed mapping of the aspects involving the ESG agenda in both BRICS initiatives, in order to identify – in the institutional documents and reports – the role of these two mechanisms in ESG aspects.

Chapter 10 "Development Effectiveness: The Role of Multilateral Development Banks and Their Evaluation – Reference and Insights for New Development Bank" by Xiaochen Hou looks at the role of Multilateral Development Banks (MDBs) from the perspective of development effectiveness, compares and contrasts the evaluation mechanisms of MDBs, and points out that MDBs should closely integrate their development objectives with their policy frameworks to develop corresponding evaluation indicators. Through evaluation, MDBs can control the project process and gradually achieve development goals, thus playing a more significant role in international development, which is indeed an outlook deserving of more scholarly attention.

Chapter 11 "Export Sophistication and Industrial Upgrading: A Study of Energy Vehicles in BRICS" by Xuwen Cao and Rajah Rasiah offers the insight into the energy vehicles export industry in BRICS from 2015 to 2021, measuring the export sophistication of energy vehicles in BRICS with panel data. Considering that industrial upgrading is a long-term dynamic economic process, analyzing the export sophistication of energy vehicles with a dynamic panel model of industrial upgrading is necessary. The results show that the export sophistication of energy vehicles has a significant positive correlation with industrial upgrading in BRICS from an economic perspective. Export sophistication is critical in upgrading export trade technology structure as an internal influencing factor. In contrast, external factors such as R&D, FDI investment, and GDP growth are less influential. As a result, BRICS industrial upgrading could benefit from the exportation of energy vehicles.

Last but not least, Dr Zakia Tasmin Rahman, Dr Ruhi Lal, and Prof Ravinder Rena in Chapter 12 "New Development Bank in India: Growth, Development and Futuristic Prospects" describe the role of NDB in India, the growth and development of NDB, and to explore the future prospects of NDB in India.

The plans and strategies of NDB are studied thoroughly: the member nations and emerging nations of the world can get the advantage of infrastructural development, sustainable growth and development. NDB accelerates development in a flexible and effective way: various infrastructural developmental projects were undertaken. Initiatives like financial support for adopting various developmental technologies and strategies should be from medium- to long-term priority.

Chapter 2

Challenges and Feasibility of a Democratic Global Financial Governance[1]

Murilo Gaspardo[a] *and Daniel Campos de Carvalho*[b]

[a]São Paulo State University (UNESP), Brazil
[b]Federal University of São Paulo (UNIFESP), Brazil

Abstract

Considering a normative conception of democracy based on the values of autonomy and inclusiveness, there are many reasons to argue that a democratic global financial governance (GFG) is necessary. However, from an empirical approach, the democratization of GFG seems to be very hard to implement. Taking that into consideration, we discuss the challenges and the feasibility of a democratic GFG. We argue that both the skeptics' negative response and the positive one based on abstract premises are unsuited. A democratic GFG will only be feasible if its institutional framework has as reference a concept of democracy which is compatible with the complexity of this field, and a flexible design suitable for facing its multilevel democratic deficit. The BRICS, on the one hand, are key actors for GFG reforms. However, on the other hand, we face a very unfavorable political scenario to the thematization of the GFG democratization by the BRICS. The literature on this topic is vast, but there is a lack of comprehensive studies. We seek to fulfill this gap and, in addition to our own theoretical contribution, provide a framework for future specific empirical-normative research.

Keywords: Global financial governance; democracy; normative political theory; BRICS; New Development Bank (NDB)

[1]This chapter is based on a research developed with grants from São Paulo Research Foundation (FAPESP) – Process 2016/24875 – 4.

The Multilateralism of the New Development Bank on the Sustainable Economic Growth in BRICS Nations and Beyond, 9–28

Published under exclusive licence by Emerald Publishing Limited
doi:10.1108/978-1-83662-292-520251004

Introduction

Is a democratic global financial governance (GFG) feasible? Considering a normative conception of democracy based on the values of autonomy and inclusiveness, there are many reasons to argue that a democratic GFG is necessary, for instance: the finance is at the center of the economic relations of contemporary Capitalism; financial globalization favors the growth of income, wealth and power inequality; the GFG presents low representativeness, accountability and responsiveness, as well as a great power imbalance. However, from an empirical approach, the democratization of the GFG seems to be so hard because of its own complexity and the highly specialized knowledge that it requires, the political and economic power relations, and ideological restrictions on multilateralism and democracy at the global level.

The BRICS, on the one hand, are key actors for GFG reforms. However, on the other hand, the crisis of Brazilian democracy (Nobre, 2020) and the disastrous foreign policy of President Bolsonaro (Gonçalves & Teixeira, 2020), as well as the authoritarian regimes of China and Russia and the context of the War in Ukraine and the pandemic generate a very unfavorable political scenario to the thematization of the GFG democratization by the BRICS.

Given this starting point, we must first understand how and why GFG is not democratic. Second, it is necessary to carry out a critical mapping of the answers that have already been given, that is, the existing alternatives at the theoretical, political and social fields. Confronting the problem with the available alternatives, we will be able to address our research question. We argue that both the skeptics' negative response and the positive one based on abstract premises are unsuited. A democratic GFG is feasible just if its institutional framework has as a reference a concept of democracy compatible with the complexity of this field and a flexible and networked design suitable for facing its multilevel democratic deficit. The literature on this topic and the reformist projects are vast, but there is a lack of comprehensive studies that connect the approaches of international political economy and normative democratic theory. We seek to fulfill this gap and, in addition to our own theoretical contribution, provide a framework for future specific empirical-normative research on the topic.

To do so, we employ as methodology the "clinical institutional theory" (CIT) (Wiens, 2012). Unlike the most usual normative theory that opposes the ideal normative theories formulated by the Political Philosophy and the existing political institutions and conditions, the CIT departures from the identification of institutional shortcomings (description) and its causal processes (diagnosis). The prescriptions are established based on the injustices and discontentment identified in the previous observation process, and there are considered architectural and engineering problems. Those ones refer to institutional arrangements' designs in accordance with certain values and political purposes, while these ones deal with the technical issues that such designs involve (the application of scientific principles to determine which conditions institutions must fulfill to endure the different pressures and restrictions under which they perform). The combination of these approaches allows to reject both projects that are inconsistent with the underlying values and those that prove to be dysfunctional (or not very plausible), as well as anticipating weaknesses and making repairs. The prescriptions are temporary, contingent, and experimental, adapting to the *political pressures* observed in the institutions' performance.

The main research technique employed was a systematic bibliographic review, through analysis of reference works, cross-citations, all issues of specialized journals selected within the established time frame (January 2008 [considering the "Global Financial Crisis"] to January 2018 [10 years after that]) and journal indexers. On a complementary basis, we collected documents on websites produced by two types of sources: (1) G20, international, and transnational organizations; (2) nongovernmental organizations and social movements that act in the spheres of global democracy and finance. In the first case, they are norms, legal projects, reports and declarations; in the second, they refer to different forms of written manifestations with normative character.

In addition to this introduction and the final comments, this chapter is divided into three parts: (1) global financial governance and its democratic deficit, (2) alternatives at the theoretical level, (3) alternatives in the political and social spheres.

Global Financial Governance and Its Democratic Deficit

Globalization is a complex and contradictory phenomenon. It refers to the growing interaction and interdependence between the peoples, with economic, cultural, environmental, and social nature, whose remote origins are in the first *Homo sapiens*' migrations but which took on a qualitative and quantitative particular form since the economic, political, and technological transformations of the 1970s. The development of many countries, the reduction of poverty, and the expansion of liberal democracy observed in recent decades can be largely credited to globalization (Bhagwati, 2007). On the other hand, it is a hierarchical, asymmetrical and unequal phenomenon, that is also used as a rhetorical tool to try to legitimize relations of economic, political and ideological domination (Falk, 1999). With the advance of the nationalism in recent years and because of the pandemic of the new *Coronavirus*, there are speculations about the "end of globalization." However, the choices of national states to try to address these challenges individually does not change the condition of interdependence – the pandemic itself, climate change, and finance are examples of this.

Global governance is the response constructed by states and nonstate actors to endeavor to regulate globalization and the distribution of its costs and benefits, to offer global replies to problems arising from interdependence, by a polycentric way and with diversified institutional frameworks. Unlike the idea of government (hierarchical, centralized, with the ability to legitimately enforce its decisions using the violence), governance is based on cooperation and coordination of actions between different levels and institutions, which does not eliminate conflicts and power relations (Hale & Held, 2011; Rousenau, 2002). This reading of international relations, of a liberal matrix, has as its rival interpretation the theory of imperialism, built from Marxism. According to this approach, the structures and processes of global governance would not exist to address common issues arising from interdependence but would be instruments of a "non-territorial" form of imperialism founded on geopolitical competition (Callinicos, 2009). In this sense, global governance institutions express the unequal power relations existing in international politics (Buelvas & Mendioroz, 2014). On the other hand, despite the limits and weaknesses inherent to their nature at the international level, institutions are also capable of constraining and conditioning political action, limiting the power of the most powerful states and economic actors.

Financial globalization is one of the main aspects of contemporary globalization because of its intensity and influence on the economy as a whole, as well as on power relations. The financialization of the economy presents three fundamental features: (1) the finance acquired dominance and autonomy in relation to production and trade, (2) the value of financial assets became higher than other forms of property, and (3) the inequality of income and wealth resumes its historical growth trend (Stiglitz, 2015; Strange, 1994). The financial globalization, in turn, is explained by six factors: (1) structural changes in Capitalism; (2) political decisions to open global capital flows to reply to the pressures resulting from these transformations; (3) increasing transnational operations of financial conglomerates, banking, and nonbanking, with a very relevant role of institutional investors (such as pension funds); (4) technological development that allows real-time operations; (5) innovations in financial transaction instruments, such as the different types of derivatives; and (6) the ideological hegemony of neoliberalism (Gaspardo, 2021).

Monetary-financial governance refers to the set of rules, institutions, agreements, and political relations that regulate and shape both the international financial and monetary systems. It is one of the fundamental expressions of states' sovereignty that, through different bodies (ministries of finance, central banks, legislative branch, etc.), issue currency and regulate its value (exchange rate policy and interest rates); establish the legal framework, authorize the creation, and supervise public and private financial institutions, as well as the markets in which they operate; enforce the financial system rules; establish taxation on financial operations. Therefore, states are the primary and most important actors in GFG but not the only relevant ones. Even the most powerful do not perform satisfactorily acting alone (Davies & Green, 2008). GFG is exercised by a network comprising international multilateral organizations (global and regional – as the BRICS New Development Bank – NDB), transnational institutions, and also national and private ones, and this network was not designed in a planned way but built gradually to respond to certain issues (Young, 2017). International multilateral organizations operate through cooperation between governments, which negotiate and adjust their policies. As cooperation is difficult, it is up to multilateral institutions to try to create the conditions to facilitate it (Hale et al., 2013). The International Monetary Fund (IMF) and the World Bank are the main multilateral organizations in GFG. Another set of institutions are the so-called transnationals, which differ from international ones due to their more informal and flexible governance structure, focusing on very specialized fields, in addition to being governed by subnational authorities or nonstate actors. Some examples are the Bank for International Settlements and the Basel Committee on Banking Supervision.

It is a field whose governance combines complex and highly specialized issues with fundamental political choices because: (1) it influences the general performance of the economy and, consequently, the rates of employment and income; (2) with the growing states' indebtedness, the debt servicing, public policies, and public investments have become increasingly dependent on the raising of funds through the issuance of government bonds; (3) both the financial system's ordinary operation and the responses to its crises have distributional implications. This complex, multiform, and multilevel character of GFG makes the *engineering questions* for its democratization very hard.

Thus, it is not surprising that the concept of "democratic deficit" is related to GFG. Although it has gained space in many fields and dimensions of various natures, democratic deficit is a concept that has been used to analyze international institutional arrangements at least since the 1970s. In this domain, the notion has become a useful expression to generically designate the gap between the decision-making methods used in the exercise of power and the expectations of participation, publicity, and influence of the respective social base and related institutional agents.

Even though there are questions concerning the scientific appropriateness of using the concept in international institutions (Moravcsik, 2004), there are a variety of theoretical formulations related to the concept. To mention only a few possibilities, democratic deficit can be understood: (1) from a mainstream perspective – in which there is the perception that the strengthening of international instances leads to the emptying of the decision-making power of national populations by weakening the State, the discrediting of mechanisms that intend to guarantee some degree of democratic representation in governance beyond the National State, the detachment between the decisions by international institutions and the positioning of national public opinions, among other characteristics (Bellamy, 2006); (2) from a technocratic perspective – characterized by the absence or ineffectiveness of institutional control instruments that guarantee the decision-making transparency and the achievement of the results intended by the institution itself (Majone, 2000); and (3) from a deliberative perspective – in which at least one of these factors is absent: permanent institutional structures with decision-making and cross-supervision procedures, electoral dispute of distinct projects, collective deliberation channels with the capacity to influence decision-making (Carvalho, 2017; Follesdal & Hix, 2006). Each of these propositions sheds light on different aspects of the subject, often departing from or dialoguing more directly with the specificities of the case under analysis.

Thus, given the plurality of meanings, we have chosen to present here an "ad hoc" concept of democratic deficit that is connected to the scope of this text, in order to be more analytically accurate and maximize the results of the reflection. In this context, we argue that the democratic deficit of the GFG must be understood as a multilevel and complex phenomenon. It is multilevel because it occurs at the state level, between states, at the international and transnational organization, and in the nonsubmission of market agents' power to democratic rules and control. It is complex because in each one of these levels, there are multiple explanatory factors.

At the state level, we observe that: (1) decisions in the monetary and financial fields are immune to democratic controls, with the insulation of the technocracy (central banks and autonomous regulatory agencies) face the representative bodies; (2) the great influence of financial elite's on elections and political decision-making; (3) the constraints on the states' ability to make substantive choices in their economic policies because of trade and financial interdependence, neoliberal ideology, tax and regulatory competition for attracting capital, creditors' pressure, assessments by credit rating agencies and IMF loan conditionalities.

Considering the relations between states, we highlight: (1) the impacts of macroeconomic decisions from central countries on the others, especially the United States, China, and European Union; (2) in the same sense, we have the global impacts of the regulations issued by the US Federal Reserve, the European Central Bank, and financial regulation agencies of other central countries. There is no central authority to which they respond, so their accountability occurs only to their citizens and not to everyone affected by their decisions.

At the level of the international and transnational organizations, there are also several democratic deficit factors: (1) the asymmetry of power between states (exclusion of many states and a large part of the world population, imbalance in formal representation of those one included [voting power], and the informal power exercised by the great states); (2) nondemocratic states with a seat and high influence in the organizations; (3) private actors' lobbying, especially of the transnational financial elite; (4) organizations operation's standards and the technocracy power (lack of transparency and asymmetric access to information among stakeholders; insufficient consultations and low permeability to divergent opinions, being constituted by a closed and very homogeneous epistemic community; low responsiveness and accountability face the affected by their decisions) (Woods, 2002; Zürn & Koenig-Archibugi, 2006).

Finally, there is a democratic deficit at the GFG because of the market agents' power and their nonsubmission to democratic rules and control – in other words, the formation of areas under private self-regulation and deadlocks and deficit in the effectiveness of GFG.

These four levels of the democratic deficit in GFG are crossed by four structural constraints: (1) inequality and domination relations inherent to Capitalism in all its forms, which is intensified by financial globalization. In addition, there is no sufficiently strong counterpoint from the rest of the global population in terms of network, articulation, critical knowledge, and mobilization; (2) high technical complexity of the topics under decision-making; (3) fragmented, without central coordination, multilevel, multiform, plural, and nonsystematic features of GFG; (4) nationalist resistance to GFG democratization, on the one hand; and, on the other, the weakening of peripheral and semi-peripheral states by the political decisions taken over the past decades, which restricted the borders for choices and undermined the forces that could resist to financialization.

From a CIT perspective, any reform proposal for the democratization of the GFG must start from the multilevel and complex feature of its democratic deficit, as well as the structural restrictions to democracy in this field of the exercise of power. Considering, therefore, these conditions, we will proceed to the critical mapping of the available alternatives for political-institutional reforms.

Alternatives at the Theoretical Level

The discussion on the problem of democracy at the global level has only taken place since the 1990s. Until then, despite the consolidation of the idea that only democratic regimes were legitimate, its application was restricted to the borders of the nation-state, due to four types of arguments: (1) low political autonomy and state control over international organizations; (2) an elitist, centralized, and technically complex character of international politics, with the consequent citizens' inability to express their opinions; (3) resistance of political leaders to expand representation to the international level; (4) the belief that many of the international interdependence's issues are related to the global market, which would work better when self-regulated than under government control. Thus, democracy in the global level would refer, at most, to the meeting of democratic sovereign states for cooperation and consensual decision-making.

However, such arguments increasingly lose their strength. Relevant political decisions are made in international organizations, and the requirement for ratification within national parliaments is not enough to ensure their democratic legitimation – although formally political representatives are sovereign to decide on them, in practice, they often do not have choice, considering the costs of its rejection. Issues related to GFG are not usually discussed in electoral debates, and much less in other participatory spheres, so that indirect democratic control is feeble or nonexistent. In fact, there are many states that are not democratically governed, and even those that adopt liberal-representative systems often do not act based on democratic values in international affairs – the United States is an eloquent example. Finally, we have the democratic deficit within international and transnational organizations. Consequently, those who are affected by such decisions must have the right to participate in some way in the decision-making process that is not limited to heads of state or government's representation (Porter & Wood, 2002; Scholte, 2014). The realistic perspective also fails to consider states as the only relevant actors, neglecting the role of private agents and the complex network of international and transnational organizations (Scholte, 2012). Considering this framework, we will analyze four models of normative democratic theory that seek to offer pathways to the democratic deficit in global governance and are applicable to the finance.[2]

[2]In contrast to these models, we have the so-called radical Marxist theories, which criticize not just the global financial governance but the capitalist structure that underlies it and its contradictions. We have reviewed part of this literature (e.g., Callinicos, 2002; Hardt & Negri, 2006); however, due to our methodological approach, we will not discuss them.

The model of cosmopolitan democracy (Archibugi, 2014; Held & Maffettone, 2016) is based on the idea that there are moral obligations toward all human beings intrinsic to the human condition, regardless any nexus or features. It is a liberal political theory, grounded on individualism, egalitarianism, and universalism, which extrapolates these values beyond the nation-state borders. This results in the recognition of a cosmopolitan citizenship concomitant with the national one, which implies the right to political participation in the global level. It recognizes the relevance of power relations but emphasizes that, without institutions, hegemonic solutions and violence tend to prevail. As such relations are independent of the global governance, it is better that it exists.

In terms of institutional reforms, we find the following propositions (Gaspardo, 2021): (1) expanding the role of parliaments in international issues; (2) greater inclusion and more representative distribution of voting and governance power at the IMF, the World Bank, and other organizations; (3) establishment of mechanisms that enable the direct participation of citizens, especially the most excluded and deprived of rights, without reproducing the electoral and majority models forged for nation-states but rather adapted to global level; (4) strengthening global public opinion and its capability to influence political decisions; (5) constitution of centralized authorities (such as a "Global Financial Authority") for the coordination of rules and policies, contributing to the effectiveness of decisions, in the perspective of multilevel governance, therefore, different from ideas such as global state or federation; (6) expansion of transparency and accountability mechanisms, including horizontal ones, with controls between "powers," for example, through international jurisdictional bodies; (7) a global constitutionalism, whose enforcement would be independent of coercive mechanisms; (8) guarantee of financing sources for international organizations independent of the states' will, in order to favor their autonomous action; (9) connection of financial governance with other topics as environment, health, employment, and income distribution.

The model of cosmopolitan democracy has in its foundations a great normative power. Moving on to the propositions, based on institutionalization and law, but open to flexible forms of democracy, adapted to the multiple levels of global governance, it indicates a prospect of ambitious reforms. However, the lack or fragility of solidarity bonds in a global *demos*, the lack of motivation to participate in the global level, and the difficulties in defining the concrete conditions and criteria in which representation and participation would occur are obstacles that are hard to overcome in the current context.

Secondly, we highlight the model of global stakeholder democracy (Macdonald, 2008). Its foundations are the same as those of the cosmopolitan one, but with a greater emphasis on the constitution of a global civil society (Kaldor, 2003), which would be a space for the expression of plural voices, including that ones from the historically marginalized people. Among other actors, it would be composed of nongovernmental organizations, social movements, and global networks of activists.

Despite recognizing the value of cosmopolitan democracy as a normative imperative, Macdonald (2008, pp. 5–7) stresses that there is no feasibility for the complete implementation of such model in the near future. Thus, it would be important in orienting long-term reforms, but little applicable for the construction of immediate ones, due to the incompatibility of their universalist ideals for global politics with the fragmentation of the indeed existing society, and the infeasibility of implementing its institutional prescriptions in the short term, since they require a high degree of institutionalization and constitutionalization. So, the author advocates an alternative that aims to overcome the impasse between the inadequacy of the "community statist" democracy model and the infeasibility of "universalist cosmopolitan" projects. Its model, admittedly closer to cosmopolitan theories, is guided by the analysis of the "democratic dilemmas surrounding the power of Non-governmental Organizations (NGOs) in contemporary politics," whose answers could provide more feasible pathways for democracy in the context of a pluralist global policy. The author explains that the type of "public power" exercised by NGOs is quite different from that exercised by states – they cannot resort to violence nor have law-making capacity or a centralized organization. The legitimacy of NGOs derives from their reputation and from the legitimacy of the causes they support. The kind of NGOs' "democratic representation" also differs from the structure of state representative relations (formal electoral procedures), as they do not have a formal electoral mandate. Thus, its model of democracy is based on new concepts of "public power," "stakeholder communities," and "non-electoral representation." In summary, it proposes to open international and transnational organizations to stakeholders participation, both through formal channels (consultations, partnerships in projects' execution), as well as informal (greater permeability to international public opinion and the demands of social movements and mobilizations).

It is the most applied model in international organizations in general and financial governance in particular, although in incipient and modest experiments. Its main limitations are: (1) the scarce legitimacy of civil society actors' representation in the governance bodies, (2) the low representativeness of the excluded of globalization in NGOs and the fragility of their links with whom they intend to represents,[3] (3) the difficulty in defining stakeholder communities, (4) the narrow effectiveness of its performance in terms of influence on decision-making. Its main contributions are the promotion of public education on global finances and inclusion of topics on the global agenda with rival perspectives from the dominant ones, and not exactly in decision-making.

The third normative model is the *interactive democracy* (Gould, 2014). This model considers the political, economic, and social dimensions as interdependent and articulated; national, regional, transnational, and global levels; and participatory, electoral, and deliberative forms of democracy. In the same way of the other ones, it defends the inclusion in decision-making of all significantly affected (those who have their capacity to exercise human rights affected, especially the citizens of the "Global South," who are historically excluded from the "epistemic

[3]Therefore, the issue of political exclusion is not addressed, and there is a risk of conferring pretended legitimacy to decisions without democratic credentials.

communities" of global governance), including those made in communities to which they do not belong (such as other states and transnational corporations). This inclusion would not be limited to occasional consultations nor should it be confused with equal participation rights with community members, but it requires significant influence. Participation in this model is not just discursive but also by voting when it is necessary.

In terms of institutional designs, interactive democracy suggests new ways of expressing public opinion in international and transnational organizations, the constitution of regional or thematic "Delegate Assemblies," as well as a "People's Assembly" with real authority, highlighting its articulation since the principle of subsidiarity and the constitution of "thematic communities." As can be noticed, this approach relies heavily on the use of electronic means to promote participation and interaction.

The interactive democracy presents difficulties in institutional designing and feasibility, especially in terms of the participation of citizens other than nationals in the states' internal decisions with regional or global repercussions, and definition of concrete mechanisms and criteria for the participation. The interactive democracy model adds an important contribution to address the democratic deficit of GFG regarding the decisions of state bodies that affects people outside its borders – e.g., in the definition of regulatory rules on the banking system and the interest rate policy of the United States. However, it does not seem politically feasible at this moment.

Fourth, we have the *global discursive democracy* (Dryzek, 2010). It is a *post-Wetphalian*, postliberal, and postelectoral model, but it maintains the general principles of democracy, notably those of political equality and popular control. Unlike the liberal model, the realization of these values does not take place through the aggregation of individual preferences (vote) but through the public discussion about preferences. The deliberation must be authentic (free from pressure and well informed), inclusive (opportunities and skills for the participation of all affected), and consequent (effective influence on the decision's outcome). It is structured through the transmission of opinions from public spheres to spheres of power, as well as accountability (not just electoral) and meta-deliberation (deliberation on the very organization of the deliberative system). It is emphasized that participation in the public sphere must not only be inclusive and reflective but also effective – deliberation, at some point, needs to be transformed into law and public policies. It would be a more suitable model for network-based governance systems, in which the actors involved in decision-making processes are diffuse and do not respond to specific and determined constituencies, such as GFG.

The main proposition of this model in terms of institutional designs is the shaping of "Discourse Chambers," applicable to the bodies of GFG, which would be representative of speeches ("discursive representation"), not of people, and it would constitute an answer to the *scale problem* (the deliberative processes would be viable only in small groups of people), usually pointed out as a weakness of this model. Such *Chambers* would be complementary to the representative bodies (including those representing the states) and could take their decisions both by consensus and by vote. The model also advocates mechanisms that allow informal and flexible contact between public opinion and decision-making bodies, such as: (1) transparency and dissemination of specialized knowledge, (2) inclusion of professionals with different backgrounds than Economics in financial governance organizations – incorporating different points of view in the debates, (3) different institutionalized ways of expression, such as public hearings with authorities of those organizations, when they should justify their decisions, and (4) the creation of independent bodies to mobilize public opinion. These kinds of institutional innovations would encourage the expression of dissent, without the requirements of a strong institutionalized system, such as the cosmopolitan model, which would make the discursive model more feasible and operational. The kind of accountability made possible by the global financial public sphere cannot be structured on vertical bases but on horizontal ones, through strategies that enable it in the context of existing institutions, without, however, privileging elites to the detriment of popular forces nor ignoring democratic demands at the national level (Germain, 2007).

Communicative action would be the only possible form of democratic control over decision-making networks as we have in the level of GFG. Among other things, it would allow the expression of the positions of citizens from subordinate states, social movements, and "subordinate counter-publics" in the processes of global governance. However, it is necessary to transform public opinion into a "political power," that is, to combine legitimacy and effectiveness. It is a difficult task in the truly political conditions of the transnational public spheres, featured by inequalities, exclusions, and the absence of mechanisms to guarantee the enforcement of decisions, but it is a goal to be pursued (Fraser, 2014).

There is a dialogue between the proposals of Fraser (*transnational deliberative democracy*) and Dryzek; however, the first presents a greater emphasis on elements of substantive equality and effectiveness of the deliberative processes, which implies, even, the aforementioned demand for *new transnational public powers* with the capacity to enforce decisions taken in a democratic public sphere.

Among the main shortcomings of this model is the fact that, at the very time of decision, discursive democracy is not able to guarantee the real and proportional influence of those excluded from globalization. There are also operational and political difficulties in identifying the discourses and designating their representatives. To the usual criticism that the model presupposes an unattainable rational consensus in very unequal and plural contexts, its advocates answer that the deliberative spaces can also be pluralistic and open for dissent's expression.

Finally, we reviewed a set of proposals from the Economy and the International Economic Law (e.g., Duran, 2017; Stiglitz & Members of a UN Commission of Financial Experts, 2010; Vestergaard & Wade, 2012). It is possible to note a dialogue with the perspectives of global democracy based on states (more equitable representation of states in financial governance organizations), cosmopolitan democracy (strengthening the power of global institutions and the international law, or the creation of a "Global Financial Authority" and an "Economic and Social Security Council" at United Nations), global stakeholder democracy (participation of civil society organizations), and global discursive democracy (incorporation of different discourses in decision-making through the involvement of ministers from different areas). However, there is no effective dialogue between normative democratic theories and the disciplines dedicated to the analysis of institutional reform projects of the GFG. While those are very abstract, these do not consider the issues of the democratic deficit in depth. Promoting a constructive rapprochement between these two perspectives is work that still needs to be done.

Alternatives in the Political and Social Spheres

The reform of the international financial system and the institutions responsible for its governance has become central to the agenda of states and international organizations (political sphere) due to the very often financial crises that have occurred since the 1980s, but especially after the *1997 Asian Crisis*. In this context, the so-called *New International Financial Architecture* (NIFA) was proposed, which represented an attempt to revise the rules that govern the system, but without implying structural changes in global financial capitalism. However, NIFA has not prevented the growth of the economy's vulnerability in terms of systemic risks, financial volatility, and crises in emerging economies. In addition, there was an increase in constraints on States' political autonomy (Soederberg, 2005). The absence of effective outcomes made the theme lose its prominence for a while. However, the concern about the serious problems of GFG has returned to the scene with even greater relevance due to the *2008 Crisis*.

In this new context, the most important changes at GFG's architecture were the emergence of the Group of 20 (G20) as the main *locus* of political coordination and the transformation of the Financial Stability Forum (FSF) into the Financial Stability Board (FSB). The IMF, in turn, remained the most important global institution for macro-financial supervision (Avgouleas, 2012). In terms of power balance, the main debate is about how to make the World Bank and IMF management more democratic, which can be organized into five axes: (1) review of quota and voting power distribution, (2) the process of electing its executive directors, (3) improving accountability mechanisms, (4) increasing the transparency of decision-making and the institutions' operations, and (5) expansion of opportunities for civil society's consultation.

However, both at the IMF and at the World Bank, the reforms implemented were much more modest than announced. Although developing countries as a whole have increased their voting power in relation to global GDP, their share is significantly less than what was agreed: 3% lower in the World Bank and 2.6% in the IMF. Nevertheless, even if such reforms had been materialized, they would still be very far from the goals pursued, as the over-representation of developed countries in the direction of institutions would remain, as well as a considerable disproportion of the voting power of countries in relation to their participation in global GDP (Vestergaard & Wade, 2015).

The creation of the FSB represented a progress in relation to the FSF. Meanwhile, the problems of effectiveness and political legitimacy persist. The FSB has no institutional power and cannot enforce any state to implement the normative standards that it approves, much less to impose sanctions. As it does not find institutional support in an international treaty, there is no formal representation from states, which also weakens their institutional capacity. Its composition remains restricted, it presents distortions in representativeness of the states, and it lacks accountability mechanisms. The FSB continues to exclude the representation of the poorest parts of humanity and is led by the richest countries and by the persons who dominate technical knowledge in the field of financial regulation (Jones & Knaack, 2019).

It is noteworthy that, from negotiations initiated in 2012, the BRICS have made efforts to build an alternative institutional apparatus related to international financial governance. Thus, in 2014, the agreements that would create the "Contingent Reserve Arrangement" (CRA) and the "New Development Bank" (NDB) were signed. Following IMF's style, CRA is a monetary fund that can be called upon if one of the member states needs liquidity due to problems in its balance of payments. With an initial amount of US$ 100 billion, CRA would, in theory, create a new piece of the international institutional framework, thus increasing the diversity of institutions capable of reacting to one-off or systemic liquidity crises and repositioning the role of the BRICS members in international financial governance (Griffith-Jones, 2015).

Regarded as the main financial initiative undertaken by the BRICS, NDB is a multilateral development bank that concentrates on infrastructure and sustainable development. It is the first attempt to structure a global development bank with a leading decision-making role for emerging economies and focused on loans exclusively for developing countries. A feature of NDB's management is emblematic of the search for a more democratic GFG, and it has an impact on the bank's operation. The five founding states of NDB (Brazil, Russia, India, China, and South Africa) have the same financial contribution to the bank's constituent capital and the same decision-making power (voting weight), with decisions being made by simple majority or qualified majority, without the need for consensus or the possibility of veto due to the size of the participation quota – as occurs, for instance, in the World Bank, IMF, and the Asian Infrastructure Investment Bank (AIIB).

Similarly to CRA, NDB attests to a clear dissatisfaction by a part of the National States community regarding consolidated structures of GFG (Batista Jr., 2022) – not only in terms of decision-making but also in relation to managerial practices of traditional institutions (such as the well-known "conditionalities" imposed by the World Bank and IMF for granting resources). NDB's choice to initiate its activities with the five founding partners and only consider the possibility of developed countries' presence after its initial phase is due to the fact that such participation "tends to hinder the definition of different policies and guidelines from those followed by the main existing multilateral banks, such as the World Bank and others, which are controlled by developed countries" (Batista Jr., 2016).

However, both BRICS' initiatives have faced serious difficulties in becoming feasible. CRA has not yet managed to solve essential practical aspects, such as the establishment of physical headquarters or the definition of an economic monitoring standard. NDB, on the other hand, faced "all sorts of internal and macro-problems and soon crystallized into a sideshow" (Batista Jr., 2022). Some of NDB's challenges include: (1) the institutional cost of not having a fixed body of senior managers and relying on national representations, (2) the limited number and low impact of supported projects and loan programs, (3) the difficulty in replacing the dollar in its operations with the national currencies of the founding partners, and (4) the delay in strategic expansion to include new member countries.

Thus, the supposed institutionality enlargement – which would promote the greater protagonism of new decision-makers and reduce, at least in part, the inequality within National States – does not effectively exist. The practical inoperability makes the rhetorical promise of "democratization" tied to CRA and NDB unfeasible beforehand. Even if the structures connected to the BRICS were fully functional, their impact would be limited and one-dimensional, especially if we consider the complexity of the legitimacy crisis of GFG already pointed out in this text. Furthermore, as also mentioned above, there is nowadays an unfavorable political scenario to the thematization of the GFG democratization by the BRICS – among other reasons due to the decline of some BRICS members' global influence. Nonetheless, due to structural conditions of the international system, the alliance among the BRICS members tends to remain in place, even if with ups and downs (Batista Jr., 2022), and initiatives and issues related to GFG may be strengthened or rescued, depending on the global scenario. In this regard, a new wave of economic cooperation involving the BRICS may occur in the future, especially given the current pressure to disarticulate the international monetary system and the increased interest in attacking the dollar and euro dependence (an issue that interests China, for example, due to the intensification of trade competition with the United States and Russia, owing to the freezing of part of the latter's international reserves as a consequence of the Ukraine war).

In the assessment of Hale et al. (2013, pp. 172–176), the weaknesses in the governance of the global financial system remained after the reforms undertaken in response to the 2008 Crisis, as it continues to operate with soft law standards, and to dependent on the collaboration of national governments and the spontaneous adherence of market agents. There is no supranational power capable of enforcing the rules. Furthermore, governance has become even more fragmented due to the creation of new transnational institutions and regional regulatory organizations. Because of the enlarged membership in the bodies, multipolarity has expanded, and the growing divergence of interests between states (notably between the United States and China) hinders the cooperation and to overcome institutional inertia.

Thereby, a historic opportunity to restructure GFG institutions was lost, as only partial and incremental changes took place, during a time when there was a favorable context and great efforts were mobilized, including within the level of the United Nations' General Assembly. Thus, the structure of the system remained intact (Held & Young, 2013). These conclusions also are applied to the democratic deficit. Despite small and incremental advances, the vast majority of the world's population remains without voice and power in GFG. As noted by

Levine (2012, pp. 40–41), the measures adopted did not allow an effective and well-informed participation, neither by the general public nor by their elected representatives, remaining the "monopoly of knowledge and information necessary to evaluate their performance" in regulatory institutions, either because of its secret feature or because of its complexity. Regulators keep their independence from the public but not in the face of private financial institutions.

The emphasis on the issues of inclusion and representation of states more proportional to the *weight* of their economies is important but not enough to address the problem of democratic legitimacy, among other reasons, because: (1) many governments are not democratically elected; (2) even when they are chosen through formal democratic procedures, they do not necessarily represent the interests of the population as a whole, not even the majority; (3) some progress made in the distribution of voting rights may serve to better reflect the economic importance of emerging countries and the multipolarity, but it does not change the representativeness deficit of the globalization's "losers" – it is only attributing more power to the new "winners" (especially to China). Transparency is a prerequisite for democratic legitimacy, but it does not constitute it in itself. Consulting the "society" is also an improvement over the previous *status*, but there are at least two problems: (1) how and with which criteria is defined who will be heard? What is their representativeness? (2) mere consultation is not the same as decision-making power nor does it guarantee real and equitable influence, when it is compared, for example, with the strength of financial corporations' lobbying.

There is a risk that these reforms may serve as an instrument to confer a pretended democratic legitimacy to GFG, promoting the emptying of struggles for democracy and global justice, without any substantive shift in power relations. The domination "center – periphery" remains intact (China must be considered a central country), and the interests of those excluded from globalization continue to be disregarded. Ultimately, these reforms did not even address the GFG's democratic deficit at the state and interstate levels; its focus is just on international and transnational organizations. Therefore, the reforms carried out and designed by the G20 and the GFG organizations did not address satisfactorily neither the *architectural* nor the *engineering* issues of its democratic deficit.

Another source of projects for reforming GFG governance could be the NGOs and the social movements. Our study, in addition to the pertinent bibliography (for example, Castells, 2013; Porta et al., 2009), comprised news and documents produced by social movements that emerged in the wake of the 2008 Crisis, namely: *Occupy Wall Street* (USA), *Pots and Pans Revolution* (Iceland), and *Indignados* (Spain). We have adopted the same procedure with some international NGOs that operate within the GFG: *Association for the Taxation of Financial Transactions for Aid of Citizens (ATTAC)*, *Finance Watch*, *New Rules for Global Financial*, *Tax Justice Network*, and *Make Finance Work*.

Systematic projects for institutional reforms were not found in these sources. Its main contributions are in denouncing injustices resulting from financial globalization and defending some kind of *real* democracy and social justice, as well as the experiences of political engagement of those who participate in these movements and the cultural transformations they can trigger. If, in principle, social movements could constitute a promising field for the production of more plural and creative projects to give "voice" and real power of influence to the "losers" of globalization in GFG, the complexity of the issues previously highlighted and the empirical findings do not confirm this hypothesis. The movements do not present minimally systematized alternative programs but just some experiences of new forms of organization and deliberation, which maybe can inspire institutional designs that allow a closer connection between episodic mobilizations and social movements with the institutions' decision-making. NGOs working in the field of GFG, on the other hand, present quite concrete projects for substantive reforms. However, on the decision-making reforms, they just present generic ideas of greater representativeness, democracy, transparency, and accountability. Their greatest contribution is to make the debate on global finance and its governance more plural, in the constitution of the incipient *global financial public sphere*.

Analyzing systematically the mapped alternatives and considering both *architectural* and *engineering* criteria, we observed that not every response to the democratic deficit of GFG will come from the level of international and transnational institutions. States continue to play the main role, either because of their ability to intervene in the economic domain domestically or because of the centrality of the *Great Powers'* governments leadership for global governance's performance. Even those from the "South," to varying degrees, depending on the size of their economies and institutional capacity, keep a relevant margin of choice. For example, reducing the dependence on international capital to finance public debt and investments, at least in part, can be achieved through national fiscal and tax policies. This is the Brazilian case e.g. It is true, however, that in smaller states and with more fragile economies, there is not the same degree of autonomy.

Power relations, whether between states or social classes, which cross the different levels of GFG, are obstacles to democracy, but this does not mean that institutions and law do not matter, that they do not help to shape processes more or less democratic. If there are substantive alternatives (such as taxation and control over capital), there must exist inclusive institutions that allow them to be put into competition. It is not a case of denying technical knowledge, but, as there are disagreements between experts, it is necessary to ensure that different positions have equal conditions in a pluralist arena.

Regarding participation in GFG, in addition to the already highlighted issue of highly specialized technical knowledge that citizens, in general, do not have, another fundamental factor is that they may not want to participate, also because they often have all their time and energy consumed by the daily survival. There is no sense, therefore, in advancing the analysis and construction of projects in the perspective of a "direct democracy" or "participatory democracy" in GFG. On the other hand, a conformist position that considers enough the expansion of transparency, consultations, and accountability to an extremely narrow global civil society (or within the epistemic finance community) would not prove to be acceptable in a normative approach of an inclusive democracy.

Given this, the alternatives in the field of *global discursive democracy*, with the limits already pointed out, seem the most promising, both in terms of framing the normative assumptions of an inclusive democracy concept (*architectural issues*), as well as operational adequacy (*engineering issues*) to a field of governance structured in a network such as finance, and with a multidimensional and complex democratic deficit. The discursive processes in themselves can help in education about the topic of financial globalization and its governance, as well as in social and political mobilization for its reform.

The political and institutional design challenge would be to establish cycles and channels for mobilizations and deliberations in a transnational public financial sphere that would not only influence the decision-making of international and transnational organizations but also the citizens of the "Great Powers" and, consequently, their Governments and financial regulators. As the states, particularly the most powerful, continuous to be the main actors in GFG, the deliberative processes proposed by global discursive democracy could be a channel for the voices of the excluded from all parts of the world to influence domestic decisions of the Great Powers. There remains, however, the great challenge of inventing institutional designs that facilitate and encourage the transformation of deliberation into power in multiple arenas at different levels of governance.

All of these institutional alternatives are still at an early stage, constituting prospects for long-term transformation in the historic struggle for inclusion and autonomy that characterizes democracy. Creativity and adaptation of institutional designs to the specificities of GFG are necessary, as well as being able to articulate horizontal mobilization and institutional arenas. In this way, experimentalism, the diversified combination of models (discursive, cosmopolitan, global stakeholder, and interactive), and some sense of pragmatism are indispensable.

Final Considerations

As we have shown, the democratic deficit of GFG has four inter-crossed dimensions (within states, between states, in international and transnational organizations, and the market agents' power and their nonsubmission to democratic rules and control), and four structural restrictions (inequality and capitalist domination, high technical complexity, fragmented, multilevel, multiform and nonsystematic features of GFG, and nationalist resistance).

Moreover, mapping the existing political-institutional alternatives, we note that: (1) social movements and NGOs play a fundamental role in contesting the status quo and defending counter-hegemonic values; nevertheless, they have not been able to formulate consistent alternative projects, systematic and capable of mobilizing sufficient political support to be realized; (2) within the organizations themselves, what we found were some advances in terms of transparency, consultations, accountability, which, however, occur before a restricted and specialized audience; (3) on the distribution of power itself, the reforms are not very ambitious and limited to change the balance of forces between states, which, in essence, means little in terms of democratization because this change is not taking place in the direction of the excluded of globalization but to the new winners, particularly China. What adds to global democracy giving more power to a very powerful autocratic government? (4) there is a little more programmatic boldness within the sphere of normative democratic theory, but the models also have limitations, contradictions, and their own proponents claim that they are incipient and long-term projects.

Despite this scenario, a negative answer about the question of a democratic GFG would block the possibilities of understanding the different models and degrees of democracy, that it is a historical and unfinished process (not a question of "all or nothing"), and which has already made possible significant political, social, and economic achievements. On the other hand, a categorical affirmative answer about the submission of GFG to popular control would be naive, inconsistent with the observed reality and innocuous for social and institutional transformations. There is a deficit of legitimacy intrinsic to Capitalism, especially in the field of global finance, which points the question of democracy in its substantive sense. Every institutional design will suffer from similar difficulties, less because of its operational gaps and more because of the very logic of the international capital flow and the historical paradoxes of democracy around issues of legitimacy, effectiveness, and its relationship to specialized knowledge. Therefore, the institutions of GFG must be understood in their complexity, in their contradictions and potentialities. The same applies to the proposals for its reform, which are more likely to prosper if they do not start from ideals, but from an analysis of their democratic deficit, and simultaneously consider the issues of architecture and engineering, in addition to the driving forces that could carry on the reformists' projects.

References

Archibugi, D. (2014). The architecture of cosmopolitan democracy. In G. W. Brown & D. Held (Eds.), *The cosmopolitanism reader* (pp. 312–333). Polity Press.

Avgouleas, E. (2012). *Governance of global financial markets – The law, the economics, the politics*. Cambridge University.

Batista Jr., P. N. (2016). Brics – Novo Banco de Desenvolvimento. *Estudos Avançados*, *30*(88), 179–184.

Batista Jr., P. N. (2022). *The BRICS and the financing mechanisms they created*. Anthem Press.

Bellamy, R. (2006). Still in deficit: Rights, regulation, and democracy in the EU. *European Law Journal*, *12*(6), 725–742.

Bhagwati, J. (2007). *In defense of globalization*. Oxford University Press.

Buelvas, E. P., & Mendioroz, Á. S. (2014). Retos de la gobernanza global frente a una multipolaridad creciente. In E. P. Buelvas & H. Gehring (Eds.), *Suramérica en el scenario global: gobernanza multinivel y birregionalismo* (pp. 23–84). Editorial Pontificia Universidad Javeriana.

Callinicos, A. (2002). Marxism and global governance. In D. Held & A. Mcgrew (Eds.), *Governing globalization: Power, authority and global governance* (pp. 249–266). Polity Press.

Callinicos, A. (2009). *Imperialism and global political economy*. Polity Press.

Carvalho, D. C. d. (2017). *Direito e déficit democrático na União Europeia*. Prismas.

Castells, M. (2013). *Redes de indignação e esperança: movimentos sociais na era da internet*. Trad. Carlos Alberto Medeiros. Zahar.

Davies, H., & Green, D. (2008). *Global financial regulation: The essential guide*. Polity Press.

Dryzek, J. S. (2010). *Foundations and frontiers of deliberative governance*. Oxford University Press.

Duran, C. V. (2017). Monetary policy: Making fragmentation work. In T. Hale & D. Held (Eds.), *Beyond gridlock* (pp. 48–64). Polity Press.

Falk, R. (1999). *Predatory globalization: A critique*. Polity Press.

Follesdal, A., & Hix, S. (2006). Why there is a democratic deficit in the EU: A response to Majone and Moravcsik. *Journal of Common Market Studies*, *44*(3), 533–562.

Fraser, N. (2014). Transnationalizing the public sphere. On the legitimacy and efficacy of public opinion in a post-Westphalian world. In N. Fraser & K. Nash (Eds.), *Transnationalizing the public sphere* (pp. 8–42). Polity Press.

Gaspardo, M. (2021). *Democracia e governança financeira global*. Alameda Editorial.

Germain, R. D. (2007). Global financial governance and the problem of accountability: The rule of public sphere. In A. Ebrahim & E. Weisband (Eds.), *Global accountabilities – Participation, pluralism, and public ethics* (pp. 45–64). Cambridge University Press.

Gonçalves, W., & Teixeira, T. (2020). Considerações sobre a política externa brasileira no governo Bolsonaro e as relações Brasil – EUA. *Sul Global*, *1*(1), 192–211.

Gould, C. C. (2014). *Interactive democracy – The social roots of global justice*. Cambridge University Press.

Griffith-Jones, S. (2015). Financing global development: The BRICS New Development Bank. *DIE-GDI*, *1*(15), 1–4.

Hale, T., & Held, D. (2011). Editors' introduction: Mapping changes in transnational governance. In T. Hale & D. Held (Eds.), *Handbook of transnational governance – Institutions and innovations* (pp. 1–36). Polity Press.

Hale, T., Young, K., & Held, D. (2013). *Gridlock – Why global cooperation is failing when we need it most*. Polity Press.

Hardt, M., & Negri, A. (2006). *Multitude – War and democracy in the Age of Empire*. Penguin Books.

Held, D., & Maffettone, P. (2016). Legitimacy and global governance. In D. Held & P. Maffettone (Eds.), *Global political theory* (pp. 117–142). Polity Press.

Held, D., & Young, K. (2013). From financial crises to the crises of global governance. In D. Held & C. Roger (Eds.), *Global governance at risk* (pp. 170–201). Polity Press.

Jones, E., & Knaack, P. (2019). Global financial regulation: Shortcomings and reform options. *Global Policy Journal*, *10*(2), 193–206.

Kaldor, M. (2003). *Global civil society – An answer to war*. Polity Press.

Levine, R. (2012). The governance of financial regulation: Reform lessons from the recent crisis. *International Review of Finance*, *12*(1), 39–56.

Macdonald, T. (2008). *Global stakeholder democracy – Power and representation beyond liberal states*. Oxford University Press.

Majone, G. (2000). The credibility crisis of community regulation. *Journal of Common Market Studies*, *38*(2), 273–302.

Moravcsik, A. (2004). Is there a "democratic deficit" in world politics? A framework for analysis. *Government and Opposition*, *39*(2), 336–363.

Nobre, M. (2020). *Ponto final – a guerra de Bolsonaro contra a democracia*. Todavia.

Porta, D. d., Kriesi, H., & Rucht, D. (Eds.) (2009). *Social movements in a globalising world*. Palgrave Macmillan.

Porter, T., & Wood, D. (2002). Reform without representation? The international and transnational dialogue on global financial architecture. In L. E. Armijo (Ed.), *Debating the global financial architecture* (pp. 237–256). State University of New York Press.

Rousenau, J. (2002). Governance in a new global order. In D. Held & A. Mcgrew (Eds.), *Governing globalization: Power, authority and global governance* (pp. 70–86). Cambridge Press, Polity.

Scholte, J. A. (2012). A more inclusive global governance? The IMF and civil society in Africa. *Global Governance*, *18*, 185–206.

Scholte, J. A. (2014). Reinventing global democracy. *European Journal of International Relations*, *20*(1), 3–28.

Soederberg, S. (2005). The new international financial architecture – An emerging multi-level structure of neo-liberal discipline. In A. Baker, D. Hudson, & R. Woodward (Eds.), *Governing financial globalization: International political economy and multi-level governance* (pp. 189–209). Routledge.

Stiglitz, J., & Members of a UN Commission of Financial Experts. (2010). *The Stiglitz report – Reforming the international monetary and financial systems in the wake of the global crisis*. The New Press.

Stiglitz, J. (2015). *The great divide: Unequal societies and what we can do about them*. Norton & Company.

Strange, S. (1994). From Bretton Woods to the casino economy. In S. Corbridge, N. Thrift, & R. Martin (Eds.), *Money, power and space* (pp. 49–62). Blackwell.

Vestergaard, J., & Wade, R. H. (2012). Establishing a new Global Economic Council: Governance reform at the G20, the IMF and the World Bank. *Global Policy Journal*, *3*(3), 257–269.

Vestergaard, J., & Wade, R. H. (2015). Still in the Woods: Gridlock in the IMF and the World Bank puts multilateralism at risk. *Global Policy Journal*, *6*(1), 1–12.

Wiens, D. (2012). Prescribing institutions without ideal theory. *The Journal of Political Philosophy*, *20*(1), 45–70.

Woods, N. (2002). Global governance and the role of institutions. In D. Held & A. Mcgrew (Eds.), *Governing globalization: Power, authority and global governance* (pp. 25–45). Polity Press.

Young, K. (2017). Finance: Risk and progress. In T. Hale & D. Held (Eds.), *Beyond gridlock* (pp. 28–47). Cambridge Press, Polity.

Zürn, M., & Koenig-Archibugi, M. (2006). Conclusion II: The modes and dynamics of global governance. In M. Zürn & M. Koenig-Archibugi (Eds.), *New modes of governance in the global system: Exploring publicness, delegation and inclusiveness* (pp. 236–254). Palgrave Macmillan.

Chapter 3

Finance, Governance and Sovereignty After COVID-19: A Normative Argument for the Need to Democratise Global Finance

Robert Hanson

University of Minho, Portugal

Abstract

Voting power in crediting organisations plays a huge role in determining a country's fiscal power and access to capital, determining who has power and access to capital when it comes to crisis management. In this chapter, I explore the impact it played during the COVID-19 pandemic to highlight the need to democratize global capital when it comes to global crisis management. Parallels will be drawn between the pandemic and the climate emergency to demonstrate how the democratic deficit in global capital translates to disastrous policy-making in the medium and long term for all parties. In response to this, I argue for the democratisation of global capital and highlight how the New Development Bank can provide the necessary force for this essential shift. Pre-empting the common antagonism regarding pooling national sovereignty to supernational organisations and richer countries unilaterally surrendering their privileged position, I will also highlight how continued poor crisis management threatens all nations' national sovereignty in the long-term, given the existential threats of the climate emergency and future pandemics.

Keywords: Cosmopolitanism; democratization; liberalization; climate justice; capitalism

In this chapter, I explore how the COVID-19 pandemic has given us renewed cause to reflect on the nature of national sovereignty, and what it means to value it in an era of global crises and certain crediting International Organisations (IOs). I do so by focusing on the role disproportionate voting power in crediting

The Multilateralism of the New Development Bank on the Sustainable Economic Growth in BRICS Nations and Beyond, 29–46

Published under exclusive licence by Emerald Publishing Limited
doi:10.1108/978-1-83662-292-520251005

IOs played during the pandemic in projecting certain nation states' (NSs') short-term financial interests at the expense of tackling the virus' threat to every NSs' national sovereignty. It will be my argument that the pandemic has demonstrated that a commitment to valuing *national* sovereignty in an era of global crises entails a commitment to democratizing global finance by pooling sovereignty and capital into more democratic crediting IOs.[1]

My argument is presented in five parts.

In the first section, I will outline the concept of *national* sovereignty and the relevance of participation in crediting IOs in determining a NS's *relative* national sovereignty. The second then highlights the relevance voting power in certain crediting IOs had when it came to responding to the COVID-19 pandemic. Two points that I will focus here on are: (1) how NSs with disproportionately high voting power were able to form a voting bloc to ensure policies favour their short-term interests and (2) how their voting power bolstered their financial sovereignty. These will be used to explain why our response to COVID-19 proved needlessly antagonistic to every NSs' medium- and long-term sovereignty. In the third section, I will then draw parallels between our response to COVID-19 and climate change to demonstrate that this is a general issue with undemocratic crediting IOs when it comes to crisis response.[2]

Conceding that it is unlikely that those with disproportionately high voting power will concede this in these crediting IOs, I will then explore how a new crediting IO, the New Development Bank (NDB), has endeavoured to avoid making these mistakes in its voting distribution, and how it offers a promising alternative to the dominating but flawed system. The fourth section will detail how the NDB's voting distribution has allowed more effective policymaking than other, less democratic crediting IOs because of its commitment to more democratic representation. Meanwhile, the fifth section focuses on what needs to be changed if the NDB is to be a bigger force for necessary change, with my recommendations being to: expand the membership and have membership entail a greater pooling of sovereignty and finances. This will be used to inform my argument that to value *national* sovereignty in a world of global crises and

[1]I have chosen "a commitment to *national* sovereignty" as the normative perspective for this chapter, given that a fear of losing national sovereignty by pooling it into IOs is a common rationale for keeping power within the NS. David Held consistently made this point during his career, particularly when he referred to our fixation with *national* sovereignty in an era of global crises as "paradox of our times." This chapter will agree with Held's position and present COVID-19, climate change and the current status of global crises governance as validating Held's positions regarding what is wrong with the current political settlement and what needs to change. For Held's position, see: Held, D., 2010, "Reframing Global Governance: Apocalypse Soon or Reform!" in Brown, G.W. & Held, D., *The Cosmopolitan Reader*, Polity Press, pp. 293–311.

[2]Bobylev, S. & Grigoryev, L., make this comparison between COVID-19 and climate change policymaking and the implications of the current system and, like me, make a case that the pandemic has given BRICS a renewed sense of purpose given the fallout of the pandemic on the developing world in their 2020 article.

undemocratic finances NSs should pool their respective national sovereignty into more democratic crediting IOs, given the threat the status quo poses to every NS's national sovereignty, including those currently profiting from the status quo.

This chapter should be read as a piece of applied philosophy, with its aim being to explore the concept of national sovereignty IOs and what it means to value national sovereignty in an era of global crises era. It should also be noted that the NDB is only being used to further validate the claim that undemocratic capital is problematic for every NS's national sovereignty in the medium and long term. The NDB is not without criticism, including criticisms that it is insufficiently democratic. However, the purpose of this chapter is merely used to highlight the avoidable shortcomings of established crediting IOs and when it comes to effective policymaking for global crises because of their disproportionate voting power.

Sovereignty in the 21st Century

Starting with some definitions. Sovereignty refers to the capacity of an agent to conduct itself as it wills. Financial sovereignty, meanwhile, refers to the capacity of an agent to conduct itself given its financial limitations.[3] The NS refers to a political entity that governs over a certain territory. National sovereignty, therefore, refers to the capacity for an NS to conduct itself as its government wills within its territorial limitations. The financial sovereignty of an NS, meanwhile, refers to the capacity of an NS to conduct itself as it wills, given its financial situation.

Now, in an open market, an agent's financial sovereignty cannot be gauged without also referencing the financial sovereignty of other agents, given that a wealthier agent will be able to outbid poorer agents. In a global capitalistic market of NSs, therefore, an NS's relative national sovereignty cannot be properly understood without referencing its and other NSs' relative access to capital.

Something that impacts an NS's access to capital is its *perceived* access to capital. This is because the more an NS is perceived as having access to capital, the lower the perceived risk with investing in and/or lending to the respective NS, making it more likely that others will invest and/or lend to them.

Valuing one's respective NS's national sovereignty requires making decisions that optimally protect and promote one's NS's relative national sovereignty. In the global capitalistic market, this therefore requires one to take an active interest in securing and improving one's NS's access and perceived access to capital.

One thing that can bolster an NS's access and perceived access to capital is its participation in IOs with the capacity to lend and/or invest in its members and influence market forces. These are what will be referred to as crediting IOs.

---

[3]Li, G. & Zhou, H., 2015, "Globalization of Financial Capitalism and its Impact on Financial Sovereignty," *World Review of Political Economy*, Vol. 6, No. 2, p. 117. Here, the authors focus on the question of the right of an NS over its capital; however, I am chiefly concerned with the power an NS (does not) have because of its access to capital.

Participation in most IOs requires NSs to pool some of their sovereignty. Pooling sovereignty is where two or more agents (individuals, communities, NSs and/or IOs) agree to surrender some of their sovereignty to a shared entity by agreeing to the conditions of a given contract/treaty/relationship/membership. In exchange, the NS is granted influence (or sovereignty) over other members via their participation in the common legislature and a common bargaining position when dealing with non-members. For example, Germany's membership of the European Central Bank (ECB), World Bank (WB) and the International Monetary Fund (IMF) each comes with certain financial and budgetary commitments. In exchange for this "loss" of (financial) national sovereignty, Germany can influence what these IOs invest in, allowing them to nudge markets into formulations that suit the German economy. Equally, membership grants Germany access to the funds pooled by the membership of these various IOs. Finally, Germany's access to each of these IO's funds lowers the perceived risk of any one of them investing in and/or loaning to Germany, giving Germany privileged access to funds in each of them because of its membership of all of them, further bolstering Germany's financial sovereignty.[4] One therefore cannot understand an NS's relative national sovereignty nor what is in the interests of an NS's national sovereignty without factoring in its (non-)membership of various crediting IOs and the implications (non-)membership has for an NS's sovereignty.

This is equally demonstrable when one considers the implications of non-membership of an IO when an NS is dealing with a member of an IO.[5] For example, membership of the European Economic Community (EEC) gives the member a collective bargaining position when dealing with non-members. For example, to understand the Republic of Ireland and the United Kingdom's relative sovereignty over the island of Ireland and what is in the two NSs' financial interests, one must factor in Ireland's participation in the EEC and the United Kingdom's non-participation in it. This is because the existence of the EEC and the Republic's participation in it gives the Republic a common bargaining position against the United Kingdom and compels the United Kingdom to treat its relations with the Republic as significant to its (financial) relationship with the entire EEC.[6] To understand an NS's relative national sovereignty and what it is in the interests of its (financial) sovereignty, one must therefore include in their analysis the existence of and various NSs' participation in various IOs.

As well as membership of an IO, voting power within one is important for understanding an NS's relative (financial) sovereignty. For example, the EU and the United Kingdom combined have 29.6% of the voting power in the IMF and

---

[4]Dreher, A., Sturm, J.E., and Vreeland, J.R., also highlight how perceived influence in one IO will impact an NS's sovereignty within others in their 2015 article.

[5]Peter Dietsch (2011) made a similar point in "Rethinking Sovereignty in international Fiscal Policy," going so far as to say that Westphalian ideas of NSs as purely sovereign over their territories have "been rendered meaningless" in the contemporary global order and are unlikely to return unless the world returned to being less interconnected. pp. 2109–2111.

[6]Mary Murphy provides a detailed analysis of this situation in her 2021 article "Northern Ireland and Brexit: Where Sovereignty and Stability Collide?"

26.9% of the voting power in the WB. Once we add the members of the European Free Trade Alliance, the United States and Canada to the list, we have a voting bloc of similar and highly interconnected economies, with therefore similar economic interests with over 50% of the votes in both IOs meaning they can dictate the IMF and WB's policies.[7,8] This unofficial bloc of strongly interconnected economies with similar interests can therefore shape what the IMF and WB do with the funds contributed by the IOs' global membership, greatly expanding these NSs' sovereignties on a global level.

Voting power within a crediting IOs does not just influence an NS's perceived and actual access to capital, but it also dictates the extent to which an NS can influence the development of certain policies and markets to serve their domestic financial interests. This is because IOs oversee projects over a larger territorial area than any one NS. For example, the IMF's Poverty Reduction and Growth Trust (PRGT) has an annual budget of ~$1.7 billion for ecologically and economically sustainable projects.[9] Given the distribution of the voting power, the attractiveness of a project to European and North American NSs is a significant variable in determining the likelihood that a project will get funded and the terms for making cash available. Given these NSs' voting power, they are able to ensure the IMF favours policies that serve their own markets' interests, giving them the means to shape the development of other markets for their own financial interests. Voting power within crediting IOs is therefore highly important when attempting to understand the state of global governance and finance in the 21st century, as well as how these IOs can enhance the sovereignty of (some) members.

Moving beyond political tools, we must also recognize the relevance of non-agential variables for an NS's relative sovereignty, especially in an era of pandemics and climate change. For example, disease threatens an NS's sovereignty because it will: (1) limit what a given NS's citizens can do, (2) impact the perceived health of the NS's economy and (3) shape the NS's relative bargaining power when interacting with other agents. For example, a disease-ridden NS will be perceived as relatively weak and risky to invest in as compared to an NS with a health population, giving the former a weaker bargaining power and therefore less sovereignty than the latter enjoys.

In an era of global, non-agential threats like climate change and pandemics, IOs have attracted positive attention even from those who are sceptical with the idea of pooling their NS's national sovereignty into them. This is because they offer us a means to: coordinate our responses to non-agential threats, collaborate toward mutually beneficial goals and hold NSs accountable for their (in)actions.

Focusing on climate change, one NS achieving net zero is admirable but ultimately pointless if other NSs do not endeavour to do likewise. IOs offer us a means to incentivise other NSs to do likewise and hold NSs accountable for failing to do likewise. For example, membership of the EU entails accepting

---

[7]https://www.imf.org/en/About/executive-board/members-quotas.

[8]Suchodolski, S.G. & Demeulemeester, J.M., 2018, "The BRICS Coming of Age and the New Development Bank," *Global Policy*, Vol. 9, No. 4, pp. 580–581.

[9]https://www.imf.org/en/About/Factsheets/IMF-Support-for-Low-Income-Countries.

certain ecological regulations and EU oversight to ensure compliance.[10] Furthermore, as the EU, the members are granted a common bargaining position to push non-EU countries and IOs to adopt certain ecological commitments and give the EU oversight over their implementation. For example, the EU's recent treaty with MERCOSUR/MERCOSUL included a joint commitment to certain ecological practices and the creation of a joint commission to evaluate both parties' practices over environmental matters, a commission with disciplinary powers should a party be found to not be conforming to the regulations.[11]

Without certain IOs, NSs would be more unaccountable for their actions and less incentivised to accept responsibilities over certain global issues. We are compelled to appreciate how this would threaten every NSs' national sovereignty eventually and, therefore, why a commitment to valuing national sovereignty entails recognizing the shortcomings of more independent NSs and why pooling sovereignty can be consistent with valuing one's NS's national sovereignty.

This brings us to the question of whether our IOs are adequately set up to justify the sovereignty they request from NSs, and how they might be improved to better serve national sovereignty.

Global Governance, Finance and Representation During COVID-19

COVID-19 disrupted every NS's national sovereignty. In the process, the pandemic revealed the potential and shortcomings in our political settlement when it comes to how we protect and promote national sovereignty.

The presence of the virus, a non-agential variable, had direct impacts on the economic activity of every NS, as deaths and fear of infection (and death) impacted people's economic activity. This led politicians to introducing various policies in response to the virus and these fears, policies designed to: curb infections and deaths, fund vaccine research and, later, acquire vaccines.

From a perspective of valuing national sovereignty, the optimal course of action would have been global, egalitarian vaccine distribution. This would have minimised the chances and duration of infection, especially in poorer countries, decreasing the chances of escape variants developing and spreading, and thereby diminishing the chances of a prolonged pandemic. This is what was recommended by the WHO.

Despite this recommendation, by March 2021, 20% of the global population had access to 95% of the produced vaccines, with a strong positive correlation

---

[10] Jack, B., provides a comprehensive and critical overview of the EU's environmental policies and enforcement procedures in his 2011 article in *Environmental Law*, highlighting the power membership entails ceding to the EU's courts.

[11] The treaty gave both parties the right to environmental oversight in the other's jurisdiction and had disciplinary procedures for non-compliance See: https://circabc.europa.eu/ui/group/09242a36-a438-40fd-a7af-fe32e36cbd0e/library/63854154-7f3f-45d6-bfe6-53e330818fd0/details.

between vaccine access and gross domestic product (GDP) per capita of the recipient's NS.[12] With poorer countries unable to access vaccines and being less able to fund treatment, they became hotbeds for escape variants decimating their populations and economies before spreading to other NSs. The results of this were as the WHO predicting: (1) more people died, (2) global economic activity and recovery compromised, (3) the gap between rich and poor NSs expanded, (4) poorer NSs now more exposed to the risks associated with future pandemics and, therefore, (5) every NS is now more exposed and vulnerable to future pandemics than they needed to be.

This brings me two interconnected questions: what role could crediting IOs have played, and what role did voting power play in enabling this situation to come about? In answering these, I will present my argument for the need to democratising global finance through democratic crediting IOs.

One thing that the IMF and WB could have done is to bulk purchase vaccines to be distributed on a global scale and on an egalitarian basis, emulating what the WHO recommended and what the ECB did for its members.[13] Doing so, however, would have robbed wealthier NSs of their fiscal advantage to secure vaccines for their own people. As wealthier NSs form an effective voting majority in the IMF and WB, such a policy was therefore unlikely to ever be adopted.

This presents the IMF and WB as less helpful than they could have been. However, we should also acknowledge how the disproportionately voting power granted to certain NSs by the IMF and WB enhanced these NSs' fiscal power which, in turn, enabled them to pursue the policies that led to greater inequality in terms of vaccine access.

Recall the positive impact perceived access to credit has on an NS's financial sovereignty. Again, recall that Germany is perceived as having probable and privileged access to IMF and WB funding because of its high voting power, and that Germany's economic interests greatly overlap with other wealthy NSs. This reduces the perceived risk with taking out contracts with Germany, for example, a large contract for vaccines, and therefore enhances Germany's fiscal power when sourcing vaccines. Voting power within the IMF and WB therefore not only undermined the possibility of these IOs being used more effectively to combat the virus, it also passively enhanced fiscal advantage of wealthier NSs to source vaccines.

If we now look at the implications of this, we see that the results were not even beneficial for the medium- and long-term interests of these wealthier NSs. As previously stated, a lack of access to vaccines in poorer NSs led to these NSs becoming hotbeds for escape variants that prolonged the pandemic. In turn, this increased the damage the pandemic can and did do to the global economy. Moving to the longer term perspective, we now have poorer NSs that are even more compromised and vulnerable to future pandemics and other economic hits,

---

[12]Tatar, M., et al., "International COVID-19 Vaccine Inequality amid the Pandemic: Perpetuating a Global Crisis."

[13]https://www.ecb.europa.eu/home/search/coronavirus/html/index.en.html.

making them increased threats for the global economy and diminishing their value as prospective trading partners for wealthier NSs. Furthermore, because of these variables, their credit rating has diminished, deceasing their access to capital, making it harder for them to recover and be both more pandemic prepared and low-risk trading partners. The result of this is therefore a probable spiral of decline in these poorer NSs, as their reduced economic prospects reduce their perceived access to capital, which reduces their economic prospects, *ad infinitum*.

Framing these NSs as potential trading partners for the wealthy NSs, these actions have now diminished poorer NSs' value as potential and future trading partners, which is not in the medium- or long-term economic interests of these wealthier NSs looking for trade as a means to grow economically. This is not to say that we should critique global governance relative to how it serves the interests of developed NSs. I merely raise this point to highlight how the current system does not *even* serve the medium- and long-term interests of those wealthier NSs whom crediting IOs privilege with effective control and enhanced credit ratings via greater voting power. As things currently stand, we have supposedly global crediting IOs who, because of their voting distribution, enable policies relative to whether they are conducive to the immediate wants of a select few countries regardless of whether the policy is the most effective for responding to a given crisis *even* for these privileged countries.

What COVID-19 revealed is how voting power in crediting IOs can and did translate into poor policymaking for *global* crisis management. Wealthier countries with high voting power in the IMF and WB did not exploit these advantages in a way that served even their own medium- and long-term interests.

We should acknowledge that without the IMF and WB, wealthier NSs would still have had the economic advantage over their poorer counterparts. However, we must be mindful of how the voting power of wealthier NSs in the IMF and WB enhances their economic advantage and enabled them to pursue counterproductive policies for the world economy and their own medium- and long-term economic interests and (financial) sovereignty.

The pandemic has therefore provided us with a case study to re-examine what sovereignty, finances and governance looks like in this era of global issues and crises, as well as to critique what we need to reform given a commitment to national sovereignty. Voting power in crediting IOs is an important variable that brings these three concepts together in the 21st century. With the pandemic, we see that even if one is committed to prioritising their NS's *national* sovereignty, one must acknowledge the relevance of IOs in determining their respective NS's relative sovereignty, and how (in)action, voting power and the method of policymaking by IOs can enhance and protect as well as undermine and threaten one's respective NS's sovereignty.

Comparing COVID-19 and the Climate Emergency

Before I get on to the topic of the NDB, I will demonstrate why the story of COVID-19 is comparable to the situation concerning global governance over climate change. This is to demonstrate that voting power within these IOs is not just an issue when it comes to pandemic policymaking but in other global issues, and particularly with our biggest threat, climate change.

Firstly, it should be noted that the IMF and WB are the main source of funding for both COVID-19 and climate change, and that they treat them as comparable issues given that COVID-19 became part of their sustainable development initiatives.[14,15] What follows is a reflection of how the policies and perspectives these IOs have adopted favour the unofficial group of wealthier NSs with high voting power within the IMF and WB at the expense of what would be most conducive to responding to the climate emergency. I will then conclude this section arguing that, like with COVID-19, we see the same theme of policies being adopted that reflect the short-term interests of these NSs but at odds with their medium- and long-term interests, allowing me to again cast this policymaking procedure as counterintuitive.

We should also acknowledge what would be the most effective policy to adopt in response to climate change. Like with COVID-19, this would be a policy of "each according to their ability and each according to their needs." This would make access to capital and resources relative to what is needed to combat climate change by making those most able to contribute the most responsible to fund ecological projects.[16] Already, we can see why such a policy is unlikely to come to fruition in the IMF and WB given that this would see the wealthiest NSs, some of which have effective control over the two IOs, having to contribute the most, given their relative ability to source and use capital.

Alternatively, the issue of financing the climate emergency could be framed in terms of emissions debt. This would hold NSs financially accountable for their polluting activities, including their historical contributions.[17] However, the IMF and WB focus on current emissions and consider NSs as responsible for emissions originating from within their NS borders, regardless of whether these emissions are due to the economic demands of another NS. This perspective favours NSs with historically high emissions and who can and have afforded to outsource their production to other NSs. For example, according to the current perspective, the United Kingdom is responsible for just over 1% of emissions, once we ignore its historical contributions as a global, coal using empire and emissions due to industries it has outsourced to other NSs.[18] Changing this would require favouring policies that would be disadvantageous to wealthy NS who owe their wealth to previous ecologically damaging practices and/or those who can and have afforded to outsource emission producing activities to

[14]https://www.imf.org/external/pubs/ft/ar/2021/eng/downloads/imf-annual-report-2021.pdf.

[15]https://www.worldbank.org/en/who-we-are/news/coronavirus-covid19/world-bank-support-for-country-access-to-covid-19-vaccines.

[16]Callinicos provides a detailed outline of what this would look like in greater detail for global financing generally in their 2002 piece "Marxism and Global Governance."

[17]See Pickering, J. & Barry C., 2012, "The Concept of Climate Debt: Its Moral and Political Value."

[18]Bell, D., 2011, "Global Climate Justice, Historical Emissions, and Excusable Ignorance," *The Monist*, Vol. 94, No. 3, pp. 391–411.

other NSs. Unfortunately, this describes many NSs that make up the voting majority in the IMF and WB, making it unlikely to change.

So, what do the IMF and WB offer as a way of responding to climate change, and what does this mean when it comes to how the issue is framed in terms of responsibilities?

Most notably, the IMF and WB offer developmental loans to NSs. As loans, as opposed to grants, this casts the NS as responsible for financing its move toward sustainable economic activity, and which the IMF and WB are willing to assist with if doing so is considered a prudent investment: that it will yield profits for the investors.

Making matters worse is that, as a loan, fiscal viability has been permitted to play a significant role in funding decisions, including how vulnerability to climate change impacts an NS's perceived fiscal value.[19] Under this perspective, the worst thing to be if one wants funding for climate change initiatives is a poor NS threatened by climate change, given that one has little to offer as collateral, and what one can offer has its value threatened by climate change.

The IMF and WB do have a policy for poorer NSs wanting to source developmental loans: market liberalisation as a condition for funding. This effectively sees NSs having to open up their economies to foreign investors in exchange for access to credit.[20] As a policy, this serves the interests of wealthy individuals and NSs because it gives them the means to acquire new sources of revenue that might otherwise have been protected by protectionist policies. It is therefore unsurprising that wealthier NSs would favour such a policy, and, by proxy, it would be the policy of the IMF and WB which is effectively governed by wealthier NSs. With the condition of market liberalisation for developmental loans, we therefore see how crediting IOs expand the political and fiscal sovereignty of wealthier NSs by becoming a means for these NSs to compel poorer NSs to adopt certain policies that favour these wealthier NSs' (short-term) economic interests.

From a climate science perspective, this is ecologically disastrous as it makes poorer NSs even less economically capable to afford green initiatives in the medium and long term. Focusing on the conditions of market liberalisation, the poorer and more vulnerable to climate change an NS is, the more market liberalisation will probably be demanded for the loan. Given the assumption that climate change will continue, a poor and vulnerable NS will likely need more assistance in the future. However, at this future point, this NS will have outstanding debts, own less of its resources to put up as collateral and will only have been receiving some of the wealth

[19]Both the IMF and WB factor Stand and Poors and Moody's credit rating into their understanding of an NS's economic value and risk when assessing NSs for developmental loans, ratings that favour asset rich NSs with open markets, circumstances that are most favourable for asset and capital rich countries. See S&P Global, 2020, art. 17, 20, 22; Moody's Investors Service, 2021, pp. 4–7.

[20]Dreher, A., Sturm, J.A. & Vreeland, J.R., 2015, "Politics and IMF Conditionality," pp. 121–122.

extracted from its territory, given that foreign investors will likely take a percentage.[21] These variables will diminish their credit rating and chances of securing capital (even with the harshest economic conditions), making default and market failure more likely. The condition of market liberalisation therefore does serve the short-term economic interests of wealthier NSs by giving them the means to use their fiscal power to expand their portfolios. However, it also makes it more likely that the markets they invest in will fail, negating the value of their investments. As a policy, it therefore does not even serve these wealthy NSs' medium-to long-term economic interests given the progression of climate change and what this is doing to the market value of poorer and more vulnerable markets.

It was for reasons like these that the Morales government of Bolivia re-nationalised key industries and focused on paying off its debts to the IMF to be free of its IMF commitments concerning market liberalisation as a way of avoiding this induced spiral of decline. Since 2019, Bolivia has no outstanding debts with the IMF, allowing revenue earned in the NS to be reinvested into the country rather than go to foreign investors, boosting Bolivia's credit rating and access to capital, which the government used to invest into welfare and ecological projects. The results were improved social and ecological conditions and, therefore, better long-term economic prospects thanks to re-nationalisation.[22,23] For NSs less resource rich than Bolivia, however, they often have to work with the IMF, accept the conditions of market liberalisation, with the risks of more entrenched inequality and an increased chance of market failure.

Much like COVID-19, climate change is proving a great unequaliser, and this growing inequality is undermining our chances for overcoming this existential threat. We could respond to through collective financing, and this is something that is offered via the world's two biggest crediting IOs, the WB and IMF. However, the potential of the IMF and WB to finance our way out of the climate emergency is undermined by the way with which political power has been distributed within them and what policies this has led these IOs to favour with climate change financing. Wealthy NSs form an effective majority for policy-making and profit from having high voting power within these crediting IOs. There is therefore little incentive for these wealthier NSs to surrender their disproportionately high voting power and, therefore, little chance for the IMF and WB to have sufficient political force to change the way they are governed. Without this force, we are therefore left with the majority of global finance being governed in such a way that ecological failure is inevitable.

---

[21]This process has been highly criticised as driving up wealth inequality and pushing countries to economic and ecological failure. See Lang, 2021.

[22]Naqvi, N., 2021, "Renationalizing Finance for Development: Policy Space and Public Economic Control in Bolivia," *Review of International Political Economy*, Vol. 28, No. 3, pp. 472–474.

[23]It must be stated that Bolivia was able to achieve this because of its possession of highly valued resources. Other NSs do not have this luxury meaning that when the need for capital arises, they will be compelled to consider ceding sovereignty to the IMF and foreign investors via market liberalisation out of necessity.

The New Development Bank

Climate change will eventually provide these wealthier NSs with sufficient incentives to use the IMF and WB more effectively to combat climate change, as the problems and costs associate with climate change directly reach their own markets. Unfortunately, this may prove too late to avoid ecological failure. Even if these NSs act in time to avoid ecological failure, the longer they wait, the more expensive climate restoration becomes, undermining their future economic prospects and, by virtue, their national sovereignties. How then do we incentivise reform more quickly? One option: introducing competition.

As Suchodolski and Demeulemeester noted, the creation of the NDB partially resulted from a growing dissatisfaction among certain NSs over a lack of fair representation in existing crediting IOs, a perceived unwillingness within these IOs to change this and a desire for truly sustainable investment. Prior to the creation of the NDB, the IMF and WB did not need to concern themselves with this dissatisfaction. Afterward, however, these two IOs suddenly found themselves with a competitor. So, how does these new competitors compare to the IMF and WB when it comes to policymaking and voting?

On voting power, votes in the NDB are proportionate to the number of shares a member purchases. Recognising the different sizes of the original five economies, it was decided that each member would purchase the same number of shares at the same price and receive equal voting power to ensure no one NS could use its greater fiscal power to effectively control the Bank's policymaking. These shares equated to 55% of the voting power, which could form a voting bloc that creates the same problems as we saw in the IMF and WB.[24] However, unlike the situation with the IMF and WB, here we have five relatively unconnected economies spanning across four continents, subject to different economic pressures, and decisions are made via a simple majority, and no member has a veto.[25] Each of these variables makes it less likely that there will be policies that are uniquely in the interests of the original 5, meaning it is less likely that this will be a voting bloc with comparable problems to the ones within the IMF and WB.

This commitment to ensuring fair representation can also be seen throughout the discussions concerning the creation of the physical bank. Here, the decision was made that the physical bank would be located in China so as to immediately demonstrate the Bank had the backing of the group's biggest economy, thereby boosting the Bank's economic profile. Recognising how this may give China

[24]https://www.ndb.int/wp-content/themes/ndb/pdf/Agreement-on-the-New-Development-Bank.pdf, p. 4.

[25]The creation and functioning of both BRICS and the NDB has often been met with great surprise given these variables. See Cooper, A.F. & Farooq, A.B., 2015, "Testing the Club Dynamics of the BRICS: The New Development Bank from Conception to Establishment." Historically, these variables have been cast as an obstacle; however, they were clearly surmountable obstacles. Here, I cast them as a strength: a means to better ensure several members cannot take effective control over these IOs because the membership does not favour any one region, culture or economic perspective.

greater influence over the Bank, key positions within the Bank were distributed among the other four members.

On policymaking, there are two variables that should be acknowledged as significant departures from the IMF and WB systems. Firstly, that policies are chosen based upon the decision of a simple majority of geographically and culturally distant NSs. Secondly, there is a greater commitment to not interfering with an NS's national sovereignty.

On the voting method, this means that those looking for funding do not have to concern themselves with the fact that policies and decisions ultimately reflect what is in the interests of a bloc of wealthy NS. This means that a project is evaluated based upon its economic and ecological impact and not relative to its value as a potential asset for a wealthy investor. There is therefore less of a chance for decisions to fuel global inequality or for poverty to be an obstacle to needed finance in the NDB than with the IMF and WB.

One of the Bank's commitment is national sovereignty; this can be seen by the fact that the Bank funds projects, not NSs, and endeavours to fund projects in the local currency when possible. On the former, as projects are funded, there is not a default mechanism for having political conditions attached to funding a project as there is in the IMF and WB. The fact that a project is economically and ecologically viable is practically authoritative in financing decisions in the NDB compared to within the IMF and WB, meaning NSs are offered a source of funding that will not come with, for example, conditions of market liberalisation. On the commitment to try and fund projects in the local currency, this simple decision is significant for the NS's sovereignty. By funding a project in USD, as is standard in the IMF and WB, this pegs part of the NS's economy to the United States' economy, making this part of their economy subject to the interests of the United States' interests. Funding the projects in the local currency, however, allows the NS to retain this amount of fiscal autonomy and therefore sovereignty.

As we compare the NDB with the IMF and WB, we are therefore provided with two very different crediting IOs. The distribution of votes in the IMF and WB encourages these IOs to be more concerned with profit maximisation and market liberalisation than combatting climate change. The NDB, as it currently stands, does not have this risk because of the way votes are distributed, the composition of the membership and the method with which projects are evaluated. Furthermore, the NDB has demonstrated a greater commitment to respecting national sovereignty through its approach to financing projects.

From the perspective of an NS seeking finances for sustainability projects, the NDB therefore offers them a less politically invasive option than the IMF and WB, an attractive option. Gone are the demands for market liberalisation and the probability of increased wealth inequality, and in their place comes the possibility of fair consideration and representation. The NDB changes the political landscape because it offers an alternative with these sought-after commodities, an alternative the IMF, WB and their members do not offer and must now consider whether they should offer given that every time the NDB offers an NS credit that is an opportunity these IOs and NSs have lost out on to expand their influence.

Reforming the NDB and Global Governance

This brings us to the question: if the NDB is such a promising alternative, why do the IMF and WB still reign supreme, and what can be done so that the NDB might become a greater force for change within and beyond these IOs?

The dominance of the IMF and WB can partially be explained by their fiscal potential. The IMF's revenue budget in 2022 was $1.2 billion, while the NDB's is but $117 million in 2022.[26,27] The number of projects the NDB is able to finance is therefore dwarfed by the IMF's capacity to fund projects, meaning a lot of NSs will still depend upon IMF loans to finance projects.

To resolve this issue, the NDB could continue its agenda to expand the membership, given that new members pay into the bank for shares and voting power, and there is an incentive for new members to purchase many shares given that these will translate to voting power. This, however, does come with issues concerning sovereignty. From the prospective member's perspective, they lose some fiscal sovereignty, as they transfer money that they get to use into an organisation that will then control these finances. Meanwhile, from the perspective of an existing member, expansion diminishes their influence over the decision-making process.

However, we must recall that *national* sovereignty cannot be understood in a vacuum: a state's relative national sovereignty and prospective national sovereignty are relative to both the politics beyond their borders and the non-agential threats within the world. The options are not between states retaining and protecting their national sovereignty or pooling it into IOs. Instead, the choice is between committing some of their (financial) national sovereignty to the NDB or leave it vulnerable to: the continued poor international governance, the potential need for finances in the future, and the predatory nature of wealthier NSs in the global market.

As things currently stand, the main crediting IO for an NS to turn to when facing an economic hit and requiring financial assistance are the IMF and WB. As previously stated, the worst thing to be when it comes to sourcing capital from them is a poor NS with a terrible bargaining position and little influence over the decision-making process. Without an alternative, one's options are to lose sovereignty to whatever caused the unexpected economic hit or to cede sovereignty to the whims of the IMF and/or WB, with the possibility of never being able to reclaim said sovereignty. The bigger the membership and, more importantly, the bigger the capital invested into the bank, the less likely a member state will have to depend upon the IMF or WB. Furthermore, the bigger the NDB's budget, the better the members' bargaining positions should they decide to still engage with the IMF and WB, given their perceived access to NDB funding. From this perspective, investing into the NDB therefore manifests as insurance against being in a vulnerable position with the IMF and WB.

---

[26]https://www.imf.org/en/News/Articles/2021/05/27/pr21145-imf-executive-board-approves-fy-2022-fy-2024-medium-term-budget.

[27]https://www.ndb.int/wp-content/uploads/2022/01/NDB-Budget-disclosure-2022.pdf.

Furthermore, it should be seen as an investment into fairer financial governance and proportionate sovereignty, as opposed to diminished sovereignty for the sake of the aforementioned bloc of NSs in the IMF and WB. This is more decidedly an issue for those NSs not in the bloc of NSs with effective control over the IMF and WB as, should the need for financial support come, one should want to ensure their creditor reviews their case in terms of providing support as opposed to expanding another group's financial and political influence.

Looking beyond what expanding the membership would bring to the members' national sovereignty; we also must acknowledge how making the NDB a bigger creditor will introduce greater competition to the IMF and WB, incentivising the IMF and WB to reform. Assuming the members of the IMF and WB with effective control over these IOs want to continue to use these IOs as a means to forward their financial and political interests, they will need to ensure NSs take out financing agreements with the IMF and WB. The existence of the NDB already highlights the desire amongst various NS to work with an IO committed to fair representation and the appeal of financing with minimal political interference. With the NDB more able to provide financing options with these much sought-after political commodities to a greater number of client states, the more the IMF and WB will have to consider offering similar perks if NSs are to choose IMF or WB financing. This is because the IMF and WB will find themselves in increasing competition with the NDB, which offers financing with less political interference.

As the gap between rich and poor NSs gets bigger, choosing not to invest into an IO committed to fairer representation can only be cast as allowing one's NS's sovereignty to be subject to a group of wealthy NSs, given the nature of governance in the IMF and WB.

My second and more controversial recommendation is having membership of the NDB requiring a greater pooling of national sovereignty into the NDB.

The EU is a prime example of why *national* sovereignty cannot be understood without referencing participation in IOs. At the time of writing, it is the most integrated IO in the history, with members sharing common laws and participating in a customs union. This limits what any one member can do but offers protections and a collective bargaining position for all of them when negotiating with non-members. For example, Malta with a population of under 600,000 people has trade treaties with third parties who negotiated not with Malta but with an organisation that represented 16.7% of the world's GDP. Competition between member states is reduced because of the shared laws, and these shared laws mean that non-member NSs cannot prey on the weakest member to lower their standards for the sake of investment. As a result of this, the world has to engage with the EU as the EU, with its collective bargaining position.

Now compare the EU (+UK) to the founding members of the NDB. These countries represent 31.4% of global GDP and 42.4% of the world's population. Within the IMF and the WB, these countries only have 14.2% and 12.9% voting power, respectively. They can form part of a voting bloc within the IMF and WB; however, given the distribution of the votes, this would be a relatively impotent bloc.

Outside of the IMF and WB, however, BRICS offers a credible bargaining position given it accounts for nearly a third of global GDP. Considering what the

EU is capable of doing with its smaller economic bargaining position and BRICS, in theory, could push for more, providing they assume a common bargaining position. A common bargaining position does require pooling sovereignty into the IO, however, for the sake of collective protection for their national sovereignty. Take labour laws, for example. A common commitment to a living wage should not be too controversial: it is effectively the members committing themselves to ensuring their own citizens can survive. With BRICS and the NDB manifesting as cooperating but not integrated economies, third parties can divide and conquer: invest in the NS with the lowest labour value, cultivating competition between the members in a race to the bottom. Together, they deny third parties this option, at least in their own territories, and do not lose a competitive edge between them nor investment to one another because they have committed to the same position.

This development does not need to be anything as grand like a comprehensive customs union but something that merely demonstrates the group as a cohesive entity with shared aims that other NSs and IOs must recognise as something they may have to contend with. This alone would impact global governance and finance, as it reshapes the economic status and perceived prospects of various NSs that have, until now, denied a fair status in the world's bigger crediting agencies.

Concluding Remarks

We live in an interconnected world where some issues cannot be contained within national borders and where collaboration is often necessary for us to better protect and promote our respective NSs' national sovereignty, hence the rise of the IO as fora for collaboration and collective oversight. Unfortunately, our preoccupation with protecting our *national* sovereignty makes us prone to be sceptical of "surrendering" part of it to these IOs. However, as the COVID-19 pandemic and the ever-worsening climate change situation demonstrate, there is a growing need for more democratic global financial governance if we are to truly protect our respective NSs' national sovereignty in the long term.

In this chapter, I used COVID-19 to highlight the existential threat posed from poor global financial governance to poorer NSs' sovereignty in the medium- and long term, a trend I presented as evident in climate change financial governance. In both cases, I presented how this is an issue partially born from how votes are distributed in the IMF and WB, and why this is an issue that is unlikely to change, again, given how votes are distributed.

I then turned to the NDB and explored how its voting distribution and policymaking procedure make it a promising response to these criticisms over global financial governance and a more attractive alternative to the IMF and WB for those who put primacy on *national* sovereignty. I then concluded by engaging with the NDB's limitations, focusing on its relatively small economic size and low integration when compared to other IOs, limitations that could be overcome via the decision to expand the membership and have membership entail greater pooling of sovereignty into the Bank. Again, pre-empting the concerns of those committed to their NS's national sovereignty, I reiterated the point of the threat posed to every NSs' national sovereignty from poor governance over certain global issues and repeated the connection between poor policymaking and disproportionate voting distribution. With these variables in mind, I cast the NDB as a means to protect one's NS's national sovereignty against these threats.

The purpose of this chapter was not to extol the virtues of the NDB but to highlight why a commitment to NS entails democratising global finance. The NDB merely served as a counter-example to other, less democratic crediting IOs, demonstrating how the lack of proportionately distributed voting power translates to less effective policymaking.

References

Bobylev, S., & Grigoryev, L. (2020). In search of the contours of the post-COVID sustainable development goals: The case for BRICS. *BRICS Journal of Economics*, *1*(2), 4–24.

Callinicos, A. (2002). Marxism and global governance. In D. Held & A. McGrew (Eds.), *Power, authority, and global governance* (pp. 249–266). Polity Press.

Cooper, A. F., & Farooq, A. (2015). Testing the club dynamics of the BRICS: The New Development Bank from conception to establishment. *International Organizations Research Journal*, *10*(2), 32–44.

Dietsch, P. (2011). Rethinking sovereignty in international fiscal policy. *Review of International Studies*, *27*, 2107–2120.

Dreher, A., Sturm, J. A., & Vreeland, J. R. (2015). Politics and conditionality. *Journal of Conflict Resolution*, *59*(1), 120–148.

EU. https://circabc.europa.eu/ui/group/09242a36-a438-40fd-a7af-fe32e36cbd0e/library/63854154-7f3f-45d6-bfe6-53e330818fd0/details

Held, D. (2010). Reframing global governance: Apocalypse soon or reform! In G. W. Brown & D. Held (Eds.), *The cosmopolitan reader* (pp. 293–311). Polity Press.

Jack, B. (2011). Enforcing member state compliance with EU environmental law: A critical evaluation of the use of financial penalties. *Journal of Environmental Law*, *23*(1), 72–95.

Lang, J. (2021). The economics of the democratic deficit: The effects of IMF programs on inequality. *Review of International Organizations*, *16*(3), 599–623.

Li, G., & Zhou, H. (2015). Globalization of financial capitalism and its impact on financial sovereignty. *World Review of Political Economy*, *6*(2).

Moody's Investors Service. (2021). https://ratings.moodys.com/api/rmc-documents/395819

Murphy, M. (2021). Northern Ireland and Brexit: Where sovereignty and stability collide? *Journal of European Studies*, *29*(3), 405–418.

Naqvi, N. (2021). Renationalizing finance for development: Policy space and public economic control in Bolivia. *Review of International Political Economy*, *28*(3), 447–478.

NDB. https://www.ndb.int/wp-content/themes/ndb/pdf/Agreement-on-the-New-Development-Bank.pdf

Pickering, C., & Barry, J. (2012). On the concept of climate debt: Its moral and political value. *Critical Review of International Social and Political Philosophy*, *15*(5), 667–685.

S&P Global. (2020). https://disclosure.spglobal.com/ratings/en/regulatory/article/-/view/sourceId/6485398

Suchodolski, S. G., & Demeulemeester, J. M. (2018). The BRICS coming of age and the New Development Bank. *Global Policy*, *9*(4).

Chapter 4

BRICS: A Comprehensive Mechanism Bringing Changes Into the World Financial System and International Climate Diplomacy

Eka Khorbaladze

Centre on Contemporary China and the World, Hong Kong

Abstract

BRICS has evolved from a "dialogue forum" focused on global economic governance to a "comprehensive coordination mechanism" handling a broad multilateral agenda. The group has faced significant challenges, including the 2008 global financial crisis, the COVID-19 pandemic, and the 2022 Russia–Ukraine conflict, which have influenced its strategies. In response, BRICS has launched key initiatives such as the New Development Bank and the BRICS Contingent Reserve Pool to support infrastructure and sustainable development, enhancing global economic stability. Climate change is a central issue for BRICS, with member countries actively pursuing environmental policies and green technologies to achieve decarbonization and carbon neutrality. Since 2011, BRICS has presented a unified stance in international climate negotiations, advocating for sustainable economic growth while opposing measures that could impede development. The alliance also addresses global challenges like combating money laundering, advancing anti-corruption efforts, and ensuring food security and energy access. BRICS has made notable progress in deepening economic cooperation and reforming international financial institutions, increasing the representation of emerging and developing markets. The group's strategic initiatives and policy frameworks aim to foster greater global collaboration, address systemic risks, and promote equitable growth. By leveraging its collective strengths, BRICS continues to enhance its role in shaping global

The Multilateralism of the New Development Bank on the Sustainable Economic Growth in BRICS Nations and Beyond, 47–64

doi:10.1108/978-1-83662-292-520251006

governance and addressing both financial and environmental challenges, striving for a balanced and inclusive international order.

Keywords: BRICS; NDB; climate change; finance agenda; governance

Introduction

The wide spread of "new regionalism" (the theorists of "new regionalism" see the future structure as a complex system of intersecting institutionalized and informal associations – "regions" defined not by physical boundaries but by common tasks), the identification of an effective form of global governance, the search for new forms of interaction in an increasingly complex world, as well as a qualitative new development of interregional cooperation and the emergence of large-scale transregional "megaprojects" are important megatrends of the modern world politics.

In the context of an unprecedented growth of geopolitical risks in the world, there is an increasing awareness that the old architecture of the world order is being replaced by a new configuration of international relations and regional blocs. One of the most important driving forces of this kind of transformation of the world economy is the countries of the Global South, which create their own institutions, regional integration associations, and financial settlement systems. Among the leaders of these processes are the largest emerging markets, primarily the BRICS countries.

BRICS (Brazil, Russia, India, China, and South Africa) are often referred to as the "concert of non-Western powers" or the "club of revisionist powers" (Roberts, 2015). BRICS was formed as a result of an attempt to create a zone of transregional functional interaction outside the control and influence of the West, to form a demonstration model of a more democratic global governance of a polycentric type. This was achieved thanks to the accumulation of influence, potential, and interests of the largest world and regional powers, which have similar geopolitical and geo-economic parameters in certain favorable historical and world political conditions.

This chapter discusses the role of the BRICS as a multilateral agenda of cooperation on international arena and highlights the key directions for development; moving forward, it covers sphere of finance cooperation; next paragraph is dedicated to climate policies of BRICS member states, are distinguished differences and similarities between them; considering already done in finance and climate directions some recommendations for further development are given.

BRICS Multilateral Agenda of Cooperation

The BRICS was formed against the backdrop of expanding discussions about the justice of the world order (especially in connection with the spread of the practice of unilateral actions in world politics), the escalating North-South problem (in particular, the IBSA (India, Brazil, and South Africa) countries that formed the highest level dialogue spread the idea of South-South cooperation for development), in the context of the global economic crisis, as well as the real growth of the economies and political ambitions of the BRICS countries. Thus, the BRICS countries, as evidenced by the analysis of the joint declarations adopted as a result of the annual summits, initially formed a number of common principles and priorities that, from their point of view, could ensure the reform of the world order in a "fair" way (A Fair World Order): the rule of international law and the UN, the rejection of unilateral actions, ensuring sustainable development to the developing world, reforming existing and creating new global, transregional and regional financial and economic institutions, fair representation of developing countries in international institutions, expanding transregional cooperation at all levels.

It should be noted that over the years of its existence – since 2009, when the first summit took place – the group of countries has managed to build up a significant potential for interaction: the New Development Bank (NDB) and a pool of conditional foreign exchange reserves were created; expanded cooperation in other areas: BRICS Academic Forum, BRICS Network University, Business Forum, Urbanization Forum, Banking Forum, Youth Forum, Twin Cities and Municipalities Forum (Losev, 2019; Toloraya, 2015), introduction of the BRICS Pay payment system (Stuenkel, 2016, 268 p.) were established. All this certainly indicates the start of the process of institutionalization of the BRICS.

The strengthening of network interaction within the framework of the association indicates a significant interest both at the state level of business circles and civil society in preserving the association. According to Corresponding Member of the Russian Academy of Sciences S. Afontsev, in a matter of years, the BRICS has gone from an abbreviation to a full-fledged international association, which manifested itself in the creation of the development bank which has the potential to become a new international financial mechanism in the global governance system (Afontsev, 2015).

The BRICS phenomenon began to be seen as a manifestation of the network structure of modern world politics, as well as the network structure of the global governance system. In search of an answer to the imbalance in the global economic system and the chaotic processes in the postbipolar world, the BRICS formed a new system of cooperation – a predominantly informal multifactorial system of interconnected and mutually influencing relations.

From the point of view of the external environment, the BRICS is a transregional association with a "representative" character. This is due not only to objective factors, since the BRICS is formed by the largest regional powers, each of which has the resources and potential to act on behalf of the region or regional association but also by real initiatives, for example, in supporting the large-scale BRICS+ initiative (or BRICS-Outreach) designed to involve regional integration blocs in the orbit of cooperation.

The BRICS agenda covers a large number of areas and a wide range of issues. Currently, in addition to issues of global governance in the economic sphere, as well as the issues of fundamental principles for the development of the world political system, the dialogue of the participating countries is focused on the broad agenda of "pluralistic security" – from poverty alleviation and sustainable development to internet governance and the fight against new challenges. At the annual summits, topical issues of the world politics are included in discussion: for example, the declaration of the BRICS summit in 2018 reflected such issues as the settlement of the Middle East conflict, the consequences of the humanitarian crisis in Yemen, the political situation in Afghanistan and Syria, the denuclearization of the Korean Peninsula (Johannesburg Declaration of the Tenth BRICS Summit, 2018), etc. This indicates that BRICS seeks to form a dialogue on problems and crises of the widest range – of a global, regional, or transregional nature. In addition, all BRICS countries are in the process of searching for a new growth drivers and effective modernization models. The exchange of experience and the launch of joint initiatives within the framework of the BRICS provide significant support to national development models (Stuenkel, 2016, 256 p.). Thus, the set of tactics used in the BRICS includes various techniques – from the strategy of mobility and competition to various types of creativity.

The BRICS has an undoubted potential for embedding in the network format of global governance. One of them is organizational. All five countries are members of key trade, economic and monetary organizations, whether it is the World Trade Organization (WTO), the International Monetary Fund (IMF), or the Group of Twenty, ensuring their influence in the global economy. Political influence is due to the fact that China and Russia are permanent members of the UN Security Council, while everyone else claims this status; all are regional leaders and have undoubted military power. Three states are nuclear powers; Brazil and South Africa belong to the so-called "threshold states." The BRICS format allows five countries to coordinate their positions and act with a single platform within other associations and organizations. This is most clearly manifested in the activities of the G20, on the margins of which the BRICS came up with joint initiatives and positions (on food security, agriculture, etc.), as well as, although to a lesser extent, within the UN (questions on the role of the EU in General Assembly, on Libya).

No less important is the fact that strengthening of ties in the BRICS is also ensured by the expanding social and humanitarian cooperation within the association. Creation of the BRICS Business Forum, forums on healthcare, science and education, sports, tourism, youth affairs, the Forum of twin cities and municipalities, the Council of Regions of the BRICS countries, etc., indicates the formation of a complex multilevel network of interaction not only in the state, but also in nonstate level, as well as a hybrid forms of interaction between state institutions and nonstate actors of the BRICS countries. Such heterogeneity and dynamism of connections contributes to the maintenance and development of the polylogue culture.

Finance Cooperation Within the BRICS

The key factor in the development of the modern world economy is the intensification of international trade and investment activities. The BRICS is an important interstate association for determining the vector of development of world economic relations due to the fact that its members have significant economic, investment, raw materials, and demographic potential; they account for about 30% of global gross domestic product (GDP) at purchasing power parity (PPP), 16% of world trade, 12% of outgoing investments, and they cover 40% of the world's population and 29% of the global territory (The World Bank, 2019), taking an active part in the activities of international financial institutions and working to reform the system of global governance and maintain the stability of the international trading system.

One of the key areas for cooperation is enhancing trade and investment ties by increasing the number of free and preferential trade agreements. This includes reducing barriers to foreign direct investment in strategic sectors and easing restrictions on the movement of capital between BRICS member states and regional groups. Currently, trade relations between BRICS members are being strengthened, which confirms the existence of significant potential for further development of cooperation and creates prerequisites for enhancing economic growth in the member states. For example, in May 2018, an agreement was signed on trade and economic cooperation between the Eurasian Economic Union (EAEU) and People's Republic of China (PRC): the parties continue to discuss options for developing interaction in terms of linking the EAEU and the PRC's Belt and Road initiative. The aim is to create a new liberalization mechanisms and optimization of trade relations, ensuring the interconnection of infrastructure and free movement of capital in order to implement the joint idea of forming a free trade zone between China and the EAEU in the future. As part of cooperation with the Latin American region, in December 2018, a memorandum of understanding was signed between the EAEU and the South American association Mercosur, which determines the framework for future relations between the parties, on the basis of which priority areas of cooperation will be selected for joint work to expand economic and trade ties between states (TASS, 2018). In addition, Mercosur expressed desire to sign an agreement on a free trade zone with the EAEU (Eurasia Expert, 2018), and members of this association are actively cooperating with the Eurasian Economic Union in the direction of trade liberalization.

Within the framework of the BRICS finance cooperation agenda, several significant trends can be identified. A promising institution contributing to the enhancement of BRICS economic growth and unlocking investment potential is the BRICS Export Credit Agencies Association. Currently, this cooperation is primarily technical, focusing on the exchange of experience and best practices. Nevertheless, representatives from the member countries acknowledge the vital role this group of organizations plays in promoting trade within the association and supporting exporters from the five member countries. As part of the BRICS+ initiative, the possibility of significantly expanding the role of this initiative through joint support of projects for the supply of products from the BRICS to third countries is being discussed, which is confirmed by the provisions of the memorandum of understanding and cooperation between the export credit agencies of the BRICS countries, signed within the framework of the VI BRICS Summit in 2014.

Another important trend is cooperation between development banks and other development institutions established by the BRICS countries, which lays the foundation for expanding investment cooperation by pooling resources in order to implement large-scale sustainable development projects in the BRICS countries. At the same time, the central role in this process should be played by the New Development Bank (hereinafter referred to as the NDB), which is able to take a leading position in supporting the development of the activities of the BRICS economic entities through commitment to the principles of equality and mutually beneficial cooperation, focus on creating prerequisites for sustainable social and economic growth of the BRICS, as well as through the use of various – including innovative and financing – instruments. For example, as part of these operations, the NDB decided in April 2017 to provide a $300 million loan to the Brazilian Development Institute to implement several renewable energy projects. In May 2018, the NDB signed a memorandum of understanding with the Development Bank of Southern Africa (DBSA) (The New Development Bank, 2018a), and in July of the same year, the NDB management decided to allocate 300 USD million for the development of projects in the field of renewable energy sources (The New Development Bank, 2018b).

Expanding the use of national currencies, creating their own reserve currencies and payment systems is also an up-to-date trend within the BRICS. There are factors pointing to the possibility of using the BRICS countries as a platform for more active use of the national currencies of the member states (in particular, the ruble, yuan, and Indian rupee) in trade and investment transactions, which will ultimately reduce the share of the US dollar and euro in mutual settlements of the parties, as well as significantly simplify their interaction. The turnover of mutual trade in the BRICS national currencies is gradually increasing. For example, in 2018, the share of settlements in rubles between Russia and India was 20% for exports and 21% for imports. The volume of project financing by the BRICS Development Bank in the currencies of the member states continues to grow: in October 2017, the NDB decided to finance projects in China in the amount of 5 billion yuan (GBTIMES, 2017). In May 2018, NDB announced its intention to place a bonded loan in the same currency in the amount of 5 billion (Reuters, 2018). Another currency used by the NDB for operations is the Indian rupee. In the future, the NDB intends to expand borrowing in the BRICS markets and, in particular, place bonds in the amount of about $300 million in the currency of India, which has a developed offshore rupee market. However, in the long term, an important condition guaranteeing the expanded use of more national currencies within the BRICS framework is their stability: over the past few years, developing countries have experienced a period of high exchange rate volatility, which creates serious risks for the implementation of the set of goals (for example, in July 2018, the devaluation of the South African rand was 7%, the Brazilian real – 10%, and a moderate devaluation of the Chinese yuan was recorded; The International Monetary Fund, 2018). The expansion of the use of the BRICS national currencies is important for strengthening the positions of the countries of this association in the global financial system. In turn, the internationalization of the national currencies of the BRICS states acts as the most important condition for the implementation of this initiative. At present, of all the countries of

BRICS, the PRC currency (yuan) holds the largest share in the total volume of international payments – 1.61% (RMB Tracker, 2018). Consequently, the further development of trade and investment relations of the BRICS participants, subject to the use of national currencies, will allow in the future to significantly increase the volume of gold and foreign exchange reserves of central banks by including additional currencies of partner countries in their composition. In addition, the expansion of the foreign economic activity of the BRICS and their partners by simplifying the procedure for mutual settlements can be facilitated by the implementation of the initiative to create a new international payment card system in the BRICS and BRICS+ format (Plas Magazine). Currently, four BRICS countries already have national payment systems (hereinafter referred to as NPS): Russia has a national payment card system Mir, India has RuPay, Brazil has ELO, and China has established own international payment system China UnionPay. However, none of the listed NPS, with the exception of China, has a strong external position.

Participation in the process of formation of regional and international financial centers is one more trend. Experts point the possibility of strengthening cooperation between BRICS and other regional blocs through the formation of international financial centers (hereinafter referred to as the IFC) through the circulation of shares of the BRICS and BRICS+ companies on the exchanges of partner countries. Currently, the Exchange Alliance is functioning, created by the BRICS interstate group and providing cross-listing of derivative financial instruments for stock indices of five countries, which are traded on the participants' platforms in national currencies (Official website of the Alliance of Exchange Stocks). Considering the results achieved, it can be concluded that the BRICS and BRICS+ mechanisms, firstly, contribute to the activation of economic growth in developing countries and, secondly, lays the foundation for the development of integration processes throughout the developing world.

Multilateral trade agreements with settlements in the national currencies of the BRICS countries are last but not the least most important trend within BRICS format of cooperation. At the same time, the following will contribute to the increase in demand for national currencies:

- implementation by central banks of prudential measures aimed at maintaining currency stability – establishing more stringent requirements for loans denominated in foreign currencies compared to loans denominated in national currencies, application of more stringent foreign exchange liquidity risk ratios compared to international standards, development of additional requirements for provisioning for possible losses on loans and equivalent assets;
- conclusion of bilateral swap agreements in national currencies between the BRICS and BRICS+ central banks designed to support international trade relations;
- creation of clearing centers for settlements in BRICS+ national currencies in order to simplify the use of participants' currencies in international economic activity;

- maintenance of the trade balance between the partner states, i.e., maintaining close volumes of exports and imports to ensure the stability of trade in national currencies and eliminate the need to regulate the volume of trade with usage of US dollar;
- pursuing a coordinated monetary policy by harmonizing the legislation of the countries in the field of foreign exchange regulation and foreign exchange control, as well as easing control over the movement of capital.

Simplification of regimes for foreign investors contributes in ensuring the sustainable development agenda for collaboration. The optimization of financial cooperation between the BRICS+ countries is facilitated by:

- creation of a fair (nondiscriminatory) legal system to ensure a flexible and open regulatory regime by eliminating the shortcomings of national legislation in terms of protecting property rights and reforming the judiciary;
- improvement of the tax regimes of the participating states, aimed at increasing their attractiveness for foreign investors by clearly defining the general framework of tax procedures, including the audit, collection and organization of the activities of tax authorities, and guaranteeing a balance between the rights of taxpayers and tax administration;
- formation of conditions for the development of investment activities, which imply consistency and predictability of the investment policy, and an increase in the transparency of the investment environment due to the expansion of exchange trading between the BRICS and BRICS+ countries, the introduction of strict requirements for professional participants in the securities market and the procedure for the operation of trading floors, and also due to the convergence of national regulatory standards with international standards;
- ensuring the development of urban infrastructure, improving its quality and accessibility in order to create the necessary conditions for attracting investment through the creation of new jobs and the development of financial services in national currencies.

Climate Policies of BRICS Member States: Differences and Similarities

The increase in the concentration of greenhouse gases in the Earth's atmosphere is the main factor in destabilizing the climate of the planet. Among the world leaders in greenhouse gas emissions, the BRICS countries occupy a significant place. In 2018, these countries produced 43% of all anthropogenic CO_2 emissions (16.6 billion tons), which is almost twice as much as that of the G7 countries (8.8 billion tons) and five times more than EU countries (Crippa et al., 2019).

By the beginning of the third decade of the 21st century, the BRICS has turned into a global ecological "leviathan," on whose "behavior" the life of the whole planet depends. The rapid economic development of the countries of the group since the early 1990s (with the exception of Russia) was inextricably linked with an increase in the consumption of natural resources and an increased impact on the environment. In 1991–2017, consumption of energy and material resources by these states increased in absolute terms from 14.4 to 49 billion tons (The Material Flow Analysis Portal, 2020). The use of resources by China increased 6 times, India – 2.5 times, Brazil – 2 times. At the same time, CO_2 emissions increased during this period in China by 332%, in India – by 300%, Brazil – by 122%, and South Africa – by 60% (in Russia, it decreased by 33%).

The continued economic growth of the BRICS countries, necessary to achieve the sustainable development goals by 2030, will further increase carbon emissions. And, as a result, without a comprehensive and deep involvement of the group in solving the climate problem, the stabilization of the global geosystem is impossible. In 2015, the countries of the group signed the Paris Agreement. From this moment, their positions in international climate diplomacy are moving away from the principle of "renunciation of obligations" to reduce greenhouse gas emissions to the principle of "common but differentiated responsibility." The commitment by the Chinese side to achieve carbon neutrality by 2060 clearly demonstrates significant shift in international climate policy. In other BRICS countries (primarily India, Brazil, and South Africa), the green economy is also developing rapidly. India occupies one of the leading places in the world in terms of the pace of construction of renewable energy sources (RES). Russia in these processes is assigned the role of an "outsider" of the BRICS group.

The BRICS countries have played and are playing an important and active role in shaping international climate policy. However, their position was assessed until 2015 as "restraining" decisive action in this area. Until 2011, the BRICS countries did not have common positions on global climate policy issues. At the beginning of the negotiation process within the framework of the Conference of the Parties (COP), they were in various groupings of states with common interests. Russia was included in the group of countries committed to reduce greenhouse gas emissions by 2000. Brazil, India, China, and South Africa, on the contrary, until 2015 were not bound by any international obligations in this area. Historical factors, the structure of the economy, national, social, and cultural characteristics, as well as low GDP per capita, the Human Development Index (HDI), and a huge lag behind the West in the social sphere are directly reflected in this position. Until 2011, especially India and China categorically refused to take on any obligations to limit emissions. In addition, they insisted on technological and financial assistance from developed countries. It is thanks to the persistence of China and India that the COP in Copenhagen (2009) decided to establish a Global Green Fund for Environmental Modernization and Climate Adaptation of Less Developed Countries.

Russia, as a country with a high dependence of the economy on the extraction and export of hydrocarbon raw materials, has followed (and still adheres to) a climate policy that protects its oil and gas complex. Russia's interests coincided with the goals of the Organization of the Petroleum Exporting Countries (OPEC) (1st Conference of the Parties in 1995), and later with the JUSSCANNZ countries, with which the Russian side forms the so-called "umbrella group" in the negotiation process. This subgroup is characterized by a skeptical position regarding the causes of global warming and the effectiveness of certain tools in combating it.

At a conference in Lima, the BRICS countries recognized the proclaimed principle of the "common but differentiated responsibility" in stabilizing the planet's climate, and already in 2015, they signed the Treaty of Paris and ratified it in 2016. Each of these states submitted a national climate strategy to the UN.

The common positions of BRICS countries on the issue of global climate change and the fight against it were first announced at the III BRICS Summit in China in 2011 (Rusakova, 2016), when the final document emphasized the will of the BRICS countries to promote the implementation of the UN Climate Convention, and increasing cooperation between countries to adapt economies and societies to climate change. In 2012, Article 30 of the Final Declaration of the IV Summit noted that BRICS countries are determined to play their role in the global fight against climate change and to contribute to global efforts to combat climate change through sustainable and inclusive growth, rather than through the imposition of restrictions on development (Delhi Declaration, 2012, p. 6).

Orientation toward further economic growth through the introduction of a new, environmental technology has since become the "core" of the climate policy of these countries.

At the next summits of the BRICS countries, the topic of global climate change was increasingly included in the circle of the main political issues discussed. The declarations adopted at the summits in Ufa (2015), Goa (2016), Xiamen (2017), Johannesburg (2018), Brasilia (2019), and Moscow (2020) expand the unified position of countries in the field of global climate policy through common aspirations in the framework of sustainable development, the balance of social, economic, and environmental growth, and the development of "clean" energy sources and "green" technologies.

The position of the BRICS countries in international climate diplomacy is characterized, on the one hand, by upholding their right to "development" (further economic growth and increasing CO_2 emissions), on the other hand, by understanding the need for environmental modernization of their economies, strengthening energy and resource efficiency of own production, wide introduction of "clean," "green" technologies, environmental protection. This largely determines the national climate policy of these countries, which is increasingly moving away from the doctrine of "growth at any cost" to a policy of "quality growth," where environmental, social, and economic goals do not contradict each other but create a complex unity.

However, there are noticeable differences among the BRICS countries in assessing the importance of climate policy and green technologies in the development of states. At the summits chaired by China, India, and Brazil, these topics were one of the priorities (Larionova, 2015). On the contrary, under the chairmanship of Russia and South Africa at the BRICS summits, the topics of global climate change and the "green economy" were paid less attention.

The national climate policy of the BRICS countries is formed on the basis of the interaction of a whole complex of both external and internal factors. In initiating local measures to reduce greenhouse gases and adapt societies to climate change, a significant role is played by the global climate regime (since 2015 – the Paris Agreement), which creates a legal framework for the formation and implementation of national policy in the field of climate. The financial mechanisms for climate stabilization in the North-South system (CDM, REDD, Green Climate Fund) formed at the COP further stimulate the formation of climate policy in developing countries, including the countries of the grouping. At the same time, the national climate policy of the BRICS countries covers numerous intertwined internal socioeconomic, political, demographic, and environmental factors. In India, South Africa, and Brazil, many social problems (poverty, hunger, unemployment, lack of housing, sanitary conditions) are particularly acute. And as a result, their elimination is a priority of the sustainable development policy of these countries without which it is impossible to solve them (upholding the right to economic growth of these countries was especially clearly demonstrated at the 25th COP in Madrid in December 2019) (UN News, 2019). However, economic growth causes significant internal environmental problems, so the ecological transformation of the economies of these countries to achieve climate goals is considered by their leaders as a tool for solving these national problems.

China is the world leader in anthropogenic carbon emissions; in 2018, the country produced 11.3 billion tons of CO_2 (27.5% of global emissions), which is almost 9 billion tons more than in 1990 (Crippa et al., 2019). Economic growth has become the main cause of a sharp deterioration in the purity of air, water, and soil in many regions of China. The progression of population diseases associated with poor environmental conditions forced the leadership to rethink the concept of economic development, which was reflected in China's five-year development plans. In particular, the program of the 11th five-year plan (2006–2011) outlined tasks to eliminate environmental problems and reduce the consumption of natural resources, declared the transformation of the Chinese economy in the direction of a cyclical economy (closed economy), and the creation of an energy-efficient and environmentally conscious society (Government of China).

In the 12th five-year plan, adopted in 2011, the word "transformation" already receives a specific semantic content:

> The transformation of the mode of economic development should focus on the importance of creating a resource-saving and environmentally friendly society to save energy, reduce emissions greenhouse gases and combating global climate change. We must develop a closed circular economy and new decarbonization technologies. (China Direct, pp. 2–3)

In the 13th five-year plan (2016–2021), environmental modernization has become a priority among the seven main directions of the country's development. The transition to the "new economy" is enshrined in government legislation: the Circular Economy Promotion Law (2009), the Energy Conservation Law (2007), the Green Production Law (Cleaner Production Promotion Law, 2003), spatial planning and conservation laws (Land Administration Law, 1999; Environmental Protection Law, 2015).

In 2015, China signed the Paris Agreement and made voluntary commitments to reduce greenhouse gas emissions: according to these commitments, the peak of CO_2 emissions in the country will be reached in 2030, which is approximately 17.6 billion tons. After 2030, this indicator is expected to decrease.

The results of the implementation of the plans for the ecological transformation of the Chinese economy have no analogues in the world today. The capacity of produced renewable electricity increased in the country in the period 1996–2019 from 3 to 464 GW, which accounted for 32.2% of the world's renewable energy capacities. In 2019, China became the world leader in the production of solar electricity (204 GW) and wind energy (236 GW). In the same year, the capacity of Chinese alternative renewable energy was 1.2 times higher than that of all EU countries, 2.2 times the United States, 5 times India, and more than 6 times Japan (Renewables, 2020).

The ecological transformation of the Chinese energy sector is going hand in hand with the unprecedented pace of electromobilization of the population in the world, the development of climate-neutral models of living and production. At the same time, China is implementing a large-scale greening program for the country's desert territories (the so-called China Green Wall). In the period 2013–2020, the government allocated 34.5 billion US dollars for the creation of new forest areas, and by 2050, forests should be planted in the west of the country on an area comparable to the territory of Western European countries (more than 400 thousand sq. km) (Telepolis, 2020).

India's National Action Plan on Climate Change (Government of India) was adopted in 2008 as the main political document defining India's national climate policy. It outlines eight main directions aimed at reducing greenhouse gas emissions and adapting Indian society to changing external conditions. Among the directions are the development of solar energy, improving the energy efficiency of society, improving the sustainability of the human environment, increasing the efficiency of water use, protecting the Himalayan ecosystem, new forest plantations, sustainable agricultural policy, and the creation of a climate change research fund.

Considerable attention is paid to climate transformation in development programs for a number of industries. According to the national green economy development strategy, the share of renewable energy by 2030 should be 40% (Renewables, 2020). It is planned to build "solar parks" (25 parks by 2022), develop wind power (60 GW), hydro and bioenergy, as well as the construction of nuclear power plants (up to 63 GW in 2032) (Green Growth and Sustainable Development in India, 2015).

As part of its efforts to create a sustainable human living environment, the Government of India intends to build about 100 smart cities that will improve the quality of life in a changing climate. Plans are outlined for recycling solid waste within a closed economy, wastewater treatment. Particularly noteworthy is the Green India Mission, which proposes the expansion of forest areas to 6 million hectares (Government of India).

Brazil's national climate protection policy began to take shape at the end of the first decade of the 21st century. In 2009, the Parliament adopted a resolution on the national climate protection policy. In 2012, the Law for the Protection of the country's primary forests came into force, and in 2015, Brazil signed the Paris Agreement. In 2016, a national strategy for climate stabilization was adopted, according to which the measures planned by the government will lead to a reduction in CO_2 emissions by about 16% by 2030 (United Nations Framework Convention on Climate Change). It is planned to increase the share of renewable energy sources to 45% by 2030, increasing the energy efficiency of production and transport, introducing "clean" technologies into industry, increasing the production and consumption of biofuels, and expanding the area of forests by 12 million hectares.

South Africa ranks first in Africa for carbon emissions. In 2018, the level of emissions amounted to 477 million tons of CO_2 in absolute terms, an increase of 165 million tons compared to 1990 (Crippa et al., 2019). According to the national strategy, South Africa is committed to controlling CO_2 emissions in the period 2025–2030 within the limits of 398–614 million tons (NDC Registry UNO). A wide range of planned indicators indicates the existence of various scenarios for the country's economic development. Like other BRICS countries, South Africa is focusing on the development of a "green economy" in achieving climate goals. The country demonstrates particularly significant potential in the field of renewable energy, ranking third in the world in terms of the amount of incoming solar energy per unit of territory and possessing an impressive potential for wind energy production.

However, in terms of the pace of development of alternative energy, South Africa is a noticeably inferior to China, India, and Brazil. The problem is that part of the South African population (15%) does not have access to electricity at all. More than 43% of the country's population is classified as "energy" poor, only partially able to pay electricity tariffs, which negatively affects investment in alternative sources. While the share of renewable energy in the overall structure of electricity production in 2019 was only 3.1%, in 1996–2018, its production increased from 60 million kWh to 6.4 billion kWh43. According to government plans, the share of RES will increase by 2030 to 9% (Renewables, 2020).

The climate policy of Russia began to take shape in the early 1990s, which predetermined the creation in 2009 of the Climate Doctrine of the Russian Federation, according to which Russia undertakes to implement a comprehensive climate policy, takes measures to adapt to climate change, mitigates anthropogenic impact on climate, strengthens international cooperation in this area, and reduces greenhouse gas emissions by 2020 by 25% compared with emissions in 1990 (Climate Doctrine of the Russian Federation, 2009).

Compared to other BRICS countries, Russia's domestic climate policy is characterized by excessive "restraint" in carrying out "green" transformations and only timid steps toward environmental modernization. Thus, in the Russian Federation, it is planned to increase the share of alternative energy sources to 4.5% by 2024, further development of nuclear energy as climate neutral is being stimulated. At the same time, one of the huge problems is the dependence of economic and social life on the extraction and export of fuel resources, since the fuel and energy complex is the "foundation" of the Russian economy (about 60% of its commodity exports) (Rosstat).

Equally important is the significant reduction in Russia's share of global CO_2 emissions due to the already felt negative effects of climate change. Droughts, fires, and floods cause enormous financial damage to both individual regions of Russia and its economy as a whole and lead to social and political destabilization of the country. It should be expected that the frequency of these phenomena (forest fires, droughts, floods, etc.) caused by global climate change will increase. However, BRICS joint efforts to manage with the problems of the climate change can significantly contribute to Russian and other BRICS member-states policies.

Recommendations

The BRICS countries' role in global financial institutions does not explicitly reflect their increased economic weight in the world economy. As shown by the already implemented and still discussed among the BRICS initiatives, member states are actively looking for their place in the global financial and economic order. To bring changes into the world monetary and financial system, they are making efforts in two directions: trying through consolidated pressure to increase their competence and specific weight in decision-making in existing institutions of the global economic management, as well as simultaneously create new financial institutions. In general, the vector of efforts of the BRICS countries is aimed at raising their positions and the positions of other developing countries in the international arena. This seems to be not an easy task; however, following suggestions might be helpful on this way:

- increasing role of BRICS national currencies in the international monetary and financial system;
- integration of payment systems and cards;
- creation of the BRICS own independent rating agency.

Speaking about climate agenda, as for the third decade of the XXI century, BRICS member states are the world leaders in greenhouse gas emissions (more than 40% of global CO_2 emissions). Without a comprehensive climate transformation of the societies of its member countries, achievement of the main goal of the Paris Agreement (keeping the growth of global average air temperatures by 2100 at the level of 1.5–2°C) is not feasible.

BRICS countries stand for sustainable economic growth through the introduction of new, environmentally friendly technologies, and against restrictive measures, hindering their economic development. China, India, Brazil, and South Africa are undertaking numerous environmental transformation projects aimed at decarbonizing their economies and achieving carbon neutrality. Particularly profound changes are noticeable in the energy sector.

All in all, BRICS countries are "key" players in international climate diplomacy. For further effectiveness:

- it is necessary to think about the assistance that countries can provide to their partners within the organization (sharing new "green" technologies, experiences, common efforts to develop new models of economic development that take into account economic constraints, etc.);
- it is necessary to provide other organizations with information about the developments that are in the BRICS;
- BRICS could use the conceptual shell of the "green economy" foundation;
- the main mission of the BRICS should be aimed at offering some ideas and developing models of economic growth that take into account environmental constraints. The primary source of environmental problems is growing consumption, so it needs to be restrained, and BRICS needs to bring this issue to the global discussion;
- it is a vital coordinated work on the development of international standards for green finance (in the BRICS countries, it is the cheapest way to reduce emissions).

Conclusion

The current world political situation and the state of inter-economic cooperation between the peoples of different countries are among the important external factors that continually influence changes in the BRICS agenda.

The BRICS countries have made outstanding achievements in the field of financial and economic cooperation. First, the BRICS countries continue to deepen their economic cooperation. Second, the creation of appropriate mechanisms marked the beginning of a new stage of financial cooperation among the BRICS countries. In this regard, the establishment of economic institutions in 2014, particularly the NDB and the Pool of Conditional Foreign Exchange Reserves, is a critical step for the institutionalization of the association. Third, the advancement of the BRICS countries in the reform of international financial institutions has resulted in an increase in the representation of emerging market and developing countries. In addition, BRICS alliance offers effective solutions to many global issues, such as combating money laundering, anti-corruption cooperation, climate change, food security, and energy, which helps to enhance the role of BRICS in global governance. The interaction of development banks in the implementation of large-scale investment projects creates the conditions for financing development programs that are important for the national economies of partner countries on more flexible terms using a variety of instruments to ensure sustainable socioeconomic growth of developing countries.

BRICS countries are the "key" players in international climate diplomacy, having been speaking since 2011 with a unified position in international negotiations under the Convention on Climate Change (17th Conference of the Parties). This position was voiced in the Declaration of the III BRICS Summit as a “common but differentiated responsibility” of the countries of the world in the fight against global warming. The members of the group insist on their right to further economic growth, eliminate internal social problems, and improve the welfare of the population. Their climate doctrines and national goals differ from those in the developed countries of the world. In addition, among the countries of the group, there are significant differences in the degree of assessment of the threat of global climate change and the need for environmental modernization (decarbonization) of the economies of states, which is reflected in the structure of the declarations of the BRICS summits. Most of the participating states are planning to increase greenhouse gas emissions by 2030 while carrying out extensive activities for the environmental modernization of their farms. At the same time, the countries of the group are rapidly modernizing urban and transport infrastructure, increasing the energy and resource efficiency of production and increasing the share of “clean” technologies. Cooperation in this area between states will continue to deepen.

References

“A Fair World Order”, the most common wording in BRICS declarations and statements by the leaders of the member-countries. Data and other conclusions of the BRICS in the annual declarations on the results of the summits of the member-countries: Joint Heads of State on the results of the I and II BRICS summits in Yekaterinburg (2009) and Brazil (2010). http://www.nkibrics.ru/. Accessed on 06 12, 2022.

Afontsev, S. (2015). Global economic management: New challenges and initiatives. In V. Baranovsky & N. Ivanova (Eds.), *Global management: Opportunities and risks/ otv* (315 p.). IMEMO RAN.

China Direct. *Delegation of the European Union in China: China's 12th five-year plan 2011-2015.* https://cbi.typepad.com/china_direct/2011/05/chinas-twelfth-five-new-plan-the-full-english-version.html. Accessed on 07 18, 2022.

Climate doctrine of the Russian Federation, President of Russia. (2009). http://kremlin.ru/events/president/news/6365. Accessed on 07 19, 2022.

Commodity structure of exports of the Russian Federation. Rosstat. http://old.gks.ru/wps/wcm/connect/rosstat_main/rosstat/ru/statistics/ftrade/. Accessed on 07 25, 2022.

Crippa, M., Oreggioni, G. D., Monforti-Ferrario, F., Muntean, M., Schaaf, E., Guizzardi, D., Solazzo, E., Duerr, M., Perry, M., & Vignati, E. (2019). *Fossil CO2 and GHG emissions of all world countries 2019.* Publications Office of the European Union. https://doi.org/10.2760/687800

Delhi Declaration. (2012). *President of Russia.* http://kremlin.ru/supplement/1189. Accessed on 07 03, 2022.

Eurasia Expert. (2018). *Mercosur wants to sign an agreement on a free trade zone with the EAEU.* http://eurasia.expert/merkosur-khochet-podpisat-s-eaes-soglashenie-o-zone-svobodnoy-torgovli/. Accessed on 06 10, 2022.

GBTIMES. (2017). *New Development Bank approves 5bn yuan loan for Chinese projects.* https://gbtimes.com/newdevelopmentbankapproves5bnyuanloanchineseprojects. Accessed on 06 25, 2022.

Green growth and sustainable development in India, towards the 2030 development agenda. (2015). https://www.teriin.org/projects/green/pdf/National_SPM.pdf. Accessed on 07 23, 2022.

India's national action plan on climate change, Government of India. http://www.nicra-icar.in/nicrarevised/images/Mission%20Documents/National-Action-Plan-on-Climate-Change.pdf. Accessed on June 22, 2022 and July 22, 2022.

Intended nationally determined contribution towards achieving the objective of the United Nations Framework Convention on climate change. UNO. https://www4.unfccc.int/sites/ndcstaging/PublishedDocuments/Brazil%20First/BRAZIL%20iNDC%20english%20FINAL.pdf. Accessed on 07 22, 2022.

Johannesburg Declaration of the Tenth BRICS Summit. (2018). http://www.kremlin.ru/supplement/5323. Accessed on 05 17, 2022.

Larionova, M. (2015). South Africa's BRICS presidency: Regional power at the helm of a Global Governance Forum. *Vestnik RUDN. International Relations*, *15*(1), 125–134.

Losev, A. (2019). *BRICS pay – The unified payment system of the BRICS countries.* Valdai Club. http://ru.valdaiclub.com/a/highlights/brics-pay/. Accessed on 05 14, 2022.

NDC Registry UNO. UNO. https://www4.unfccc.int/sites/NDCStaging/pages/All.aspx. Accessed on 07 22, 2022.

New international payment card system: BRICS. *Plas magazine*. https://www.plusworld.ru/professionals/novaya-mezhdunarodnaya-sistema-platezhnyh-kart-briks¬dalee-vezde-2/. Accessed on 06 20, 2022.

Official website of the Alliance of Exchange Stocks of the BRICS countries. http://www.bricsmart.org/index.html. Accessed on 07 01, 2022.

Renewables 2020. Global status report. (2020). https://www.ren21.net/wp-content/uploads/2019/05/gsr_2020_full_report_en.pdf. Accessed on July 18, 2022 and July 19, 2022.

Reuters. (2018). *Update BRICS development bank to issue $ 780 million in yuan denominated bonds*. https://www.reuters.com/article/chinabricsbank/update1bricsdevelopmentbanktoissue780millioninyuandenominatedbondsidUSL3N1SZ3SQ. Accessed on 05 27, 2022.

RMB Tracker. (2018). *RMB internationalisation: Where we are and what we can expect in 2018*. SWIFT.

Roberts, C. (2015). *Are the BRICS building a non-western concert of powers?* The National Interest. http://nationalinterest.org/feature/are-the-brics-building-non-western-concert-powers-13280. Accessed on 06 18, 2022.

Rusakova, Y. (2016). *Problems of international environmental security and search for diplomatic ways to overcome them at the present stage (case of contemporary negotiations on climate)*. MGIMO University.

Stuenkel, O. (2016). *The BRICS and the future of global order*. Lexington Books.

TASS. (2018). *Mercosur and the EAEU signed a memorandum of understanding.* https://tass.ru/ekonomika/5924097. Accessed on 06 02, 2022.

Telepolis. (2020). *Chinas Grüne Große Mauer*. https://www.heise.de/tp/features/Chinas-Gruene-Grosse-Mauer-4638653.html. Accessed on 06 27, 2022.

The 11th five-year plan: Targets, paths and policy orientation, Government of China. http://www.gov.cn/english/special/115y_index.htm. Accessed on 07 12, 2022.

The International Monetary Fund. (2018). *World economic outlook update. Less even expansion, rising trade tensions.*

The Material Flow Analysis Portal. (2020). *Domestic extraction of world in 1970—2017.* http://www.materialflows.net/visualisation-centre/data-visualisations/. Accessed on 07 07, 2022.

The New Development Bank. (2018a). *Memorandum of understanding between the New Development Bank and the Development Bank of Southern Africa on general cooperation.*

The New Development Bank. (2018b). *Greenhouse gas emissions reduction and energy sector development project. Project summary for public disclosure.* https://www.ndb.int/wpcontent/uploads/2018/07/DBSASouthAfrica.pdf. Accessed on 07 09, 2022.

The World Bank. (2019). *World Bank Group flagship report. Global economic prospects. Darkening skies.*

Toloraya, G. (Ed.). (2015). *BRICS Academic Forum (7th)* (518 p.). NCR BRICS.

UN News. (2019). *Results of the conference in Madrid: Small steps, but still there is progress.* https://news.un.org/ru/interview/2019/12/1369571. Accessed on 07 12, 2022.

Chapter 5

De-dollarization, the New Development Bank, and BRICS Trade Currency Changing Multilateralism and Geopolitical Arrangements

Ndivhuho Tshikovhi[a], *Fulufhelo Netswera*[a] *and Bruno De Conti*[b]

[a]Durban University of Technology, South Africa
[b]University of Campinas, Brazil

Abstract

The US dollar (USD) has served as a global reserve currency over the past eight decades without contest. Also referred to as the Petrodollar, the US dollar has been perceived as a hegemonic currency that is detrimental to the economic aspirations of the developing world for many years. Recent efforts by developing countries to diversify their currency reserves away from the US dollar have raised serious anxieties in the Global North as much as it has raised hopes about the new dawn for the economies of the Global South away from unfettered US dollar dominance. However, a possible transition from the US dollar as a reserve currency worldwide is far more complex as the emerging economies, especially Brazil, Russia, India, China, and South Africa (BRICS), have not necessarily embraced a singular stance beyond the general acceptance that the status quo can no longer hold. The potential decline of the US dollar's role in global finance presents a conundrum that deserves dedicated scholarly inquiry. The implications of the de-dollarization for the BRICS nations at this juncture are opportune enough to deserve an academic inquiry. Therefore, this study examines the role of the BRICS banks in the rising power of de-dollarization.

Keywords: De-dollarization; BRICS; NDB; finance; currency; US dollar; multilateralism

The Multilateralism of the New Development Bank on the Sustainable Economic Growth in BRICS Nations and Beyond, 65–79

doi:10.1108/978-1-83662-292-520251007

Introduction

De-dollarization refers to the process by which countries reduce their reliance on the US dollar in international trade and finance (Ize & Yeyati, 2006). The US dollar has long been the dominant currency in global markets, serving as the primary medium for international trade, a major reserve currency for central banks, and a benchmark for commodity pricing. This dominance has afforded the US significant economic and political influence worldwide (Yeyati, 2021). However, several nations, particularly within the BRICS group – comprising Brazil, Russia, India, China, and South Africa – are seeking to diminish this dependency. A combination of economic, strategic, and geopolitical factors drives this movement toward de-dollarization. For the BRICS nations, de-dollarization holds particular significance. These countries represent some of the world's largest and most dynamic emerging markets, collectively accounting for a substantial share of global gross domestic product (GDP) and population (Liu & Papa, 2022). The reliance on the US dollar exposes these nations to vulnerabilities, such as exchange rate risks, economic sanctions, and the monetary policies of the United States. By reducing their dependence on the dollar, BRICS countries aim to enhance their economic sovereignty, stabilize their financial systems, and foster greater cooperation within the group. Moreover, successful de-dollarization could lead to a more multipolar global financial system with significant implications for global trade and economic stability.

The hegemony of the US dollar on the international monetary system caused several controversies over the years, going back to Valéry Giscard d'Estaing denouncing the "privilege exorbitant" in the 1960s. Currently, dollar dominance means that policy in third countries, particularly emerging economies, is constrained by financial spillovers (Vicquéry, 2022). It can also be claimed that the label was the first strand of the "global role" of currencies, reflecting its standing as a significant currency in the global economy. In contrast, the second strand can also be labeled as the somewhat narrower "international role," taking into consideration the use of a currency outside its constituency of issuance country of origin. Empirical studies suggest that both concepts can be interrelated: currencies that are used heavily outside their constituencies are more likely to play a significant globally, and conversely, currencies that are globally significant are likely to be used more heavily outside their constituencies.

Notably, both notions are conceptually related; the same factors do not necessarily drive them and do not necessarily have the same implications for policy. Despite the conceptual similarity, both strands of the literature analysis have largely used the same quantitative basis, namely the use of currencies in the international debt securities market (Thimann, 2008). The main objective of this chapter is to demonstrate the limitations of how global currencies have established measures concerning multilateralism and trading globally, which affects the geopolitics in the so-called new world order. The first strand of literature on the "global role of currencies" has yet to entertain the emerging economies' voice on the potential brink of the Dolla as the main international currency for national and global trading and debt markets. This chapter adds some new perspectives, findings, and policy implications in the advent of de-dollarization.

The main objective of this chapter is to explore the de-dollarization efforts of BRICS nations, examining their motivations, strategies, and historical context behind international financial architecture. The key research questions addressed in this study are:

- What are the primary drivers behind the de-dollarization efforts in BRICS countries?
- What strategies have BRICS nations employed to reduce their reliance on the US dollar?
- What lessons are to be drawn from the past currencies and financial institutions?

By doing so, the chap contributes to the understanding of global financial dynamics and the evolving role of BRICS plus nations in the international monetary system.

Literature Review

The US dollar's pre-eminence in global trade and finance can be traced back to the Bretton Woods Conference of 1944, which established the dollar as the central currency of the international monetary system. This arrangement was based on fixed exchange rates, with the dollar convertible to gold, positioning the US dollar as the world's primary reserve currency. Even after the collapse of the Bretton Woods system in 1971, the dollar retained its dominant status due to the size and stability of the US economy, its deep and liquid financial markets, and the widespread trust in its institutions (Cohen, 2012). The dominance of the dollar has conferred significant advantages on the United States, including lower borrowing costs and the ability to run large trade deficits. It has also allowed the United States to exert considerable economic and political influence globally. However, this dominance has been challenging, as it subjects other countries to the monetary policies of the US Federal Reserve and exposes them to potential economic sanctions (Eichengreen, 2011).

Theoretical Frameworks on De-dollarization

De-dollarization can be examined through various theoretical lenses, including the concepts of currency hegemony, monetary sovereignty, and financial stability. Currency hegemony refers to the dominant position of one currency in the international monetary system, which can create vulnerabilities for other countries. Monetary sovereignty is the capacity of a state to regulate its currency and monetary policy independently, which can be compromised by reliance on a foreign currency. Financial stability theory suggests that reducing exposure to foreign currency risks can enhance a country's economic stability (Gandolfo & Trionfetti, 2014). These frameworks underscore the motivations behind de-dollarization efforts as countries seek to mitigate the risks associated with dollar dependence and enhance their economic autonomy. By diversifying their currency holdings and promoting the use of alternative currencies, countries aim to achieve greater monetary sovereignty and financial stability.

Several studies (Ize & Yeyati, 2006; Szetela et al., 2016; Yeyati, 2021) have examined the de-dollarization initiatives of BRICS nations, highlighting their strategies, successes, and challenges. China has been at the forefront of these efforts, with its strategy centered on the internationalization of the yuan (Renminbi). The Chinese government has pursued a multifaceted approach, including establishing offshore yuan markets, promoting the use of the yuan in trade and investment, and creating financial institutions such as the Asian Infrastructure Investment Bank (AIIB) to support its currency's global use (Lee, 2014). Russia has also been proactive in its de-dollarization efforts, particularly in response to economic sanctions imposed by Western countries. The Russian government has sought to reduce its reliance on the dollar by increasing the use of the ruble in trade, developing bilateral currency swap agreements, and accumulating gold reserves (Korhonen & Ledyaeva, 2010). These measures aim to insulate the Russian economy from external shocks and enhance its financial resilience. India, Brazil, and South Africa have also pursued de-dollarization strategies, albeit to varying degrees. India's approach has included promoting the use of the rupee in international trade, particularly with neighboring countries and key trading partners. Brazil has focused on regional initiatives, such as the creation of a common currency for South American nations. At the same time, South Africa has implemented policies to encourage the use of the rand in regional trade (Armijo, 2007).

The international debt market reflects about one-tenth of the global bond market (Tran, 2021). It includes all debt securities issued by nonresidents of a certain currency geographical location. The largest issuers in this market are globally operating financial institutions and corporations, such as banks and microfinance institutions. They choose internationally available and easily accessible currencies – mainly the US dollar, the EUR, and the Japanese YEN – to finance part of their operations outside their home markets. European banks and corporations dominate the international debt market for US dollars.

In contrast, the European market represented by EUR is dominated by investment banks and corporations from the United States, the United Kingdom (UK), and a sizable other European country outside the EUR area. Previously, sovereign issuers from developing economies were also significant. However, given their vastly improved financial position, only a number of people have been tapping this market on a large scale in recent years. There is a tension between the experience of US dollar hegemony pointing to a strong network that is found all over the world effects and a winner-takes-all equilibrium and the financial stability risk implied by a hegemonic supplier of global safe assets. To challenge this tension, policymakers outside the United States, such as the BRICS nations and others, have called for a more multipolar international monetary system underpinned by both technological changes in the financial infrastructure and enhanced international monetary coordination (Vicquéry, 2022). Historical parallels, based on past quantitative work on international currencies, played a crucial role in shaping a more optimistic view of multipolarity in the international monetary system.

Global Currencies and Their Depolarization Debates

The history of currencies is deeply intertwined with the development of economies and societies. Since 1450, there have been six major world reserve currency periods: Portugal (1450–1530), Spain (1530–1640), the Netherlands (1640–1720), France (1720–1815), Great Britain (1815–1920), and the United States from 1921 to today. The average currency span is 94 years (Eichengreen et al., 2018).

The gold standard originated in 1819 when the United Kingdom officially adopted gold as the basis for its currency. It provided a standard measure of value, simplifying trade and reducing transaction costs. This was followed by several countries in Europe, then Japan and the United States, as they adopted the gold standard later in the 19th and 20th centuries. Given the pre-eminence of the United Kingdom in world trade and finance, London was the center of the Investment Management Standard (IMS), which was built on the gold standard. Under the gold standard, the main objective of the central bank was to preserve the official parity between its currency and gold. It was further supported by the global trade enabled and maintained as a fixed price of gold by all participants in the system, more so during the British colonial expansion, which, in turn, ensured fixed exchange rates between their currencies (Angeloni et al., 2011).

The interwar period saw three regimes: general floating from 1919 to 1925, the gold exchange standard from 1926 to 1931, and managed floating from 1932 to 1939. The United States returned to gold in 1919, but other countries, including the United Kingdom, continued to let their currencies float freely for several years after the war. After 1925, when the United Kingdom returned to the gold standard by pegging sterling to gold at its prewar parity, the IMS evolved into a gold exchange standard, a variant of the prewar system. The new fixed-exchange-rate system added a new category of international reserves to gold, currencies fully backed by gold, mainly sterling and the dollar, in the hope of avoiding the problem of gold shortage that had at times plagued the gold standard (Eichengreen et al., 2018).

As expected, advanced economy currencies dominate in virtually all size components, and their weight in global financial markets is well above their share in global GDP (68.5%) or global trade (47.9%). These economies account for 90% of global debt securities outstanding and 80.2% of the global stock market capitalization. Financial institutions of advanced economies are dominant debt issuers, with US financial institutions alone accounting for one-fifth of the global debt market. In advanced economies, the US dollar's weight is particularly important, owing to its share in the global equity market, which is at least twice that of the euro in terms of capitalization, number of listed companies, and turnover. The evolution of currencies has been a cornerstone in the development of human societies, enabling trade, economic stability, and growth from ancient barter systems to the Danis guilder, British pound, and US dollar.

Danish Guilder, British Pound, US Dollar

The Danish guilder (rigsdaler) played a significant role in Denmark's economic history, serving as a foundational currency through various periods of financial reforms and modernization. However, the start of the European Monetary System (EMS) represented another milestone between European countries in the post–World War II period. The initial steps in that direction were taken in 1950 with the establishment of the European Payments Union, which was established to facilitate settlements of international trade transactions between European nations. The year 1951 saw efforts to promote trade relations inside the European zone through the removal of trade barriers by creating the European Coal and Steel Community. This arrangement was made possible by countries such as Germany, France, Belgium, Luxembourg, the Netherlands, and Italy, who removed restrictions on the trading of raw steel and coal (Pinsky & Kvasnicka, 1979). The EMS started its operation in March 1979 with an ambitious target of establishing a zone of intra-European exchange rates and monetary stability. The most remembered feature of the EMS is the Exchange Rate Mechanism (ERM). The first countries to participate in the ERM in 1979 were Belgium, Denmark, France, Germany, Italy, Ireland, and the Netherlands. Few then joined later: Spain in 1989, Britain in 1990, and Portugal in 1992. The participants in the ERM are required to establish a bilateral exchange rate grid, which is a set of bilateral central parity rates of the ERM currencies (Woo, 1999).

In contrast, the British pound's history reflects the broader economic and political changes in the United Kingdom. The United Kingdom and France had been the main global monetary and financial powers since the beginning of the 1800s; the role of Germany as a capital exporter only goes back to the nation's unification, which took place in 1871. Before then, Hamburg marked banco as the German factor since 1820. The Hamburg mark banco had long played a role as an international currency issued in the main silver-based financial center of Europe. Therefore, it is clear that there is no historical justification for the US dollar in the pre-1914 global currency horse race (Costigan et al., 2017). The United States was a catching-up capital importer for most of the century, with US dollar reserves only in neighboring countries such as Canada and a lower share of global reserves with the Dutch guilders and Scandinavian currencies in Europe (Rogoff, 2001). In the interwar period (1918–1939), the British sterling, the US dollar, and the French franc are considered. The German mark never approached the 5% share threshold of global reserves in the interwar period, and it was symbolized by the deep instability, including hyperinflation, the "transfer problem" related to war indemnities, and strict capital controls after the 1931 banking crisis.

During the International Monetary Fund (IMF), voting rights were shared largely based on the quotas for special drawing rights. The United States now holds 16.52% of the votes, followed by Japan with 6.15%, China with 6.09%, and Germany with 5.32%. Some other European and BRICS plus nations hold between 5% and 1%, even though most other countries are below 1.23%. Given that some important decisions – including changes in voting shares – require a supermajority of 85%, the United States (and only the United States!) can veto such decisions (Herzog, 2021).

Breton Woods and the Adoption of the Gold Standard

The adoption of the gold standard and the Bretton Woods system represent two pivotal moments in the history of global economic policy. Both systems sought to bring stability and predictability to international trade and finance, albeit through different mechanisms. The Bretton Woods system emerged from the Bretton Woods Conference held in 1944, attended by representatives from 44 Allied nations. The primary goal was to create a framework for international economic cooperation and prevent the competitive devaluations that had contributed to the Great Depression (Bordo, 1993). The idea was contingent in the sense that the public understands that the suspension will only last for the duration of the wartime emergency, plus some period adjustments. It assumes that the government will follow the deflationary policies necessary to resume payments at the original parity.

Under Bretton Woods, countries agreed to peg their currencies to the US dollar, which was convertible to gold at 35 US dollar per ounce. This created a system of fixed exchange rates, providing stability and predictability in international trade (Angeloni et al., 2011). Both the gold standard and the Bretton Woods system sought to provide a stable framework for international economic transactions, but they did so through different mechanisms. The gold standard's rigidity contrasted with the more flexible, yet still structured, approach of Bretton Woods. While the gold standard constrained monetary policy, Bretton Woods allowed for some degree of adjustment, which contributed to its initial success. The legacy of these systems is profound. The gold standard's emphasis on stability and discipline influenced subsequent monetary policies, while the Bretton Woods system laid the groundwork for contemporary international economic institutions and cooperation (Duesterberg, 2023).

Despite its successes, the Bretton Woods system faced challenges. Persistent trade imbalances, particularly with the United States running large deficits, led to concerns about the dollar's convertibility to gold. By the late 1960s, the US gold reserves needed to be increased to cover the amount of dollars held by foreign governments. This led to a crisis of confidence, and in 1971, President Richard Nixon suspended the dollar's convertibility to gold, effectively ending the Bretton Woods system (Rached, 2019). The adoption of the gold standard and the establishment of the Bretton Woods system were significant milestones in the history of global economic policy. Each system reflected the economic challenges and priorities of its time, aiming to bring stability and predictability to international trade and finance. Despite their eventual collapse, the principles underlying these systems continue to influence modern economic policies and the ongoing quest for a stable and equitable global economic order.

The Fiat Currencies and what Keeps Them Afloat. Petrodollar and Nixon 1971

For a while, the system of floating exchange rates implemented in the mid-1970s seemed well suited to achieving policymakers' goals of full employment, stable prices, and sustainable current account positions. Gradually, however, this hope dissipated, notably because the key players' macroeconomic policies were often not consistent with international monetary stability, and foreign exchange markets tended to overshoot before adjusting to equilibrium (Costigan et al., 2017).

If one asks what the term "money" means in international contexts, one immediately gets to the heart of the matter: there is no "global" currency, only the different currencies issued by the central banks of different countries. And these are not equal: some currencies, mostly the dollar and the euro, serve as global reserve currencies. They are held by public and private institutions all over the world because they are most used for international financial transactions. They are seen as stable, reliable, and liquid, and thus most useful for protecting oneself against external shocks, e.g., shifts in commodity prices. Roughly 56% of the global reserves are held in dollars, followed by over 18% in euros, and much smaller shares in Chinese renminbi, Japanese yen, British pound sterling, and Canadian and Australian dollars, respectively (Herzog, 2021).

Money is a man-made institution, and in times of challenges, when trust breaks down, it is the backing up by powerful reserve banks that keeps stabilizing the monetary system of liquidity provision within nations with closed economies and their currencies; in other instances, the national central banks can back up the system. In a globalized world without a global sovereign, powerful countries can issue liquidity that plays this role. For instance, it can decide to soften the budget constraints of some financial institutions to prevent the implosion of the system. However, it has discretion about who gets access to such lifelines (Szetela et al., 2016). There is clear evidence that at least some elements of multipolarity have already been presented as the first globalization in the 19th century. It is evident that by 1870, three blocs based on different monetary standards coexisted: the gold one around the British Empire, the bimetallic one around France, and the silver one, spanning from Eastern Europe to Asia (Thimann, 2008). French monetary diplomats attempted a harmonization of the international monetary system around the French franc in the 1860s. As the 1870 Franco-Prussian war destabilized the French external position and prevented effective cooperation with the newly formed German Empire (Flandreau, 1996), a global movement toward the gold standard occurred (Eichengreen et al., 2018).

Crucial changes took place in the functioning of the international monetary system toward the end of the 1990s. Following financial crises in the second half of the 1990s and early 2000s, where a series of developing countries, especially in Latin America but also in East Asia, gave up exchange-rate pegs and moved to flexible exchange-rate regimes to avoid large exchange-rate variations. In contrast, another group, including dominant players like China and most oil-exporting Middle East countries, maintained various kinds of fixed exchange-rate regimes. The late 1990s was also the beginning of a historically unprecedented emergence of global imbalances, both in terms of current account surpluses and deficits and reserve accumulation (Samay, 2022).

The Gold Gobbling by Emerging Economies

In recent years, emerging economies have significantly increased their gold reserves, a phenomenon often referred to as "gold gobbling." This strategic accumulation of gold reflects these nations' desire to diversify their foreign exchange reserves, reduce reliance on the US dollar, and enhance financial stability (Reinsberg et al., 2022). Nevertheless emerging market currencies continue to have a smaller weight in terms of the global financial market size than currencies of developed economies. Interestingly, stock markets are more than twice as important as debt markets, with global shares of 14.6% and 6.4%, respectively. For instance, Hong Kong and China combined in 2024 are estimated to rank fifth in global stock market capitalization, after the United States, the European area, Japan, and the United Kingdom. Almost one-quarter of globally listed firms are listed on Emerging Markets Economies (EME) stock markets, illustrating strong numerical participation in these markets. EME markets are also relatively important in terms of raising new capital through initial public offerings (IPO) (about 24%), reflecting a buoyant growth in new access to these markets and IPO activity, especially in Hong Kong and mainland China.

If EME currencies are to play a greater international role, this is likely to come first through stock markets, where they are a more important player than in global debt markets. The picture could shift somewhat once the renminbi becomes convertible, as outstanding government debt in China is relatively high in absolute terms and almost stands at the same level as in the United Kingdom (Thimann, 2008). The phenomenon of gold gobbling by emerging economies is a strategic response to various economic, financial, and geopolitical challenges. By increasing their gold reserves, countries aim to diversify their assets, hedge against inflation, enhance financial stability, and assert economic sovereignty. This trend has significant implications for global gold markets, currency dynamics, and geopolitical relations, reflecting the evolving landscape of international economic power. As these economies continue to grow and assert their influence, their strategies regarding gold accumulation will remain a critical factor in global economic policy and stability.

In the year 2007, the IMF was given a mandate for surveillance over members' exchange rates, in which the United States was supposed to inform China that the value of its currency was below the appropriate requirements by IMF systems. The discussions around the so-called "unfair currency manipulation" have had official status in US law for over two decades and in the IMF Articles of Agreement for far longer despite its protectionist status. In practice, the supposed injunction on surplus countries to revalue upward has yet to be enforced, in contrast to the pressure on deficit countries to devalue. Some would say it is time to rectify the asymmetry (Szetela et al., 2016) despite the IMF being infamous for its structural adjustment programs, which require countries to undertake policy reforms in exchange for loans. EME countries can still diversify their reserves, reducing reliance on any single currency, particularly the US dollar. Yet, not only do countries routinely fail to implement these reforms, but they also frequently return to the IMF to start the process afresh (Reinsberg et al., 2022).

BRICS Economies and the New Development Bank

The BRICS nations – Brazil, Russia, India, China, and South Africa – represent some of the largest and most dynamic emerging markets in the world.

Collectively, they account for over 40% of the global population and approximately 25% of the world's GDP (Maria et al., 2023). These countries have diverse economic structures, ranging from the manufacturing powerhouse of China to the resource-rich economies of Russia and Brazil. Despite their differences, all BRICS nations share a common goal of enhancing their economic sovereignty and reducing their reliance on the US dollar. China, the largest economy among the BRICS, has experienced rapid industrialization and urbanization, propelling it to become the world's second-largest economy. India, with its vast and youthful population, has shown significant growth in the services and technology sectors (Rached, 2019). Russia, endowed with substantial natural resources, relies heavily on oil and gas exports. Brazil, the largest economy in Latin America, benefits from its agricultural and mineral wealth. South Africa, the most industrialized economy in Africa, has a well-developed financial sector and abundant mineral resources.

BRICS countries have taken various steps to implement trade currency changes (Tiwari et al., 2021). These include establishing bilateral swap agreements, developing payment systems that bypass traditional Western-dominated networks, and creating frameworks for the settlement of trade in local currencies. For instance, China and Russia have increased the use of their respective currencies, the yuan and the ruble, in bilateral trade. Similarly, India has initiated efforts to settle trade with BRICS partners in Indian rupees. These measures aim to facilitate smoother and more secure trade transactions while reducing exposure to external economic pressures. BRICS nations have also focused on developing regional financial institutions to support their de-dollarization efforts (Vidal et al., 2022). The New Development Bank (NDB), established by BRICS countries in 2014, is a key institution in this regard. The NDB provides financial support for infrastructure and sustainable development projects in BRICS and other emerging economies, promoting the use of local currencies in its operations. Another significant initiative is the Contingent Reserve Arrangement (CRA), which provides a financial safety net for BRICS countries in times of liquidity crises. By pooling resources, the CRA aims to reduce the reliance on the IMF and the US dollar in times of economic distress (Bruno & Shin, 2020).

Promoting the use of local currencies in trade is a critical component of the de-dollarization strategies of BRICS nations. China has made substantial progress in this area, with the yuan increasingly used in trade settlements and financial transactions. The launch of the Cross-Border Interbank Payment System (CIPS) has further facilitated the international use of the yuan. Russia has also promoted the use of the ruble in trade, particularly in energy transactions with countries like China and Turkey. India has encouraged the use of the rupee in trade with neighboring countries and key partners, aiming to reduce dependence on the dollar. Brazil and South Africa, while facing challenges in promoting their currencies internationally, have nonetheless taken steps to encourage regional trade in local currencies. These efforts contribute to a gradual shift away from the dollar in BRICS trade. Chinese banks have a presence in nearly all major regions of the world and have extended financing to countries that traditional lending institutions have shied away from or shut out. Having recently helped to find two new multilateral development banks, the NDB and the Asian Infrastructure Investment Bank, along with 13 regional and bilateral funds, China's role in development finance appears to be set for continued growth (Singh, 2020).

The initiatives by BRICS, particularly through the NDB and trade currency changes, signify a shift in global power dynamics. By challenging the dominance of Western financial institutions, BRICS nations are advocating for a more balanced and equitable global economic order. The NDB serves as a tangible symbol of this shift, offering an alternative source of funding and reducing the influence of the IMF and World Bank. This development underscores the emergence of a multipolar world where multiple power centers coexist and collaborate (Cooper & Flemes, 2013). The United States and the West, along with the international financial institutions that they dominate, such as the IMF and World Bank, notoriously have required recipient countries to implement harsh policy reforms as a precondition for access to financing, often requiring nations to slash social spending, privatize public institutions, and liberalize the economy in order to meet those conditions (Fischer et al., 2003). The emergence of alternatives, such as the NDBs, brought about a new international financial institution to counter the United States and the West's financial dominance.

BRICS' efforts to enhance financial cooperation and create alternative financial mechanisms have implications for global governance (Hao, 2020). The NDB and trade currency initiatives position BRICS as influential players in shaping international economic policies. By promoting principles of inclusivity and sustainability, BRICS nations advocate for reforms in global governance structures that better represent the interests of emerging economies. This approach challenges the traditional Western-centric model and calls for a more democratic and participatory framework in global decision-making. BRICS nations leverage their financial initiatives to bolster regional influence. The NDB's investments in infrastructure projects enhance connectivity and economic integration within regions, strengthening BRICS' geopolitical standing (Braga et al., 2022). For example, China's Belt and Road Initiative (BRI), supported by the NDB, extends its influence across Asia, Africa, and Europe. Similarly, Brazil's involvement in regional infrastructure projects enhances its leadership in South America. These efforts underscore BRICS' strategic use of economic tools to enhance their geopolitical influence.

The changes in the NDB and BRICS trade currencies represent significant advancements in promoting financial autonomy and sustainable development. These initiatives challenge the dominance of Western financial institutions and advocate for a more inclusive and equitable global economic order.

Challenges and Opportunities for BRICS Plus Nations in a De-dollarized World

Despite the progress made by BRICS nations in their de-dollarization efforts, several challenges remain. These include:

- Economic Challenges include the limited acceptance of local currencies in global markets, exchange rate volatility, and the need for robust financial infrastructure.
- Political Challenges: Geopolitical tensions, domestic political instability, and resistance from established financial institutions and markets.

The successful de-dollarization of BRICS nations presents several opportunities, including:

- Economic Sovereignty: Enhanced control over monetary policy and reduced vulnerability to external shocks.
- Financial Stability: Diversification of foreign exchange reserves and reduced exposure to dollar fluctuations.
- Global Financial System: Promotion of a multipolar financial system, reducing the dominance of the US dollar and fostering greater global economic stability.

The de-dollarization efforts of BRICS nations have the potential to reshape the global financial landscape, promoting greater economic sovereignty and stability.

Conclusion

This chapter has explored the de-dollarization efforts of BRICS nations, analyzing their motivations, strategies, and outcomes. The key findings of this study suggest that the motivations are born out of the desire to enhance the BRICS nation's economic sovereignty, reduce vulnerability to US monetary policy and sanctions, and promote financial stability. Both economic and geopolitical considerations drive the pursuit of de-dollarization. De-dollarization strategies employed by BRICS countries have varied in their attempt to reduce their reliance on the US dollar. These strategies include establishing trade agreements and currency swaps, developing regional financial institutions, and promoting the use of local currencies in trade and investment. Each country has tailored its approach to its specific economic and geopolitical context. Evidently, for centuries, currencies have been seen – beyond their economic functions – as symbols of sovereignty. In the current environment of globalization, currencies are often seen as symbols of the economic and financial strength of economic areas in an international context.

Furthermore, this chapter has argued that the size of the underlying economy, as well as the size and stage of development of its financial markets, together with the soundness of the respective governance structure are the relevant variables in the geopolitics of the day. The analysis of the currencies and their genesis indicated a structural development containing information that is also relevant from a policy point of view. Policymakers in BRICS and the West are continuously reforming their economy to international trade and capital flows, the development of the domestic financial market in terms of instruments, regulation, and oversight, and the credibility of the overall policy framework.

Finally, the analysis of this study has important implications for policymakers and global trade; for instance, policymakers in BRICS nations should continue to pursue measures that promote the use of local currencies in international trade and finance. This includes strengthening financial infrastructure, expanding bilateral currency swap agreements, and fostering regional financial cooperation. De-dollarization can contribute to greater financial stability by reducing exposure to exchange rate risks and external economic shocks. BRICS nations should prioritize the development of robust financial markets and institutions to support their currencies. The de-dollarization efforts of BRICS nations have the potential to promote a more balanced and stable global financial system. This shift could reduce the dominance of the US dollar and encourage greater use of multiple currencies in international trade and finance.

References

Angeloni, I., Bénassy-Quéré, A., Carton, B., Destais, C., Darvas, Z., Pisani-Ferry, J., & Sapir, A. (2011). Global currencies for tomorrow: A European perspective. *Bruegel Blueprint*, *13*(2 August 2011).

Armijo, L. E. (2007). The BRICs countries (Brazil, Russia, India, and China) as analytical category: Mirage or insight? *Asian Perspective*, *31*(4), 7–42.

Bordo, M. D. (1993). *The gold standard, Bretton Woods and other monetary regimes: An historical appraisal.* National Bureau of Economic Research.

Braga, J. P., De Conti, B., & Magacho, G. (2022). The New Development Bank (NDB) as a mission-oriented institution for just ecological transitions: A case study approach to BRICS sustainable infrastructure investment. *Revista Tempo do Mundo*, (29), 139–164.

Bruno, V., & Shin, H. S. (2020). Currency depreciation and emerging market corporate distress. *Management Science*, *66*(5), 1935–1961.

Cohen, B. J. (2012). The benefits and costs of an international currency: Getting the calculus right. *Open Economies Review*, *23*, 13–31.

Cooper, A. F., & Flemes, D. (2013). Foreign policy strategies of emerging powers in a multipolar world: An introductory review. *Third World Quarterly*, *34*(6), 943–962.

Costigan, T., Cottle, D., & Keys, A. (2017). The US dollar as the global reserve currency: Implications for US hegemony. *World Review of Political Economy*, *8*(1), 104–122.

Duesterberg, T. J. (2023). *China's economic weakness and challenge to the Bretton Woods system: How should the US respond?* Hudson Institute.

Eichengreen, B. (2011). *Exorbitant privilege: The rise and fall of the dollar and the future of the international monetary system.* Oxford University Press.

Eichengreen, B., Mehl, A., & Chitu, L. (2018). *How global currencies work: Past, present, and future*. Princeton University Press.

Fischer, S., Meltzer, A. H., Sachs, J. D., & Stern, N. (2003). The future of the IMF and world bank: Panel discussion. *The American Economic Review*, *93*(2), 45–50.

Flandreau, M. (1996). The French crime of 1873: An essay on the emergence of the international gold standard, 1870–1880. *The Journal of Economic History*, *56*(4), 862–897.

Gandolfo, G., & Trionfetti, F. (2014). *International trade theory and policy*. Springer.

Hao, W. (2020). The BRICS countries and the global financial governance. In *The BRICS studies* (pp. 130–148). Routledge. https://www.taylorfrancis.com/chapters/edit/10.4324/9780367492212-8/brics-countries-global-financial-governance-wang-hao

Herzog, L. (2021). Global reserve currencies from the perspective of structural global justice: Distribution and domination. *Critical Review of International Social and Political Philosophy*, *24*(7), 931–953.

Ize, A., & Yeyati, E. L. (2006). Financial de-dollarization: Is it for real? In A. Armas, A. Ize, & E. L. Yeyati (Eds.), *Financial dollarization. Procyclicality of financial systems in Asia*. Palgrave Macmillan. https://doi.org/10.1057/9780230380257_3

Korhonen, I., & Ledyaeva, S. (2010). Trade linkages and macroeconomic effects of the price of oil. *Energy Economics*, *32*(4), 848–856.

Lee, J. W. (2014). Will the renminbi emerge as an international reserve currency? *The World Economy*, *37*(1), 42–62.

Liu, Z. Z., & Papa, M. (2022). *Can BRICS de-dollarize the global financial system?* Cambridge University Press.

Maria, A., Ndivhuho, T., & Nirmala, D. (2023). *Global inequality: Will the BRICS countries succeed in 'steering' the global economy*. Valdai Discussion Club, Issue. https://valdaiclub.com/files/43341/

Pinsky, N. J., & Kvasnicka, J. G. (1979). The European monetary system. *Economic Perspectives, Federal Reserve Bank of Chicago*, *3*, 19.

Rached, G. (2019). BRICS and the emergent countries in the twenty-first century: Discussing contemporary perspectives. In *Revisiting regionalism and the contemporary world order* (p. 83). https://library.oapen.org/bitstream/handle/20.500.12657/53300/9783847414971.pdf?sequence=1#page=84

Reinsberg, B., Stubbs, T., & Kentikelenis, A. (2022). Compliance, defiance, and the dependency trap: International Monetary Fund program interruptions and their impact on capital markets. *Regulation & Governance*, *16*(4), 1022–1041.

Rogoff, K. (2001). Why not a global currency? *The American Economic Review*, *91*(2), 243–247.

Samay, M. A. (2022). *The dynamics of Eurasian comprehensive security, political and economic cooperation*. Budapesti Corvinus Egyetem.

Singh, A. (2020). The myth of 'debt-trap diplomacy' and realities of Chinese development finance. *Third World Quarterly*, *42*(2), 239–253.

Szetela, B., Mentel, G., & Gędek, S. (2016). Dependency analysis between bitcoin and selected global currencies. *Dynamic Econometric Models*, *16*, 133–144.

Thimann, C. (2008). Global roles of currencies. *International Finance*, *11*(3), 211–245.

Tiwari, A. K., Taufemback, C. G., & Kumar, S. (2021). A sequential Bayesian change-point analysis of BRICS currency returns. *Journal of Quantitative Economics*, *19*, 393–402.

Tran, Q. T. (2021). Economic policy uncertainty and cost of debt financing: International evidence. *The North American Journal of Economics and Finance*, *57*, 101419.

Vicquéry, R. (2022). *The rise and fall of global currencies over two centuries*. Banque de France Working Paper No. 882. https://papers.ssrn.com/sol3/papers.cfm?abstract_id=4205564

Vidal, J. A., Hoyle, D. F., Vargas, K. L., & Vásquez, V. M. (2022). Policies for transactional de-dollarization: A laboratory study. *Journal of Economic Behavior and Organization*, *200*, 31–54.

Woo, K.-Y. (1999). Cointegration analysis of the intensity of the ERM currencies under the European Monetary System. *Journal of International Financial Markets, Institutions and Money*, *9*(4), 393–405.

Yeyati, E. L. (2021). Financial dollarization and de-dollarization in the new millennium. https://elischolar.library.yale.edu/cgi/viewcontent.cgi?article=15677&&context=ypfs-documents&&sei-redir=1&referer=https%253A%252F%252Fscholar.google.com%252Fscholar%253Fhl%253Den%2526as_sdt%253D0%252C5%2526q%253Dfinancial%252Bde%252Bdollarization%252Band%252Bde%252Bdollarization%252Bin%252Bmilenium#search=%22financial%20de%20dollarization%20de%20dollarization%20milenium%22

Part II

The Role of NDB in Supporting Sustainability

Chapter 6

NDB and SDGs: Does the Bank Fulfill Its Mandate?[1]

Leonid Grigoryev and Alexandra Morozkina

HSE University, Financial Research Institute of the Ministry of Finance of the Russian Federation, Russia

Abstract

Multilateral development banks (MDBs) have long played an important role in resolving of international challenges, including though research cooperation. They are believed to be less politically engaged than bilateral development assistance programs and therefore better positioned to form the global agenda. The New Development Bank (NDB), in its turn, is an especially important player among MDBs, since it is one of the few institutions with the world's largest economies as its cofounders, but without any of the G7 economies. In 2020, it showed its ability to provide well-timed and effective loans to its members during crises, approving the first NDB Emergency Assistance Program in Combating COVID-19 in March 2020.

In this chapter, we discuss changes to the global sustainable development agenda and the NDB's contribution to sustainable development goals (SDGs) in member countries, potential instruments, and priority sectors in the longer-term and implications for the global financial architecture, given the changing global economic environment. We have looked at the alignment of NDB projects with the SDGs and concluded that the NDB primarily contributes to SDG 6, SDG 7, SDG 8, and SDG 9, with the latter leading the way with its 49 projects. This is consistent with the Bank's mandate, which highlights infrastructure as a primary sector of investment.

Keywords: NDB; SDGs; multilateral development banks; financing for development; inequality

[1]This chapter is based on the article "NDB and SDGs: Does the bank fulfill its mandate?" *Contemporary World Economy*, *1*(3), published in 2023.

The Multilateralism of the New Development Bank on the Sustainable Economic Growth in BRICS Nations and Beyond, 83–101

Published under exclusive licence by Emerald Publishing Limited
doi:10.1108/978-1-83662-292-520251009

As an innovative institution, NDB has to permanently be up to the challenge of being always new.

Marcos Troyjo,
President of the New Development Bank

Introduction

The shocks of the last years severely disrupted global sustainable development plans and require a serious reconsideration of the 2030 agenda. One of the main outcomes of this crisis is increased inequality, within and between countries. As developed countries have been focusing on their own paths out of recession, and their domestic fiscal stimuli have increased on an unprecedented scale, their assistance to developing countries in need was far more modest.

Total official development assistance (ODA) from the Development Assistance Committee (DAC) countries increased by 11% (OECD, n.d.) to $206 billion in 2022. However, the scope and complexity of global needs have increased dramatically during the COVID-19 pandemic: as per the Organization for Economic Cooperation and Development (OECD) estimates, the SDG financing gap increased up to $3.7 trillion in 2020 (Ahmad & Carey, 2021, p. 15). Both these trends – a small increase in assistance and a large increase in development financing needs – have led to a decline in the relative capacity of the ODA. The situation looks especially unfair when one looks at the geographical distribution of assistance: the share of low-income countries as recipients fell by 3.5% to $25 billion in 2020 in comparison to 2019 (Ahmad & Carey, 2021, p. 8). As one might expect, the ODA's priorities had shifted to healthcare and medical needs (especially vaccination) during the pandemic (IHME, 2021).

Disruption of the SDGs and a relative decrease in financing has led to a change in the type of challenges faced by international society, from short-term analysis and measures to deeper layers of problems in terms of adaptation to current and possible future crises and the long-term development agenda. The same applies to development cooperation: the key issue is how to provide support for a number of small countries that have been affected, or less developed countries with significant losses in income. But in the longer term, the key problem is the restoration of growth and a return to the path of development, as well as resolving issues pertaining to adaptation to crises. Regional or systemic banks are expected to follow the deep changes in the global agenda.

The bilateral and multilateral assistance agenda has been shifting in recent years. The 2020 pandemic took the world aback, and all countries had to find their own ways to fight the disease with limited international assistance, rather than it being united international effort. The global agenda started to include more healthcare issues, "new poverty," etc. (Grigoryev & Morozkina, 2022). At the same time, the issue of energy security started to grow in importance (Grigoryev & Medzhidova, 2020). In 2020–2022, global political and economic processes started running ahead of the capability of response of the multilaterals and national governments. The recovery of 2021 came at the same time as the early commodity cycle and was characterized by a delayed recovery in services, but fast growth in consumer demand. Energy and commodity prices have been growing much faster than consumer inflation in general, and there was a danger of stagflation from the 1980s returning. Before any remedies were found and employed, the Special Operation of Russia (February 24, 2022) received a dramatic response in the shape of sanctions from the North Atlantic Treaty Organization (NATO) and the EU countries. It is probably fair to say that the traditional development agenda, global governance, and the path of global economic growth may never be the same as in previous decades.

In these difficult circumstances, multilateral development banks (MDBs), as both research institutions and participants in the system of development assistance, have to play a decisive role in shaping the new framework. They are believed to be less politically engaged (Morozkina, 2019) and thus have a more balanced position in terms of global development and its financing.

This chapter considers the potential role of the MDBs and the New Development Bank (NDB) in particular in updating the sustainable development agenda globally. In the first section, the most recent trends in sustainable development framework and long-term implications are analyzed, while in the second section, the theoretical role of MDBs in sustainable development is examined. In the third part, the data sources and evaluation methodology of the NDB's role in sustainable development are explained. In the fourth section, we look at the activities of the NDB in the field of sustainable development, and in the final section, we give some recommendations on the development of NDB policies.

Latest Trends in SDGs

The shock of the COVID-19 pandemic severely disrupted global sustainable development plans in 2020–2022 and affected all the SDGs. Until 2019, the international community appeared optimistic about the then course of events (based on the UN National Voluntary SDG reports). Discussions relating to the achievement of the SDGs commonly focused on the expected success of the implementation of the SDG agenda by 2030, although, at the same time, achievements on the ground were not impressive in many respects. The recent Global Sustainable Development Report shows pathways for critical transformations needed to accelerate global efforts in terms of development (UN, 2023). The shock caused by the COVID-19 pandemic changed the anticipated early trajectory, disrupted the SDGs, and created a new list of problems to address. For example, the year 2020 demonstrated the unsustainability of some of the results that had been achieved thus far (Sachs et al., 2021). Further, the global average index measuring the performance of countries in terms of the SDGs declined in 2020 for the first time since 2015, and the pandemic and following shocks have already severely affected the first goal (SDG 1, End poverty in all its forms everywhere) as the number of the people living on less than US$1.90 per day has increased by more than 75–95 million people, while at the same time, their proportion of the world population grew from 8.7% in 2019 to 9.6% in 2020 (World Bank, n.d.). Other goals were surely also severely affected, as is shown by the UN (UN, 2023). The proportion of undernourished people increased from 8% in 2019 to 9.8% in 2021 (UN, 2023, p. 10). SDG 3 (Good health and well-being) seems to be no longer achievable with the decline in life expectancy during 2020 in most European countries (EC, 2021). Target 3.3, "By 2030, end… epidemics… and other communicable diseases" appears to be inconsistent with present realities (UN, 2015), especially given the growing number of COVID-19 deaths from 1.8 million in 2020 to 4.8 million in 2021 (Our World in Data, n.d.).

SDG 4 (Quality education) will also require correcting given the mass school closures in 2020 and the effects on education, which are yet to become clear. For example, in April 2020, schools in 173 countries were closed due to lockdowns, and in 7 more countries, schools were kept only partially open (UNESCO, 2021). Given the differences in access to digital education, school closures also increased inequality within and between countries depending on access to online education during lockdowns (Goal 10, Reduced inequalities).

In addition to the above, SDG 8 (Decent work and economic growth) showed a negative performance with rising global unemployment, up from 5.4% in 2019 to 5.8% in 2022 (UN, 2023, p. 14).

SDG 7 (Affordable and clean energy) and SDG 13 (Climate action) were, at first, seen as having gained from the lockdowns. But they did not fare better than the other SDGs in the end, with daily CO_2 emissions eventually increasing and overcoming precrisis levels no later than the beginning of 2021, and in sum being much higher than expected. Total CO_2 emissions in 2020 were only 5.4% lower than in 2019 (Liu et al., 2021); greenhouse gas (GHG) emissions in 2021 had surpassed the 2019 level not only in China but in many other countries, and globally. Coal returned in 2021, even in EU countries. That was a negative signal for the UN Climate Change Conference in Glasgow in November 2021, which was to set new, advanced goals on the climate agenda. There is no shortage of energy globally and, for the most part, regionally.

While high prices for traded energy materials reached new heights in the beginning of 2022, sanctions, and later, the partial embargo for Russia energy exports (also metals and fertilizers) brought the prices to even higher, and rigid, levels. The same should be said about grain prices, dependent also on energy and transportation costs, which in turn depend on policies for cargo shipping and the use of ports. In terms of strategic planning in the development context, we can highlight the key three current challenges: (1) the challenging situation during 2022; (2) the long-term limitation on financing, logistics, and management on the SDG agenda; (3) the change of priorities in the long run for many governments and multilaterals.

The overall effect of the 2020 crisis has been described as "catastrophic" (UN, 2021). It has increased the financing gap for developing countries to overcome the crisis and also to achieve the SDGs by at least 50%, amounting to $3.7 trillion in 2020 (Ahmad & Carey, 2021). The International Monetary Fund (IMF) has also voiced concerns regarding the vaccination gap (IMF, 2021, pp. 2–3).

Given the potential for present conditions to become endemic, and ultimately creating a "new normal," scholars such as Bobylev and Grigoryev (2020), Grigoryev and Medzhidova (2020), and Grigoryev et al. (2021) have proposed some amendments to the SDGs. They suggest that it is necessary to strengthen the concept of the value of human life in the SDGs and propose two options: first, transforming SDG 3 (Good health and well-being) to include health-related indicators from other SDGs, e.g. redistributive impact of fiscal policies (target 10.4), which, among other things, means access to healthcare facilities; second, creating an additional SDG focused on the importance of human life and the risk of epidemics and new diseases (Bobylev & Grigoryev, 2020).

For a long time, the differences between national healthcare systems reflected the institutional settings of societies and taxation systems. Since the COVID-19 pandemic, it is concerning that despite the uneven performance of healthcare systems in developed countries (and we are not talking about developing countries here) at the time of the pandemic, there have been no public calls for reviewing the above-mentioned financial and institutional healthcare framework in the new environment. Of course, it is hard to start such an overhaul in the mid of an ongoing crisis. But the absence of debate on creating more adequate systems in the future looks puzzling, though it is understandable from the viewpoint of vested interests in the existing healthcare systems: the state (state budgets), private financing, companies providing medical drugs, etc. From this viewpoint, and as seen in Table 6.1, there are more questions than answers. Huge differences in healthcare expenditures per capita among the global community have protected people from COVID-19 infections. All countries and medical organizations were doing their best to combat the pandemic, while social and financial problems now look deeper than just managerial and budgeting issues. Unexpectedly, the United

Table 6.1. Differences in Healthcare Systems, Latest Available Data[a] (2020 for Expenditures and March 2022 for the COVID-19 Effect).

	Healthcare Expenditures, Current USD per Capita, 2020	**Cumulative Number of COVID-19 Deaths, % of Population**	**Cumulative Number of Confirmed COVID-19 Cases, % of Population**	**Share of People Fully Vaccinated, % of Population, March 2022**
High-income countries, incl.	*6,176*	*0.19*	*22.3*	*74*
US	11,702	0.30	24.3	66
UK	4,927	0.25	31.5	72
France	4,492	0.21	37.8	78
Germany	5,930	0.16	25.4	75

(Continued)

Table 6.1. *(Continued)*

	Healthcare Expenditures, Current USD per Capita, 2020	Cumulative Number of COVID-19 Deaths, % of Population	Cumulative Number of Confirmed COVID-19 Cases, % of Population	Share of People Fully Vaccinated, % of Population, March 2022
Upper-middle-income countries, incl.	*527*	*0.10*	*4.9*	*76*
Russia	774	0.25	12.2	50
China	583	0.00	0.0	86
Mexico	539	0.25	4.4	61
Brazil	701	0.31	14.1	75
South Africa	490	0.17	6.3	30
Lower-middle-income countries, incl.	*95*	*0.04*	*2.7*	*50*
India	57	0.04	3.1	60
Ukraine	270	0.25	11.4	35
Philippines	165	0.05	3.4	59
Low-income countries, incl.	*34*	*0.01*	*0.3*	*11*
Ethiopia	29	0.01	0.4	18

Source: World Bank (n.d.), Our World in Data (n.d.).

[a]All countries in the World Bank database by income groups (and averages).

States and the United Kingdom also have relatively high rates of deaths during these two years, which are close to the COVID-19 mortality rates reported in Brazil and Mexico. Such correlations are worthy of a call for a review of traditional views on healthcare systems as they relate to the SDGs. At the same time, such adverse results partly explain the difference between the scale of domestic and international reactions of donor countries, as advanced economies struggled with their own difficulties. Multilateral development institutions may play a significant role in such discussions of the ways to increase the sustainability and resilience of social systems, given their expertise and more neutral role.

MDBs in Sustainable Development

The role of MDBs in sustainable development agenda has long been recognized by scholars. There are four key groups of MDB activities in relation to sustainable development recognized by researchers: increase of financing for development, incorporating SDGs in operational process (project requirements and evaluation), promotion of the agenda and norm setting, the mobilization effect on private financing.

Although sometimes MDBs are seen as marginal sources of financing for development in comparison to bilateral financing (Kenny, 2019), generally, international society sees them as an important source of development financing (Avellan et al., 2022; Griffith-Jones, 2016). The role of development banks is particularly important in crises, when multilateral finance usually plays a more counter-cyclical role (Griffith-Jones, 2016; Griffith-Jones & Gottschalk, 2012) than bilateral financial flows. This phenomenon was once more justified in 2020, when six key MDBs (the World Bank, Asian Development Bank [ADB], African Development Bank [AfDB], Inter-American Development Bank [IADB], Asian Infrastructure and Investment Bank [AIIB], NDB) quickly stepped in with a large increase in disbursements. Their collective disbursements increased by 34% in 2020, whereas ODA bilateral disbursement by the Development Assistance Committee rose by only 10% during the same period (Fig. 6.1). For example, the high rating and access to finance allowed the International Bank for Reconstruction and Development (IBRD, part of the

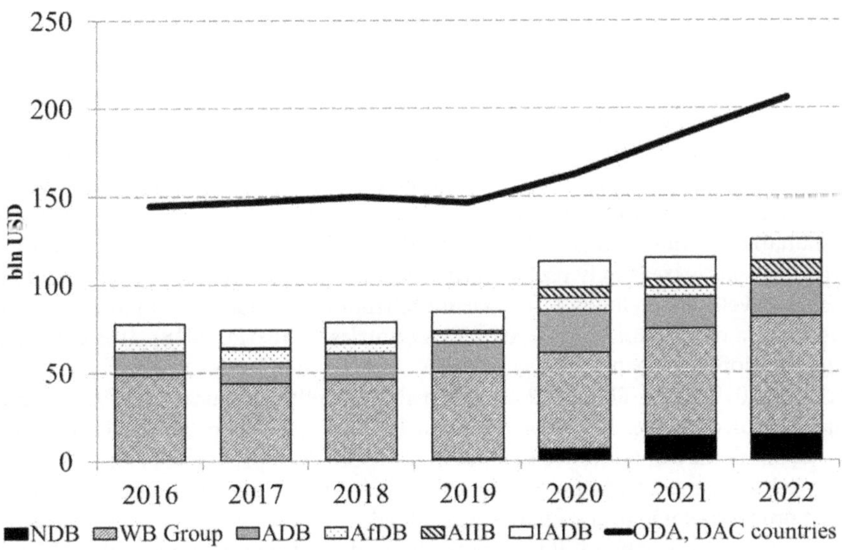

Fig. 6.1. Disbursements of the Key MDBs and ODA of Development Assistance Committee (DAC) Countries, 2016–2022, Billion USD. *Source:* World Bank (2023), NDB (2023), ADB (2023), AfDB (2023), IADB (2022), AIIB (2023), OECD (n.d.).

World Bank Group) to raise $15 billion through sustainable development bonds over a three-day period (World Bank, 2021). Of course, in absolute terms, bilateral ODA from DAC countries is by no means comparable to total disbursements of MDBs because not all of the latter flows are counted as ODA.

The second way to support sustainable development is to align the operations of the bank with it. Günther Handl concludes that MDBs have the ability and "international legal obligation to take sustainable development considerations into account" (Handl, 1998, p. 665). For example, the NDB publishes its contribution to the SDGs in its annual report (NDB, 2021) and takes the sustainability of a project into consideration as one of the criteria for approval (NDB, 2023). MDBs also use innovative financial instruments and play a role in scaling them. Mendez and Houghton (2020) highlight the role of MDBs in promotion of green bonds and emphasize that "MDBs (and other supranational agencies) were green bonds' only issuer before 2012" (Mendez & Houghton, 2020, p. 13).

Some researchers highlight the role of MDBs in development banking as norm promoters (Mendez & Houghton, 2020) and agenda-setters: "the development banks have shaped thinking about what development means and how to go about it" (Bazbauers & Engel, 2021, p. 2). MDBs have carried out substantial pioneering research in the sustainable development sphere (Bhattacharya et al., 2018), publish reports on sustainable development (Gable et al., 2015), and maintain databases. The NDB does not have any publicly available reports or databases in the sphere; however, it made an important step as promoter of the local currency bond market with bond programs in Chinese renminbi, South African rand and Russian rubles, and 20.8% of loans made in local currencies of member countries (cumulative share, NDB, 2023).

And the great majority of researchers stress the mobilization effect of MDBs in sustainable finance (Artecona et al., 2019; Avellan et al., 2022; Bhattacharya et al., 2018; Broccolini et al., 2020). This function has even been placed at the center of the sustainable development financing system. For example, the World Bank states that projects should be financed with public funding only if there is no sustainable private sector solution (OECD, 2021, p. 372), and international organizations increasingly use the term "blended finance" defined as "the strategic use of development finance for the mobilization of additional finance towards sustainable development in developing countries" (OECD, 2018). It is estimated that development bank-backed blended finance can be leveraged at 9:1 ratio (Kenny, 2019, p. 1). The NDB also contributes to the mobilization of sustainable finance: for example, based on the data for projects where the total value of a project is available, authors calculated that $33 billion provided by the NDB was allowed to finance projects totaling more than $80 billion. At the same time, we must note that some of the finance was added by local government entities, so one has to be cautious when talking about the mobilization effect and only take into account the attraction of private finance, rather than just the total project cost.

Overall, MDBs, and the BRICS' NDB in particular, play an important role in global development, especially given the challenges associated with global governance in the current geopolitical circumstances. They are obligated to participate and possibly take the lead in resolving a new set of problems amid limited resources and shifting priorities. Disruption of global logistics and supply chains – for various reasons and in various different ways – will inevitably lead to countries making new attempts to achieve autonomy and independence.[2]

The new hybrid format is coming, with the high intensity of trade regionalization, friend-shoring, and the trend toward self-sufficiency with regards to essential commodities and technologies. Investment projects will reflect not only development needs, financing, and technologies but also issues regarding sanctions, compliance, and export market restrictions. The development objectives will be extremely difficult to reach in such a tough environment.

Data and Methodology

The NDB has a special role in sustainable development. From the beginning, it was mandated to "mobilize resources for infrastructure and sustainable development projects in BRICS and other emerging and developing countries" (BRICS, 2014). As the previous section showed, it contributes to all four areas of MDB support to sustainable development.

Moreover, each one of the NDB's projects can be aligned with SDGs. The Bank itself has developed a special evidence-based method to monitor and report on the alignment of the Bank's financing with the SDGs and published these results in its annual report. This constitutes a major difference as compared with other key development banks such as the World Bank and three large regional banks (ADB, AfDB, IADB). Though they mention SDGs in annual reports, all these banks have adopted various social and environmental strategies and align their operations with SDGs, and they do not regularly publish the direct contribution to SDGs of their projects in their reports or project descriptions.

In this research, we improved the methodology proposed by the NDB. The Bank aligns each project only with one primary goal, whereas other projects have a number of goals, such as the Pará Sustainable Municipalities Project, which develops municipalities in three areas: road paving, sanitation improvement, and enhancement of digitalization.[3] As a consequence, this contributes to three different SDGs, all of which are equally important. Thus, we aligned each of the projects approved by NDB with all of the goals it can contribute to.

In order to calculate the contribution of NDB projects to the SDGs, we analyzed the list of projects publicly available on the NDB web-site. The list of projects contains 126 projects. Out of them, there are 94 approved projects, 27 proposed, and 5 canceled. For the purposes of our analysis, we took only the approved projects totaling $33 billion. Afterward, we used the following scheme:

---

[2]E.g., establishment of independent mechanisms such as new financial settlement mechanisms, bilateral and multilateral trade agreements, climate-related country-specific goals, etc.

[3]New Development Bank. Pará Sustainable Municipalities Project. https://www.ndb.int/project/para-sustainable-municipalities-project-brazil/

- First, we selected only approved projects, including technical assistance.
- Second, we aligned each of the 94 approved projects with the SDGs it can contribute to, using publicly available project description and SDG targets and indicators. We counted only direct impact, not taking into account, for example, potential economic benefit for rural households from improved road connection, or effect of improved sanitation on community health.
- Third, we summarized the number of projects and the loan amounts in the table. Since one project may be attributed to a number of goals, the sum of project value exceeds $33 billion, and the number of projects exceeds 94. In case of loan currencies other than USD, we used exchange rate on the date of project approval to convert loan value into USD.

Sector breakdown might be a primary draft of projects' contribution to SDGs, except for the COVID-19 emergency loans and multisector loans. This primary analysis shows the large number of infrastructure projects, including transport, social, and sustainable infrastructure (Fig. 6.2). On the second place, we can see clean energy with 14 projects and $4 billion. Thus, we might deduct that the main goals that NDB contributes are Goal 9 (Industry, Innovation and Infrastructure) and Goal 7 (Affordable and Clean Energy). At the same time, the sector cannot be used as a precise evaluation of project's contribution to SDG as some projects may contribute to several SDGs within one sector. For example, the Sorocaba Mobility and Urban Development Project contains measures aimed at both improvement of urban planning (Goal 11) and road infrastructure (Goal 9).[4] Another challenge with the sectorial breakdown is related to indirect association of the sector with the SDG. For example, as two out of three social infrastructure projects are related to education (Teresina Educational Infrastructure Program and Development of Educational Infrastructure for Highly Skilled Workforce), measures provided by the Judicial System Support Project are more contributing to the upgrade of physical ICT infrastructure in judicial sphere. In the next part, we will look into the alignment of the bank's operations with the SDGs in more detail.[5,6,7]

The NDB in Sustainable Development

The NDB has approved a set of documents governing its environmental and social activities, including: Environmental and social framework, environmental and social guideline, sustainable financing policy framework. They ensure environmental and

[4]New Development Bank. Sorocaba Mobility and Urban Development Project. https://www.ndb.int/project/xian-xianyang-international-airport-phase-iii-expansion-project/

[5]New Development Bank. Teresina Educational Infrastructure Program. https://www.ndb.int/project/brazil-teresina-educational-infrastructure-program

[6]New Development Bank. Development of Educational Infrastructure for Highly Skilled Workforce. https://www.ndb.int/project/russia-development-educational-infrastructure-highly-skilled-workforce/

[7]New Development Bank. Judicial System Support Project. https://www.ndb.int/project/judicial-support-russia/

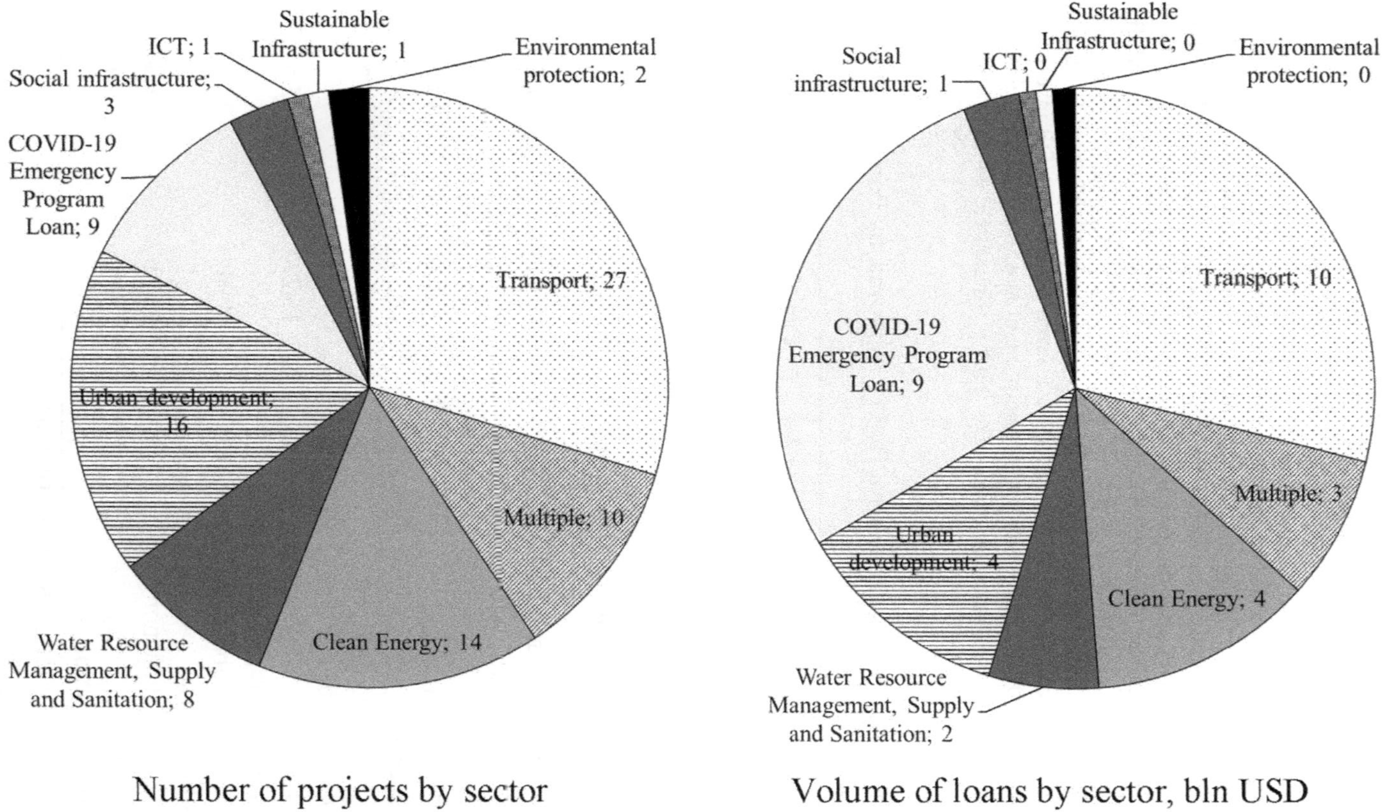

Fig. 6.2. NDB Projects by Sectcr, Number, and Volume (USD Billion), 2023. *Source:* NDB (n.d.).

social soundness and sustainability of operations and support integration of these aspects into the decision-making process, including project approval and usage of green and sustainability instruments. The basic document is the "Environment and Social Framework" (NDB, 2016), which sets the categories for projects according to their social and environmental impact: A – significant adverse impact, B – less adverse than A, C – minimal or no impact. This information is publicly available for all of the projects on NDB's portal. Also there is a rule that if the project is conducted using the financial intermediary (e.g., the loan is given to another bank or fund) and has a significant negative impact (category A), it has to be approved directly by the NDB's Board of Directors (NDB, 2016, p. 8).

NDB's portfolio directly contributes to achieving 12 out of 17 SDGs (Table 6.2). We can see that as we expected, a large portion of NDB investment contributes to SDG 9, with 49 projects containing at least one measure related to this goal. This is consistent with the bank's mandate, which highlights

Table 6.2. The NDB's Cumulative Project Approvals by Primary SDG Alignment.

SDG Alignment	**Number of Projects**	**Cumulative Approvals (USD Million)**	**Share of Total Project Value (%)**
SDG 1. No poverty	3	3,000	8.9
SDG 2. Zero hunger	1	300	0.9
SDG 3. Good health and well-being	6	4,214	12.6
SDG 4. Quality education	3	650	1.9
SDG 6. Clean water and sanitation	17	4,406	13.1
SDG 7. Affordable and clean energy	20	5,990	17.8
SDG 8. Decent work and economic growth	14	8,476	25.2
SDG 9. Industry, innovation, and infrastructure	49	15,293	45.5
SDG 11. Sustainable cities and communities	15	4,942	14.7
SDG 13. Climate action	2	600	1.8
SDG 16. Peace, justice, and strong institutions	1	460	1.4

Source: Author's calculations based on NDB (n.d.).

infrastructure as a primary sector of investment. Also, the next largest goal by the number of projects is Goal 7, as the sectorial breakdown showed, whereas by the project volume, the second place is held by SDG8.

These results are somewhat different from the SDG alignment published in the annual report. The first and main reason behind this is the methodology, which allows us to count more projects as related to a particular goal. For example, the NDB's results show 24 projects contributing to Goal 9 with $8 billion of investment. However, there are projects with a minor contribution to this goal, which are not counted, so our estimations show a much higher number, 49 projects. Unfortunately, there is no publicly available information on the financing of the subprojects, which does not allow us to be more precise in estimations of financial contributions to particular SDGs. Thus, the whole project cost is included in each goal it contributes to. Second reason is the updated data in our research, as the results in the annual report do not count 10 projects in this field approved in 2022–2023.

As a part of its sustainability strategy, the NDB publishes SDG-related targets and planned results in its annual report (Table 6.3). These expected results are available

Table 6.3. Expected SDG Impact of the NDB's Operations.

Development Indicators	**Expected Outcome**	**SDG Alignment**
Schools to be built or upgraded	58	SDG 4. Quality education
Sewage treatment capacity	535,000 m^3/day	SDG 6. Clean water and sanitation
Drinking water supply capacity to be increased	159,000 m^3/day	SDG 6. Clean water and sanitation
Water tunnel/canal infrastructure to be built or upgraded	1,300 km	SDG 6. Clean water and sanitation
Renewable and clean energy generation capacity to be installed	2,800 MW	SDG 7. Affordable and clean energy
Roads to be built or upgraded	15,300 km	SDG 9. Industry, innovation and infrastructure
Bridges to be built or upgraded	820	SDG 9. Industry, innovation and infrastructure
Urban rail transit networks to be built	230 km	SDG 11. Sustainable cities and communities
Cities to benefit from NDB's urban development projects	40	SDG 11. Sustainable cities and communities
CO_2 emissions to be avoided	5.5 million tons/year	SDG 13. Climate action

Source: NDB (2021). *Annual report 2020* (p. 9). https://www.ndb.int/governance/transparency-reporting/

only for those targets where the alignment with the SDGs and potential impact is clear and quantifiable. For example, three projects identified as having an impact on SDG 1 (No poverty) are the COVID-19 Emergency Loans.[8] One of their goals was stated as strengthening social safety nets, which coincides with targets 1.3 (Implement nationally appropriate social protection systems and measures for all, including floors, and by 2030 achieve substantial coverage of the poor and the vulnerable) and 1.5 (By 2030, build the resilience of the poor and those in vulnerable situations and reduce their exposure and vulnerability to climate-related extreme events and other economic, social, and environmental shocks and disasters) (UN, 2015). However, there were no specific estimates of the number of people affected in project documentation.

Thus, our analysis show that the NDB primarily contributes to the goals that raise the least number of question in terms of changed circumstances, such as SDG 6, SDG 7, SDG 8, and SDG 9. Similar results with highlighting SDGs 7 and 9 were obtained using a case study approach based on five NDB projects (Braga et al., 2022). Other researchers also highlight the share of projects classified as sustainable infrastructure (60.4% by the end of 2019), which is a strong signal of NDB's commitment to sustainability (Humphrey, 2020).

However, as research on the effect of crisis on the SDGs primarily shows, the main challenges are associated with goals 1, 2, 3, 4, 8, and 10. In order to be an important player in global sustainable development, the NDB must pay special attention to these fields. It is true that the bank already has some projects aimed at these particular goals, and that they are mostly directly associated with the COVID-19 Assistance Program. For example, three projects with SDG 1 association are three first COVID-19 Emergency Programme Loans to Brazil, South Africa, and India.[9,10,11] In all of the programs, there are measures aimed at maintenance of minimum income levels for vulnerable groups and improvement of social safety nets (Goal 1.3). SDG 2 becomes particularly important in current crisis under rising agriculture prices; however, there is only one project associated with this goal. However, only with a limited impact as this is a contribution to "Indian National Investment and Infrastructure Fund: Fund of Funds (FoF)".[12] FoF is focusing on key socioeconomic areas of the Indian economy; however, NDB does not have a direct influence on the project themes, and there might be no contribution to SDG 2 in the end. Five projects are associated with the

[8]New Development Bank. COVID-19 Emergency Program for South Africa. https://www.ndb.int/news/ndb-board-directors-approves-usd-1-billion-covid-19-emergency-program-loan-south-africa/

[9]New Development Bank. Emergency Assistance Program in Combating COVID-19. Brazil. https://www.ndb.int/project/brazil-emergency-assistance-program-combating-covid-19/

[10]New Development Bank. COVID-19 Emergency Program. South Africa. https://www.ndb.int/project/south-africa-covid-19-emergency-program/

[11]New Development Bank. Emergency Assistance Program in Combating COVID-19. India. https://www.ndb.int/project/india-ndb-emergency-assistance-program-combating-covid-19/

[12]New Development Bank. National Investment and Infrastructure Fund: Fund of Funds – I. https://www.ndb.int/project/india-national-investment-infrastructure-fund-fund-funds/

extremely important SDG 3; however, they include already discussed investment in FoF and COVID-19 Emergency Program Loans in South Africa and India, adding two COVID-19 Emergency Program Loans in China and Russia supporting the countries' healthcare sectors. SDG 10 is not present in NDB's projects; however, the bank's activities may have an indirect impact on those living in vulnerable rural and remote communities by improving infrastructure and therefore minimizing transfer costs.[13,14]

Microlevel analysis of NDB projects and their contribution to SDGs showed the prevalence of infrastructure and growth effect of the bank's activities. At the same time, the bank quickly stepped in during the pandemic in 2020 and provided loans aimed at social issues such as social protection, education, and healthcare.

However, at the moment, the NDB and overall system of global development assistance are facing unprecedented challenges. Multilaterals are running the crisis management and stabilization of the global economy. Increasingly probable stagflation keeps the IMF and the World Bank busy. The UN is busy dealing with the effect on the developing world and corresponding SDGs. Meanwhile, we would stress the urgency of creating some practical approaches for these new, difficult, and mostly unexpected challenges to humanity.

As the BRICS countries often position themselves as centers of expertise for the developing world, they are able to develop ambitious solutions aimed at countries in the global South and propose new ways of catching up.

Conclusions and Recommendations

In this chapter, we have examined the current state of the SDGs and some specific challenges to sustainable development, including the need to review some of the goals and adapt to a new global framework. In particular, there is an urgent need to develop SDG 3 and review the approaches to sustainable and resilient healthcare systems. There are several channels though which MDBs could facilitate this process, including direct financing aligned with SDGs, norm setting and agenda developing, and expertise in the field of the current challenges.

The NDB, as an important player in this field and the only global multilateral bank with only developing countries as members, is in unique position to become a global rule-maker. We analyzed the relationship between the bank's operations and SDGs and showed the already significant contribution of the bank toward 12 out of 17 goals, especially SDG 6, SDG 7, SDG 8, and SDG 9. However, there are several potential ways to strengthen the NDB's role in sustainable development.

---

[13]New Development Bank. NDB Emergency Assistance Program in Combating COVID-19. https://www.ndb.int/project/india-ndb-emergency-assistance-program-combating-covid-19/

[14]New Development Bank. COVID-19 Emergency Program Loan for Supporting Russia's Healthcare Response. https://www.ndb.int/project/covid-19-emergency-program-loan-for-supporting-russias-healthcare-response/

First, currently, the NDB's role as a norm setter and agenda developer might be enhanced greatly. Currently, it is limited to promotion of local bond markets, whereas it might take an active role in shaping the new SDG agenda, taking into account the current challenges uncovered by the latest global crises, including inequality, poverty, food security, and healthcare. Publishing reports on SDGs and best practices of projects alignment to SDGs are only a few possibilities in terms of playing a larger role in the field.

Second, our analysis showed that there is scope for increased transparency on NDB financing by subprojects, including different parts of the projects aimed at different SDGs. Since the NDB positions itself as a bank aimed at promotion of sustainable development, it may more clearly articulate projects' contributions to the SDGs. In some projects, this happens, but most lack this kind of data.

Third, the NDB should pay more attention to contemporary challenges facing the global society, including rising inequality. SDG – 10 is a critical junction – 2020–2021 and 2022 have brought more inequality inside and between countries (World Inequality Lab, 2022). Only if we pay special attention to these critical aspects of global development might the future of the world look brighter.

References

African Development Bank (AfDB). (2023). *African Development Bank Group annual report 2022*. https://www.afdb.org/en/annualreport

Ahmad, Y., & Carey, E. (2021). Development co-operation during the COVID-19 pandemic: An analysis of 2020 figures and 2021 trends to watch. In *Development co-operation profiles*. OECD Publishing. https://doi.org/10.1787/e4b3142a-en

Artecona, R., Bisogno, M., & Fleiss, P. (2019). Financing development in Latin America and the Caribbean: The role and perspectives of multilateral development banks. In *Studies and perspectives series – ECLAC Office in Washington, DC*. No. 19.

Avellan, L., Galindo, A. J., Lotti, G., & Rodriguez, J. P. (2022). *Bridging the gap: Mobilization of multilateral development banks in infrastructure*. IDB Working Paper Series #1299.

Bazbauers, A. R., & Engel, S. (2021). *The global architecture of multilateral development banks: A system of debt or development?* Routledge.

Bhattacharya, A., Kharas, H., Plant, M., & Prizzon, A. (2018). The new global agenda and the future of the multilateral development bank system. *International Organizations Research Journal*, *13*(2), 101–124. https://doi.org/10.17323/1996-7845-2018-02-06

Bobylev, S. N., & Grigoryev, L. G. (2020). In search of the contours of the post-COVID sustainable development goals: The case of BRICS. *BRICS Journal of Economics*, *1*(N2). https://doi.org/10.38050/2712-7508-2020-7

Braga, J. P., De Conti, B., & Magacho, G. (2022). The New Development Bank (NDB) as a mission-oriented institution for just ecological transitions: A case study approach to BRICS sustainable infrastructure investment. *Revista Tempo do Mundo*, (29), 139–164. https://doi.org/10.38116/rtm29art5. https://repositorio.ipea.gov.br/bitstream/11058/11618/9/Tempo_Mundo_n29_Artigo_5_The_new_development.pdf

BRICS. (2014). *Agreement on the New Development Bank*. https://www.ndb.int/wp-content/themes/ndb/pdf/Agreement-on-the-New-Development-Bank.pdf

Broccolini, C., Lotti, G., Maffioli, A., Presbitero, A., & Stucchi, R. (2020). *Mobilization effects of multilateral development banks*. World Bank Policy Research Working Paper #9163. https://openknowledge.worldbank.org/handle/10986/33395

EC. (2021). *Life expectancy decreased in 2020 across the EU*. https://ec.europa.eu/eurostat/web/products-eurostat-news/product/-/asset_publisher/VWJkHuaYvLIN/content/id/12645457/pop_up

Gable, S., Lofgren, H., & Rodarte, I. O. (2015). *Trajectories for sustainable development goals:* Framework and country applications. World Bank. https://openknowledge.worldbank.org/handle/10986/23122

Griffith-Jones, S. (2016). *Development Banks and their key roles: Supporting investment, structural transformation and sustainable development*. Discussion Paper 59, Bread for the World. https://www.stephanygj.net/papers/Development_banks_and_their_key_roles_2016.pdf

Griffith-Jones, S., & Gottschalk, R. (2012). *Exogenous shocks: Dealing with the only certainty: Uncertainty* (The Initiative for Policy Dialogue, Policy Brief #8). Paper prepared for the Commonwealth Secretariat, September 2012, for the Commonwealth Finance Ministers' Meeting, Tokyo, October 10, 2012. https://policydialogue.org/publications/policy-briefs/exogenous-shocks-dealing-with-the-only-certainty-uncertainty/

Grigoryev, L. M., Elkina, Z. S., Mednikova, P. A., Serova, D. A., Starodubtseva, M. F., & Filippova, E. S. (2021). The perfect storm of personal consumption. *Voprosy Ekonomiki*, (10), 27–50. (in Russian). https://doi.org/10.32609/0042-8736-2021-10-27-50

Grigoryev, L. M., & Medzhidova, D. D. (2020). Global energy trilemma. *Russian Journal of Economics*, *6*(2020), 437–462. https://doi.org/10.32609/j.ruje.6.58683

Grigoryev, L. M., & Morozkina, A. K. (2022). Pandemic shock and recession: The adequacy of anti-crisis measures and the role of development assistance. In V. Jakupec, M. Kelly, & M. de Percy (Eds.), *COVID-19 and foreign aid: Nationalism and global development in a New World Order* (344 p.). Routledge. (forthcoming).

Handl, G. (1998). The legal mandate of multilateral development banks as agents for change toward sustainable development. *American Journal of International Law*, *92*(4), 642–665.

Humphrey, C. (2020). *From drawing board to reality: The first four years of operations at the Asian Infrastructure Investment Bank and New Development Bank*. https://doi.org/10.3929/ethz-b-000411422

IMF. (2021). *Economic outlook. Recovery during a pandemic. Health concerns, supply, disruptions, and price pressures*. Washington, DC, October. https://www.imf.org/en/Publications/WEO/Issues/2021/10/12/world-economic-outlook-october-2021

Institute for Health Metrics and Evaluation (IHME). (2021). *Financing global health 2020: The impact of COVID-19*. Seattle, WA. https://www.healthdata.org/sites/default/files/files/policy_report/FGH/2021/FGH_2020_full-report.pdf

Inter-American Development Bank (IADB). (2022). *Annual report 2022. Financial statements*. https://publications.iadb.org/en/inter-american-development-bank-annual-report-2022-financial-statements

Kenny, C. (2019). *Marginal, not transformational: Development finance institutions and the sustainable development goals*. CGD Policy Paper 156. Center for Global Development. https://www.cgdev.org/publication/marginal-not-transformational-development-finance-institutions-and-sustainable

Liu, Z., Deng, Z., Ciais, P., & Tan, J. (2021). *Global daily CO_2 emissions for the year 2020*. Researchgate. https://www.researchgate.net/publication/349759072_Global_Daily_CO_2_emissions_for_the_year_2020

Mendez, A., & Houghton, D. P. (2020). Sustainable banking: The role of multilateral development banks as norm entrepreneurs. *Sustainability*, *12*, 972. https://doi.org/10.3390/su12030972

Morozkina, A. K. (2019). Official development aid: Trends of the last decade. *World Economy and International Relations*, *63*(9), 86–92. (in Russian). https://doi.org/10.20542/0131-2227-2019-63-9-86-92

NDB. (2016). *Environment and social framework*. https://www.ndb.int/wp-content/uploads/2017/02/ndb-environment-social-framework-20160330.pdf

NDB. (2021). *Annual report 2020*. https://www.ndb.int/data-and-documents/annual-reports/

NDB. (2023). *Investor presentation*. https://www.ndb.int/wp-content/uploads/2023/04/Investor-Presentation_2023.pdf

NDB. (n.d.). *List of all projects* [dataset]. NDB. https://www.ndb.int/projects/list-of-all-projects/

OECD. (2018). *OECD DAC blended finance principles: Unlocking commercial finance for the sustainable development goals*. https://web-archive.oecd.org/2022-08-19/469783-OECD-Blended-Finance-Principles.pdf

OECD. (2021). *Development co-operation report 2021: Shaping a just digital transformation*. OECD Publishing. https://doi.org/10.1787/ce08832f-en

OECD. (n.d.). *International Development Statistics (IDS) online databases* [dataset]. OECD. https://www.oecd.org/dac/financing-sustainable-development/development-finance-data/idsonline.htm

Our World in Data. (n.d.). *Our World in Data* [database]. https://ourworldindata.org/

Sachs, J. D., Kroll, C., Lafortune, G., Fuller, G., & Woelm, F. (2021). *Sustainable development report 2021*. Cambridge University Press. https://doi.org/10.1017/9781009106559

The Asian Development Bank (ADB). (2023). *ADB annual report 2020*. https://www.adb.org/documents/adb-annual-report-2020

The Asian Infrastructure Investment Bank (AIIB). (2023). *2022 AIIB annual report*. https://www.aiib.org/en/news-events/annual-report/overview/index.html

UN. (2015). *Transforming our world: The 2030 agenda for sustainable development*. UN. https://sdgs.un.org/2030agenda

UN. (2021). *The sustainable development goals report*. United Nations Publications. https://unstats.un.org/sdgs/report/2021/The-Sustainable-Development-Goals-Report-2021.pdf

UN. (2023). *Global sustainable development report 2023*. United Nations Publications. https://sdgs.un.org/gsdr/gsdr2023

UNESCO. (2021). *Education: From disruption to recovery*. UNESCO. https://en.unesco.org/covid19/educationresponse

World Bank. (2021). *Annual report 2020*. https://doi.org/10.1596/978-1-4648-1619-2

World Bank. (2023). *The World Bank annual report 2022. A new era in development.* http://documents.worldbank.org/curated/en/099092823161580577/BOSIB055c2cb6c006090a90150e512e6beb

World Bank. (n.d.). *World development indicators database* [dataset]. World Bank. https://databank.worldbank.org/source/world-development-indicators

World Inequality Lab. (2022). *World inequality report 2022*. https://wir2022.wid.world/

Chapter 7

The New Development Bank's Role in the Low-Carbon Transition: An Analysis of Institutional Strategies and Projects Financed

Rafaela Mello Rodrigues de Sá

McMaster University, Canada

Abstract

The BRICS countries' energy transition deserves attention not only for the domestic characteristics of these economies but also for their positioning on the current geopolitical context, marked by global challenges and conflicts. In this sense, it is essential to understand the role of the New Development Bank (NDB) in financing the transition. Since its foundation, the bank has been characterized by its focus on sustainable development. The first operations to each member carried out in 2016 were directed to clean energy sector. In addition, the institution strategy for 2017–2021 highlighted clean energy as one of the core areas for the NDB, and a new guideline for 2022–2026 shows a target of directing 40% of total approvals to projects that contribute to climate change mitigation and adaptation, including energy transition. Thus, the research aims to assess how the NDB contributes to the energy transition process in the BRICS countries toward a low-carbon economy, based on the projects financed and through institutional strategies analysis. From this, it is possible to assume that the NDB contributes to the BRICS transition process to a low-carbon economy, but with differences between countries. On the one hand, the NDB favors more the transition in the energy sector in China, South Africa, and Brazil; on the other hand, the institution collaborates more with the decarbonization process in India, China, and Russia. Despite this, there are still limitations and challenges that hinder the NDB from becoming one of the main sources of incentives for its member countries to reach the climate targets.

The Multilateralism of the New Development Bank on the Sustainable Economic Growth in BRICS Nations and Beyond, 103–124

Published under exclusive licence by Emerald Publishing Limited
doi:10.1108/978-1-83662-292-520251010

Keywords: New Development Bank; low-carbon transition; energy transition; BRICS; sustainable infrastructure

Introduction

The energy transition process in progress in the BRICS countries deserves attention not only for the internal characteristics of these states but also for their position in the current geopolitical context, marked by global challenges and conflicts. Considering the instability with the war between Ukraine and Russia, it is possible to note the resurgence of challenges and problems, especially involving the energy sector. The debate on energy transition, which was already in evidence on the climate change agenda, gains greater visibility, adding strategic and geopolitical elements to the energy security of the countries.

In addition, it is also important to highlight a great contemporary challenge: the goal agreed upon in the Paris Agreement, in 2015, of keeping the planet's temperature increase below 1.5°C (Paris Agreement, 2015, p. 3). Thus, the reduction of carbon emissions is essential for this goal to be achieved, so the transition to a low-carbon economy must be pursued by countries, requiring transformations and adaptations in the industrial sector, transportation sector, and especially in the energy sector.

In this sense, if on the one hand, the process of reducing emissions is called decarbonization, that is, the substitution of energy sources that use fossil fuels for renewable and clean sources in the most varied sectors, on the other hand, the transformation called energy transition is more related to the energy sector.

Based on this, there is a major challenge, which is to address the gap between the existing infrastructure, predominantly fossil-based structures, and the lack of funding available to achieve the desired level, which is to ensure higher levels of renewable energy and the use of technologies that allow greater efficiency.

The International Renewable Energy Agency highlighted in a recent report that the world would have to spend about $131 trillion by 2050 (IRENA, 2021, p. 36). For this to be feasible, the relevance of climate finance increases, and the actors that are related to this debate can make an essential contribution.

In this scenario, it is important to understand what sort of contribution the New Development Bank (NDB) has made in financing the climate-related projects, not only direct to the energy transition but also aiming to transform the BRICS countries into a low-carbon economy. The bank, since its foundation, has been characterized by its focus on sustainable development and infrastructure. After its establishment, the first NDB projects were carried out in 2016, which were all directed at the clean energy sector for each founding member.

The overall strategy for the first years of the institution highlights clean energy as one of the core areas for the NDB, and a new guideline for 2022–2026 shows a target of directing 40% of total approvals to projects that contribute to climate change mitigation and adaptation, including energy transition (NDB, 2022a, p. 28).

It is against this background that the book chapter assessed how the NDB contributes to the low-carbon transition of BRICS countries. This was conducted through reviewing institutional documents in order to understand bank's performance. At the institutional level, two documents presenting the bank's strategy were selected, one covering the years 2017–2021 and the recently released strategy focused on the years 2022–2026. Regarding the analysis of financing, on the one hand, projects focused on the clean energy sector were mapped to assess efforts toward energy transition; on the other hand, financing that contributes to the reduction of carbon emissions in various sectors were evaluated.

Therefore, this chapter is divided into three sections, which are: the first one will address the main characteristics of the energy transition process, highlighting the situation of this process in the BRICS countries, with brief comments on the energy sector scenario in each country, as well as highlighting the position of BRICS in the global energy transition agenda; the second section will analyze the NDB, from its foundation to the details of its activities in recent years, to understand the focus of the institution on financing sustainable infrastructure and examine the implications of this for the energy transition process; and the third section will present an analysis of the projects financed by the NDB, mainly for the clean energy sector, with the objective of evaluating the bank's performance and effective contribution to the energy transition in its member countries.

Based on this, it will be possible to reflect on how the BRICS bank has been acting in the sphere of sustainable finance in its first years of operation, mainly through the evaluation of its financed projects and through the analysis of institutional strategies.

The Energy Transition and the BRICS Countries

Considering the international context of climate change and the initiatives that have been pursued to address this agenda, it is worth noting that the energy transition is "a pathway toward transformation of the global energy sector from fossil-based to zero-carbon by the second half of this century" (IRENA, 2022).

Within this scenario, we can locate the energy transition in the broader process of decarbonization of the entire economy, that is, "reducing the greenhouse gas emissions produced by the combustion of fossil fuels" (Cho, 2022) in the most diverse sectors of the economy, including not only the energy sector but also industry and transportation.

In the energy sector, the most direct way to achieve decarbonization is through the increased use of renewable energy (Papadis & Tsatsaronis, 2020, p. 02). However, it is also important to highlight the role of energy-efficient technologies, which also contribute to the process.

In other sectors, such as transport and industry, the electrification process is the most common, in order to introduce electric machines and vehicles into the economy (Cho, 2022). However, actions that contribute to the reduction of carbon emissions can also be considered in this process, such as the adoption of modern and efficient transportation modes, like electric trams or metros. All these efforts are being encouraged to make it possible to achieve the international goals and the Nationally Determined Contributions (NDCs) in the Paris Agreement scope.

Despite some collective initiatives made within the BRICS grouping – such as the signing of a Memorandum of Understanding on energy economics and efficiency in 2015 and the creation of a BRICS Energy Research Platform in 2018 (Ribeiro & Abdenur, 2022) – the five countries are characterized by different stages and approaches in their transition processes.[1,2]

Brazil is marked by having one of the cleanest energy matrices among the BRICS countries, with an abundance in natural resources, favoring the implementation of hydroelectric plants and increasing the potential for solar and wind generation (Losekann & Tavares, 2019, p. 25). Moreover, the national ethanol incentive program started in the last century also shows positive results today (Montenegro et al., 2020, p. 142). In its climate goals, Brazil wants to reach 45% renewable energy in the energy matrix by 2030 (Losekann & Tavares, 2019, p. 24), so the BRICS bank could be an excellent source of resources to encourage this goal.

On the other hand, Russia is considered the world's largest producer of crude oil and the second largest producer of natural gas, besides producing large amounts of coal (Montenegro et al., 2020, p. 143). Due to the abundance of fossil fuels in Russia, the country has in this sector a source of resources for its economy, through the export of oil and gas. Thus, the process of energy transition to less polluting sources ends up in the background, demonstrating the lower level of engagement regarding this process in relation to the BRICS countries (Losekann & Tavares, 2019, p. 39).

India, in turn, while being considered the third largest energy consuming country in the world, also has the lowest per capita consumption rate of the BRICS. This is due to the issue of electricity shortages, with blackouts and supply difficulties, especially in rural and isolated areas (Losekann & Tavares, 2019, p. 36). Another characteristic of the Indian energy sector is the significant use of coal in power generation, accounting for 1/3 of India's carbon emissions (Losekann & Tavares, 2019, p. 36).

In China, coal is also considered the country's main source of energy resources. However, this use has been gradually reduced over the past few years, with the replacement by other sources. The growing demand for natural gas has created opportunities for domestic and foreign players, with partnerships with Russia. Moreover, the growth of renewable energy is also remarkable in the Asian country, which seeks to become the technological leader of this equipment in the global market (Losekann & Tavares, 2019, pp. 31–33). Thus, the Chinese interest

[1]This document demonstrates two main objectives: (1) promoting access to energy efficient technologies and (2) the possibility of institutionalizing energy cooperation within the BRICS. The Memorandum of Understanding is available at the following link: http://www.brics.utoronto.ca/docs/151120-energy.html

[2]The BRICS Energy Research Cooperation Platform is a global platform to promote sustainable energy-based development, sharing of advanced energy technologies, expansion of cooperation in educational programs, as well as exchange of statistical data and plans on the development of national energy systems and information on best practices and regulatory frameworks in the energy sector. See: https://brics2021.gov.in/energy

in accelerating the energy transition is expressive, since 1/3 of the world's wind and solar energy is installed in the country (Montenegro et al., 2020, p. 142).

The context of the energy sector in South Africa is the most challenging among the BRICS countries, due to the low availability of economic and institutional resources. The dependence on coal in its energy matrix is also one of the characteristics of the South African country. Eskom is responsible for producing electricity in South Africa; thus, it manages the electricity supplies acting throughout the process and being the main actor that may favor an energy transition process (Losekann & Tavares, 2019, pp. 18–19). In addition, it should be noted that the country's most recent energy plan has been seeking to reverse and reduce the use of coal and nuclear energy, to intensify the spread of renewables (Losekann & Tavares, 2019, p. 20). Again, the BRICS bank can serve as an instrument to support this process of change.

Considering the major differences between the BRICS countries and the divergent interests among them, the difficulty of coordination given the discrepancies in their domestic policies is clear, adding obstacles to a multilateral negotiation toward the energy transition process within the grouping (Volpon & Ribeiro, 2018, pp. 213–215).

However, the actions of the NDB can be an instrument that can enable not only a coordination between countries but also contribute with financing that will favor the transition of BRICS countries to a low-carbon economy.

Sustainable Infrastructure and the NDB

The NDB is considered one of the latest multilateral development banks (MDBs) founded, along with Asian Infrastructure Investment Bank (AIIB), since both started their operations in 2016. These institutions finance development projects around the world, being important components on the international arena. They provide financial assistance through investment projects, which include infrastructure and social projects. These institutions were created to promote economic and social development around the world (Buiter & Fries, 2002; Nelson, 2011).

Considering the scenario of the great demand for infrastructure in emerging economies, it was possible to notice a gap between the levels of funding available and what was being requested by emerging and developing countries. The persistence of this deficit could affect not only the economies' ability to provide transportation and energy services but also prevent the population's access to more sustainable forms of development, due to the scarcity of financial resources in this area. Thus, this situation could compromise the long-term development of these economies, making it difficult to create opportunities to improve the quality of life of these populations (Griffith-Jones, 2015, p. 02; Humphrey, 2020, p. 02).

MDBs, therefore, play a key role in facilitating the access of these economies to financial resources capable of meeting this significant demand for infrastructure investments, and recently with a greater focus on sustainable infrastructure and green financing. However, traditional multilateral banks have limitations both in their financial capacity and in administrative and political issues (Humphrey, 2020, p. 02). These traditional institutions, being dominated by developed countries in their governance, "intentionally neglect the infrastructure investment needs of developing countries" (Zhu, 2020, p. 79).

The persistence of this demand may be related to the fact that governments are the main borrowers for large infrastructure projects, given the low short-term profitability of these initiatives for the private sector. For this reason, the gap between demand for investment and the designated supply, especially in less developed countries, ends up creating difficulties in accessing resources for these purposes (Abadie & Welsh, 2020). On the other hand, these emerging economies were in a position of significant growth in economic terms, with an accumulated pool of international reserves and financial resources, which could contribute to solving this deficit (Griffith-Jones, 2015, p. 02).

It was within this context that the NDB was created. At this same time, the AIIB was also founded. These two institutions, which began operations in 2016, were established to respond to these challenges, complementing the efforts of the existing multilateral banks, and also being unhappy with the governance structure of the existing multilateral banks (Humphrey, 2020, p. 02). In this sense, many of the countries that used to receive development funding from these traditional institutions are now building new financial institutions, thus strengthening the voice of emerging and developing countries in the global financial architecture (Griffith-Jones, 2015, p. 02).

The BRICS bank was established in 2014 after the signing of an agreement at the BRICS Annual Summit in Fortaleza, where the countries agreed to establish a bank that would strengthen cooperation among them. The agreement states that the main motivation for establishing this new multilateral bank is related to mobilizing "resources for infrastructure and sustainable development projects in BRICS and other emerging economies and developing countries, complementing the existing efforts of multilateral and regional financial institutions" (NDB, 2014, p. 01).

The Concept of Sustainable Infrastructure in the Bank's Performance

Sustainable infrastructure projects are considered the central emphasis of the BRICS bank's first years of operation, as highlighted in the strategy document for the years 2017–2021. To realize this approach, the document presents the institution's goal of dedicating 2/3 of the financing to this sector, intending to produce positive impacts in social and environmental terms, in addition to incorporating economic, environmental, and social criteria in both the design and implementation of projects, to mitigate possible impacts (Batista Jr., 2019, p. 263; NDB, 2017, p. 07).

The centrality of initiatives aimed at sustainable infrastructure is related to a strategy of the bank, that instead of having a very broad scope, equal to existing MDBs, the institution decided to focus its efforts "on a group of sectors that is more limited in scope, although still broad enough to provide ample space to find and implement viable projects" (NDB, 2017, p. 12).

In this sense, the institution has five key areas that make up the financing portfolio, and these are: (1) clean energy, including technology projects for renewable energy and energy efficiency, as well as initiatives to reduce pollution in this sector; (2) transportation infrastructure, with financing aimed at providing better connectivity between people, markets, and services, as well as promoting affordable modes of transportation; (3) sanitation and water resource management, with projects to provide adequate drinking water and sanitation, as well as enabling technologies for efficient water resource management; (4) sustainable urban development, favoring efficient and sustainable urban environments, improving quality of life, energy use, and economic productivity; (5) economic cooperation and integration, with financing that strengthens relations between different countries, with installation of integration infrastructure such as rail and road links and port infrastructure (NDB, 2017, p. 20).

However, despite the focus on financing aimed at sustainable infrastructure, the institutional documents that constitute the bank do not present a clear definition of what this concept means, nor specific criteria that are considered for investments (Kweitel & Krishnaswamy, 2016; Mineiro et al., 2018, p. 19). This broad understanding, without much detail, ends up allowing the financing of projects that may question the bank's sustainable commitment, since the institution ends up financing projects that may generate socio-environmental impacts, which ultimately will not contribute to sustainable development.

Even if the lack of a more specific definition of sustainable infrastructure can be considered a broad and holistic approach by the institution – seeking not to limit the bank's possibilities of action – it is important to consider that the institution's executive staff needs to be careful not to fall into the trap of approving "financing for poorly designed infrastructure or extractive energy megaprojects, which may be beneficial to corporate elites but do not serve national development" (Kweitel et al., 2017).

It is in this regard that they have been suggestion of creating metrics to evaluate the potential of financing, relating sustainable development to "incentives that would encourage borrowers to think of sustainable practices not as bureaucratic formalities, but as actions linked to better outcomes" (Vazquez, 2020, p. 184).

NDB's Social and Environment Approach

Another issue that the NDB differs from other MDBs is the fact that the institution adopts the Country Systems system. This way, instead of using international safeguards – making external interference possible – the bank makes "use of borrower country legislation, regulations, and supervisory procedures whenever possible" (NDB, 2017, p. 15).

If, on the one hand, social and environmental safeguards were implemented to generate positive impacts for the financed projects, on the other hand, they would, in some cases, end up representing inflexible standards imposed by international bodies and are placed above national laws. For this reason, the approach implemented by the NDB, which would prioritize national systems, could encourage bank staff to dig deeper into national laws and regulations and could suggest changes and indicate weaknesses (Humphrey, 2016, pp. 03–07). Nevertheless, some challenges are presented by adopting this approach. In cases of weaknesses and gaps in local regulations, it is essential to define minimum standards to mitigate potential risks (Teixeira & Pimentel, 2017, p. 46).

Among these challenges, the following stand out: (1) the possibility of misalignment between planning instruments and measures to strengthen national systems, (2) the threats of setbacks in the social and environmental governance of countries that need to be considered, (3) possible flaws in methodologies to measure the benefits and results of using national systems, (4) inconsistencies and risks in the application of regulations in cases where there are financial intermediaries, and (5) possible failures in social and environmental protection and lack of effective monitoring of standards against human rights violations in the national system (Borges & Cruz, 2018, pp. 101–108).

For the Country Systems approach to be successful and effective, it is important to take into account the following issues:

- The implementation of a robust, consistent, and integrated approach, with citizen participation, access to justice, and transparency standards of public agencies and environmental rules.
- Monitor, report, and remedy potential impacts on human and environmental rights.
- Strengthen the capacities of local actors. For this, communities and nongovernmental organizations (NGOs) must have access to information about the projects, to influence the implementation and evaluation processes (Borges & Cruz, 2018, pp. 22–23).

From the above, it is also important to note that, the "Environment and Social Framework" document highlights the NDB's approach to the environmental and social management of its operations, whose central objective is to enable a framework to manage potential socio-environmental risks in the design and implementation phase of projects, and to encourage good international environmental and social practices in the institution's operations, thus strengthening national systems.

In order to mitigate risks and impacts, the participation of local actors and civil society organizations becomes significant. However, to evaluate each step of the process – from the conception, through evaluation, to the implementation of the projects – it is necessary to have detailed evidence and information. For this reason, the issue of transparency is a subject that must also be discussed.

Even though the bank's website makes available the institutional documents and the data referring to the approved projects, there are still difficulties in accessing information about the financing implementation process. If, on the one hand, the AIIB details the procedures of each project with documents made available showing not only the socio-environmental assessment carried out but also reports on the implementation process, the NDB, on the other hand, only presents information about the project during its funding application process, not disclosing details about what happens after approval. This makes it difficult for civil society groups to monitor and defend the rights of local communities.

Another criticism indicated is the absence of mechanisms that can ensure effective participation of affected communities and civil society groups in the design and implementation of projects and also in the bank's policies and strategies (Kweitel & Krishnaswamy, 2016; Kweitel et al., 2017). Despite the launch of a document addressing information disclosure issues in 2016 – "Interim Information Disclosure Policy" – the NDB still needs to consolidate and enhance a dialogue channel with civil society and with the populations affected by financing projects, in addition to making available the projects and management plans developed by clients that aim to minimize or avoid socio-environmental impacts (Mineiro et al., 2018, p. 36; Oxfam, 2021, p. 4).

With the founding of the NDB, the institution became the first MDB that claims to have a global reach that was constituted exclusively by emerging economies, without the participation of developed countries in the initial stage of construction (Batista Jr., 2019, p. 249; Zhu, 2020, p. 94). This issue demonstrates the possibility of the bank to be a transformative institution among the actors that make up the international financial architecture, contributing to sustainable development and infrastructure initiatives (NDB, 2021, n.p.).

Concerning this, it was expected that being a bank created in 2014, it would also innovate in its practices. However, the NDB's socio-environmental approach ends up showing gaps, with low transparency in the design and implementation processes of financing and an absence of mechanisms that allow the participation of affected communities, demonstrating elements that the bank still needs to consolidate and improve certain elements, which may affect the institution's approach and its contribution to the energy transition process in member countries.

Energy Transition and the NDB

Considering the characteristics presented about the creation and operation of the NDB, it is important to evaluate how its approach and the financing provided by the institution are contributing to the energy transition process of its member countries, and, more broadly, to the BRICS transition toward a low-carbon economy.

For this, it is important to evaluate not only the strategic efforts, through the institution's official documents, but also to understand how financing for clean energy and decarbonization initiatives favors the transition process.

This section will show a document and material analysis of the NDB's performance in these last years. At the institutional level, the bank's strategic documents were analyzed, identifying the institution's goals and objectives in this scope. Regarding materiality and practice, the financed projects were mapped and categorized, in order to allow an examination of the bank's initiatives toward the energy transition.

The Energy Transition in the Documents and Institutional Strategy of the NDB

In order to access the main sources of the institution's strategy, two core documents that present the main characteristics of the NDB's actions were selected: the General Strategy (2017–2021) and the General Strategy (2022–2026). Both documents portray the central objectives of the bank since its early years of operation until nowadays. From this, it will be possible to understand how issues related to the energy transition are inserted in the bank's approach.

Regarding the first strategy document released by the bank, which covers actions from 2017 to 2021, it is important to highlight the operational focus of the institution, which since the beginning of its operations has sought to establish efforts toward infrastructure and sustainable development, so that one of the main strategic goals of this period was to achieve 2/3 of the financed projects aimed at this end (NDB, 2017, p. 12).

According to the bank, this goal was achieved and exceeded in the year 2016, reaching 78% of approved financing aimed at sustainable infrastructure. Among them, the vast majority of projects were directed to renewable energy generation (NDB, 2017, p. 12). Thus, it can be understood that the NDB's goal of becoming a key player in financing this sector was pursued, at least in the first year of operation.

In addition, one of the bank's key areas is clean energy financing. From this perspective, the strategy points out that:

> NDB supports the shift to a more sustainable energy path through: i) structural transformation of the energy sector, in particular by promoting emerging renewable technologies; ii) energy efficiency, including the upgrade of existing power plants, overhaul of electricity grids and energy-efficient building techniques; and iii) reduction of air, water and soil pollution in the energy sector. (NDB, 2017, p. 20)

To this end, there may be projects that fund activities more directly aimed at energy transition, such as wind and solar renewable energy generation, but also ventures that contribute indirectly and can assist this transition process, such as energy storage systems, adaptive smart electricity grids, and solid waste-based power generation (NDB, 2017, p. 20).

Another issue that deserves attention is the institution's perception that investments in green infrastructure are becoming increasingly present in the current context, in which the "costs of solar and other renewables have reached parity with those of fossil fuel-based energy in many countries. This trend is bound to accelerate as more and more countries commit to renewables, pushing costs down" (NDB, 2017, p. 08). Thus, demonstrating the relevance of the theme in the current moment and the importance of the bank in acting in this sphere, so that "the green energy is the present-not the future" (NDB, 2017, p. 08).

After the first five years of operation, the bank updated its policies and strategies, determining new directions and actions, which are translated into the strategy document that will encompass the activities from 2022 to 2026. The document presents a balance of the results achieved during the previous strategy's scope. According to the NDB, the bank directed very diverse efforts toward several sustainable development goals (SDGs), being 29% of the projects toward SDG 9 on Industry, Innovation, and Infrastructure, 15% toward SDG 11 on Sustainable Cities and Communities, and 13% toward SDG 7 on Clean and Affordable Energy (NDB, 2022a, p. 15).

Thus, it is possible to understand that there was a priority for the clean energy and energy efficiency sectors, which contribute to SDG 7, since this area was one of those that received the most funding, according to the bank.

Regarding the actions for the next cycle, the Fig. 7.1 below shows the main topics of this new management.

As shown in the image, the clean energy and energy efficiency sector continues to be one of the pillars of the bank's activities. Regarding these energy issues, the institution states that "will continue to support its member countries' transition toward a low-emission development pathway, as guided by their NDCs" (NDB, 2022a, p. 20). Thus, the priority given to this sector will be maintained for the next five years, aiming to ensure "the deployment of clean and renewable energy at

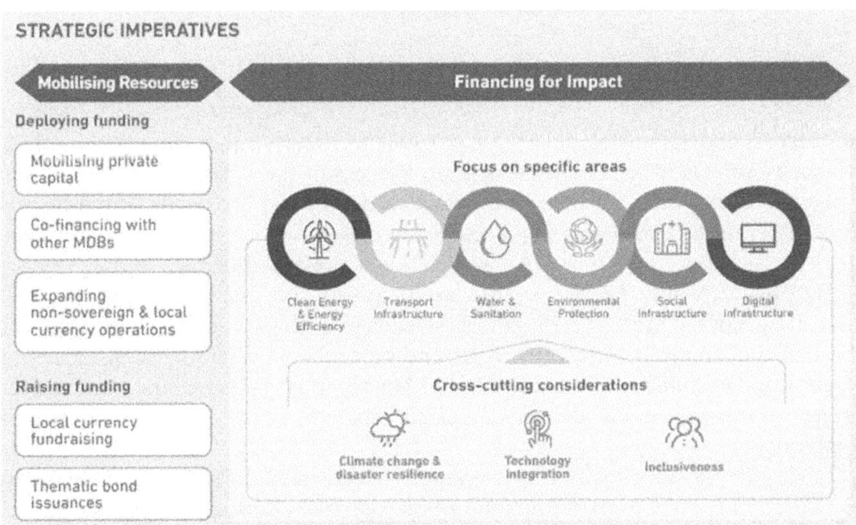

Fig. 7.1. NDB Strategic Imperatives for 2022–2026. *Source:* NDB General Strategy (2022–2026), p. 03.

scale, as well as those that enhance the efficiency of power transmission, distribution, and storage through proven and emerging transformative technologies" (NDB, 2022a, p. 20).

The issue of climate change is increasingly affecting the policies and strategies of multilateral banks. This can be noticed with the important advance that can be highlighted in the current strategy, which is the statement that "NDB will not consider financing any new coal fired capacity for power generation" (NDB, 2022a, p. 20). From this, the BRICS bank moves toward a more sustainable position and greater contribution to its members' transition to a low-carbon economy by ending coal-based financing.

Moreover, the institution also states that the goal of addressing climate change and disaster risks is one of the key considerations of operations, so that "the bank will identify and prioritize projects or components that contribute to reducing GHG emissions, support transition to lower-emission economies and help countries adapt to climate change" (NDB, 2022a, p. 21).

Finally, it is worth noting the current strategy's goal of "direct 40% of total financing to projects contributing to climate change mitigation and adaptation, including energy transition, over 2022–2026" (NDB, 2022a, p. 28).

Therefore, it is evaluated that, at least in its discourse and institutional strategy, the NDB seeks to support actions toward the energy transition of its member countries, with goals and initiatives that demonstrate this direction of the bank. However, in order to understand the real performance of the NDB in this perspective, it is relevant to analyze the data of the financing carried out in the first years of operation, to validate whether this strategic orientation is consistent with the institution's projects.

NDB Approach and Financing

In order to understand practical elements of the NDB's approach and the role of financed projects in the energy transition process in the BRICS countries, it was necessary to evaluate the financing provided during the first years of the institution's operation. From this perspective, the results of the mapping of projects carried out between 2016 and August 2022 are presented below.

In Figs. 7.2 and 7.3 above, it was identified the great relevance of three countries: India, China, and Brazil. India leads in both the number of projects and the amounts financed, with 26 projects and more than US$ 9 billion in financing. Regarding the number of projects, Brazil has recently passed China, reaching 25 projects. However, in the amounts financed, China is second, totaling almost US$ 9 billion.

One of the possible factors for the greater engagement of India and China may be related to the active participation of both countries during the negotiations for the creation of the bank, besides the regional proximity with the headquarters of the institution, which is located in China, and the first presidency of the bank was held by an Indian representative. Furthermore, it is worth mentioning the high level of dynamism of the two economies in recent years, which favors the request

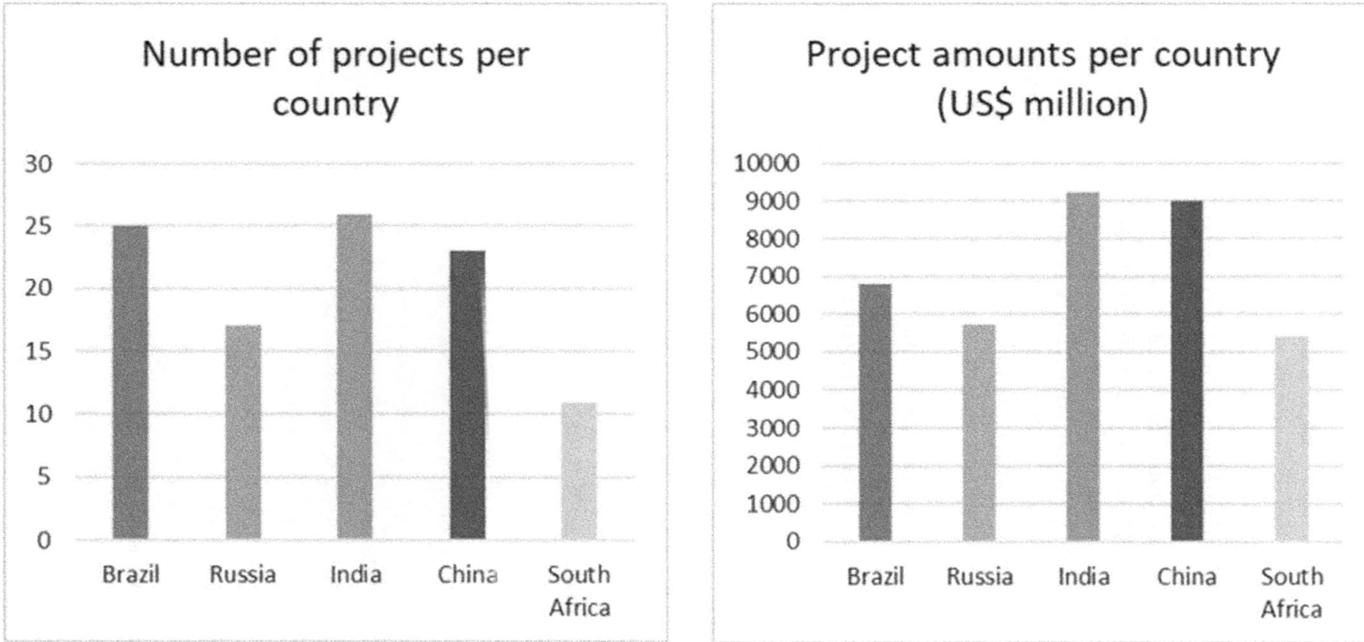

Figs. 7.2 and 7.3. Number of Projects per Country and Projects Amount per Country. *Source:* List of Projects (NDB, 2022b).

for financing in various sectors of the productive and social structure. In relation to the increase of projects for Brazil, it is worth mentioning the opening of regional offices in the Americas, one in São Paulo and another in Brasilia, which boosted the growth in the number of financing requests.

Besides assessing the direction of financing for the BRICS countries, it is also important to examine the division of sectors. In the Fig. 7.4, it is possible to identify the sectors that received the most financing from the bank.

The sector that received the most financing from the BRICS bank was transportation, encompassing works, constructions, and reforms of various modes of transportation, thus contributing to the improvement of the infrastructure of BRICS countries and promoting greater connectivity between economies. With more than US$ 11 billion directed to this area by financing 30 projects, the transportation sector stimulates and facilitates trade between the BRICS and reduce the costs related to trade by improving the quality of infrastructure in these economies.

The urban development sector was the second most financed by the bank, encompassing several constructions and improvements to the transportation infrastructure in the cities, with projects to implement subways, streetcars, and green buses. More than US$ 3.7 billion was allocated, totaling 16 projects in this area.

The third main sector that received funding was clean energy, which may be related to the high demand for more sustainable projects and a quest by countries to implement the energy transition process. The NDB financed more than 15 projects, totaling more than US$ 4 billion for this area.

The three sectors with most projects funded by the NDB are connected with the transition to a low-carbon economy, either directly with the energy sector or by decarbonization undertakings in transportation and urban activities. One of

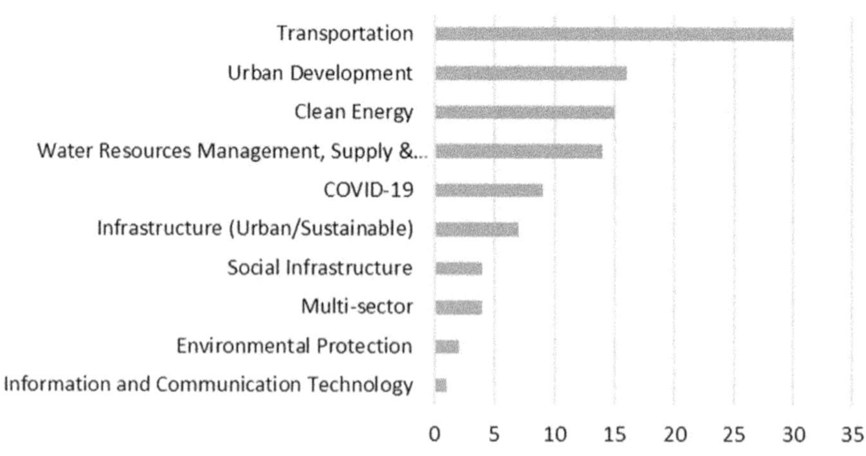

Fig. 7.4. Projects by Sector. *Source:* List of Projects (NDB, 2022b).

the reasons for this may be related to the fact that these sectors represent sustainable infrastructure projects, which is the main focus of the BRICS bank.

In this scope, in order to assess the issues related to the energy transition and the decarbonization process of the economy, a more specific mapping of the projects was carried out. Projects categorized for the clean energy sector were evaluated as directly contributing to the energy transition. In turn, some transportation and urban development projects, which somehow favor the reduction of carbon emissions in the economy, were categorized as decarbonization.

Regarding the projects aimed at energy transition, there is a big difference in the amounts financed for China and South Africa to the other three countries, as shown in Fig. 7.5. China reached more than US$ 1.6 billion with five projects. South Africa, on the other hand, obtained US$ 1.4 billion in five financings. Therefore, it is important to highlight that the contribution of the BRICS bank to the energy transition of these two countries is more expressive.

It is worth noting that despite India being the member with the largest number of financed projects, it ended up in last place, with few projects in the energy sector.

Among these projects, we identified the purposes of this financing, dividing them into six subsectors, as shown in Fig. 7.6.

As shown in Fig. 7.6 above, projects directed to renewable energy represent 50% of the financing for energy. In these cases, the projects that will be executed are not specifically described – for example, whether the investments will focus on the construction of solar or wind energy infrastructures. This is due to the fact that these projects, in some cases, are undertaken in partnership with other partner financial institutions, as is the case of financing for Brazil which has BNDES (Brazilian Development Bank) and Banco do Brazil as cofinancing institutions. From this partnership, there is the allocation of funding to the

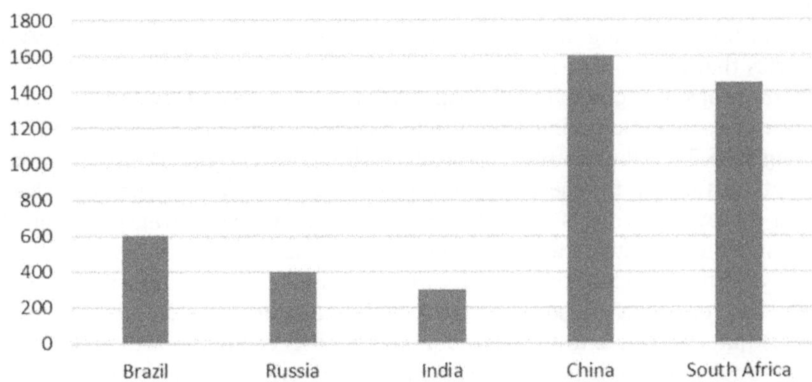

Fig. 7.5. Amounts Allocated to the Energy Transition (US$ Million). *Source:* List of Projects (NDB, 2022b).

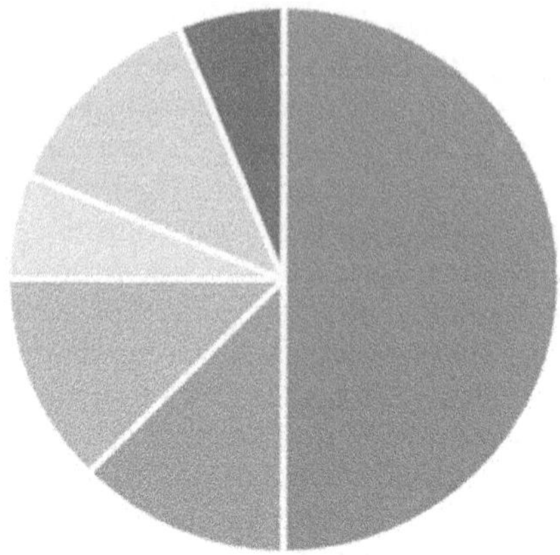

Fig. 7.6. Projects by Energy-related Sectors. *Source:* List of Projects (NDB, 2022b).

cofinancing institutions, and it is they who carry out the selection of subprojects that fit into the scope of renewable energy.

The other subsectors are more distributed. On the one hand, there are energy generation projects based on clean energy (wind and solar) and financing that support the transition (energy efficiency and storage). On the other hand, there are also contributions to initiatives based on fossil fuels, with the presence of financing for natural gas plants, with the two projects identified being for China.

Regarding financing for the decarbonization process, Fig. 7.7 shows the countries that have obtained the most resources for this area.

With projects focused on Transportation and Urban Development, India stands out in the undertakings that aim to reduce carbon emissions in the country, totaling US$ 2.4 billion in seven projects in this field. Despite not receiving large amounts of funding for the energy transition itself, the Asian country is characterized by several projects that encourage the use of cleaner transport, with the establishment of electric transport, and more efficient cities, with the construction of subways that increase the capacity of public and collective transport.

The case of China is also noteworthy in this category, with $1.5 billion in four projects that contribute to the decarbonization of its economy, with undertakings that will not only implement a modern tram network but will also carry out the replacement of natural gas-powered buses with electric vehicles.

In addition to understanding the dynamics of the NDB's performance based on the funded projects, it is also important to evaluate the institution's approaches

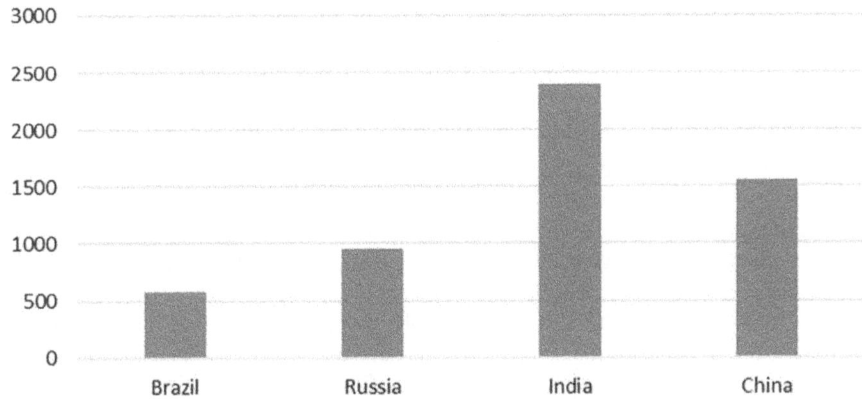

Fig. 7.7. Amounts Allocated to the Decarbonization (US$ Million). *Source:* List of Projects (NDB, 2022b).

to socio-environmental issues. In this regard, it is worth reflecting on the challenges of project implementation and the implications for the transition process. Therefore, the next section will address the limits and challenges that may affect the socio-environmental governance of the NDB.

Limits and Implications of the NDB's Operation

Regarding NDB's approach, it is worth questioning the bank's orientation toward financing that could be advantageous for business groups but would end up causing possible socio-environmental risks, not contributing to development in a broad perspective.

Thus, it is important to highlight that even in cases of financing directed to clean energy, negative socio-environmental impacts end up occurring. One of the cases that deserves evidence is the construction of wind farms that make up the Araripe 3 Wind Complex, where there are quilombola territories.

This project is a subproject that is part of the first NDB financing for Brazil, which was done in partnership with the BNDES, in which the two parties financed an amount of US$ 300 million each, to encourage the expansion of energy capacity from renewable sources.

If on the one hand, the venture was related to positive gains for the local population – with job generation, energy supply for the region's homes, and a contract that allowed the moderators who leased their land to be paid annually, becoming partners of the project – some negative impacts began to be reported by the local population, such as the impacts of the operation of the propellers in their routine, with loud noises, generating difficulties for people to sleep, besides generating effects on environmental issues, causing death of animals and a higher incidence of lightning in the region (Conectas, 2021a, 2021b, n.p.).

Furthermore, social impacts were also highlighted, since the conversations between families and the companies involved in the project occurred individually, generating a situation of distrust among residents and leading to processes of erosion of social and traditional ties of the community, besides not considering issues related to the ways of life and worldview of the residents (Conectas, 2021a, n.p.).

This case demonstrates that even in funding focused on renewable energy, it is necessary to evaluate, monitor, and question the implementation process, which can lead to "very serious effects on the lives of communities in the region when they are developed without social participation and without concern for the effects they can cause in people's lives" (Conectas, 2021a, n.p.).

One of the reasons related to these problems would be the fact that the project carried out together with the BNDES is classified as Category FI, i.e., the Brazilian development bank participates as an intermediary agency and is responsible for analyzing and monitoring environmental impacts, according to national legislation.[3] In these cases, the NDB only carries out an assessment of the gaps in the legislation and in the socio-environmental management of the responsible institution, so that they comply with all the objectives of the bank's socio-environmental framework, but respects the practices and guidelines of the bank it is financing, not intervening directly, only monitoring. However, if there are limitations and gaps in the socio-environmental management of these intermediary institutions, the risk of not effectively guaranteeing the social and environmental rights of the population could increase.

There are some cases of NDB funding for South Africa that also demonstrate gaps and problems worth mentioning, not only because of issues related to socio-environmental impacts but also because of accusations of corruption during the course of the project. One example is the funding allocated to Eskom, a South African parastatal energy company. The first project, in 2016, was intended to finance the "transmission of electricity to the grid of several privatized 'Wind and Solar Independent Power Producers' as well as for the restructuring of Soweto's electricity supply" (Bond, 2021). However, the corporation chose to privatize renewable energy production and establish relationships with European producers, generating additional costs for the residents of the Soweto region, who were further impacted by an illegal reconnection fee conducted by the corporation. This situation led to protests by unions from the affected industries (Bond, 2021).

---

[3]In its socio-environmental management, the NDB is responsible for elaborating a triage of each project to assign it a category, which can be: (a) Category A, when the project has significant environmental and social impacts that are irreversible, diverse, or unprecedented; (b) Category B, when the impacts are less adverse than those of category A; and (c) Category C, when the project has minimal or no environmental impact. There is another category that composes the bank's socio-environmental framework, which is the Category FI – Financial Intermediary, for projects where there is an intermediary agency, which will be responsible for assessing and monitoring environmental impacts, in accordance with the national legislation where the project will be implemented.

Furthermore, it is important to note that in this case, Eskom's leaders at the time held a preference for nuclear power over renewable and clean sources. These factors led the NDB to believe that the company "allocated a large portion of the $180 million loan to projects unrelated to renewable energy" (Bond, 2021). As a result, the bank eventually suspended this project, claiming the existence of corruption activities and actions that bring governance challenges to the institution. The funding was reactivated only in 2018 after its suspension. However, these actions brought impacts to the population, who experienced regular periods of power outages thanks to the failure to produce renewable energy that should have occurred.

Another case in South Africa that presented controversy was the loan in 2018 to the company Transnet, which was intended to expand the Durban container port. The controversy was over the contracting of the Italian-led CMI Emtateni consortium to do the work of cooling the port, with the participation of Shauwn Mpisane, a company that was involved in allegations of corruption in the asset procurement system. In this regard, the contract was eventually canceled under fraud in 2019 (Bond, 2021).

The company's expansion is also related to social impacts – such as the decrease of jobs in the ports due to the replacement of workers by machines – and environmental impacts, with the company's expansion and investments in fossil fuels (doubling of oil transport and refining capacity), in a context of climate change and environmental catastrophes (Bond, 2021). Moreover, the expansion of the port has been debated for years, with civil society organizations demonstrating the socio-environmental challenges and risks, such as the port's ecological degradation due to a "likely collapse of the large sandbank near the container terminal that will demolish vital bird and marine breeding areas" (Bond, 2021).

Considering Bond's (2021) analysis of these cases in South Africa, it is worth noting the danger around the NDB in moving away from projects aimed at the genuine needs of the population, to profit-oriented mega-infrastructure projects. Furthermore, the issues surrounding the implementation of the projects also portray the way in which decisions are made from the top, without greater participation or consultation with the impacted communities (Bond, 2021).

Thus, it is worth reflecting on the NDB's performance in its various areas, considering the criticisms, gaps, and challenges that the institution is facing, and the socio-environmental impacts and problems that its projects end up causing during the implementation process. Thus, we point to the need to question whether the bank is acting in a way that favors the transition of the BRICS countries to a low-carbon economy, since these challenges pointed out in the execution of the project hinder and reduce the positive results.

Conclusion

This chapter concludes that the NDB contributes to the BRICS transition process to a low-carbon economy, but with differences between countries. On the one hand, the NDB favors more the transition in the energy sector in China, South

Africa, and Brazil; on the other hand, the institution collaborates more with the decarbonization process in India, China, and Russia. Despite this, there are still limitations and challenges that hinder the NDB from becoming one of the main sources of incentives for its member countries to reach the climate targets.

The main objective of the research was to evaluate BRICS bank financing for the sectors that contribute most to the energy transition and decarbonization of various areas of the economy. A more profound understanding of the realities of each of the countries was not part of the scope of the study, but it is possible to point to ways to continue this research agenda, especially to assess whether these differences in the distribution of projects may be connected to different stages and approaches of the transition process toward a low-carbon economy in the BRICS countries. Thus, there is potential for future research that goes beyond the analysis of the institution's projects, which can evaluate the effects of these projects in the concrete realities of each country, and understand the effective contribution of the bank's actions.

It can also be concluded that, at least in the institutional and governance sphere, it is possible to find evidence of efforts toward sustainable finance, demonstrating that the NDB seeks to be in a position to support its members in these green transitions. With several goals and objectives to increase climate finance, the bank also presents a portfolio of projects that reflect, to some extent, these institutional efforts.

However, there is still a lot of room for the NDB to become one of the main sources of incentives for its member countries to achieve climate goals, especially considering the challenges and limits of the bank's actions.

As pointed out by the research, the NDB still faces problems in its socio-environmental management, with several claims, by civil society and local communities, complaining about the lack of transparency and the occurrence of impacts and conflicts in project implementation. The cases in Brazil and South Africa, addressed by the study, are just some examples of the challenges that the bank has been facing.

In this sense, it is important to highlight some recommendations for the NDB's operations:

- Delineate the concept of Sustainable Infrastructure to direct financing to projects that do not challenge the bank's sustainable commitment and can reduce socio-environmental impacts.
- Make available detailed information from all phases of the project, encompassing data on potential socio-environmental risks and elements of the implementation stage, facilitating access to information channels for civil society and local communities.
- Improve the relationship of the NDB with Intermediary Institutions in projects of Category FI, in a manner that the BRICS bank retains part of the responsibility for socio-environmental risks even after the funds are transferred to the intermediary institution.

Therefore, the evaluation of the institutional strategies and projects financed by the NDB shows that the bank is acting in a way to facilitate the transition to a low-carbon economy, but there are still limitations and challenges that need to be addressed to enhance the contribution of the institution more effectively.

References

Abadie, R., & Welsh, Y. (2020). *Global infrastructure trends.* PwC Global. https://www.pwc.com/gx/en/industries/capital-projects-infrastructure/publications/infrastructure-trends/global-infrastructure-trends-financing.html

Batista Jr., P. N. (2019). *O Brasil não cabe no quintal de ninguém: Bastidores a vida de um economista brasileiro no FMI e nos BRICS e outros textos sobre nacionalismo e nosso complexo de vira-lata.* Editora Casa da Palavra/LeYa.

Bond, P. (2021). *BRICS New Development Bank corruption in South Africa.* CADTM. https://www.cadtm.org/spip.php?page=imprimer&id_article=20169

Borges, C. D. S., & Cruz, J. C. D. C. (2018). *Country systems and environmental and social safeguards in development finance institutions: Assessment of the Brazilian system and ways forward for the New Development Bank.* Conectas Human Rights. https://publications.rifs-potsdam.de/pubman/faces/ViewItemOverviewPage.jsp?itemId=item_4041894

Buiter, W., & Fries, S. (2002). What should the multilateral development banks do? In *Annual World Bank conference on development economics – Europe.*

Cho, R. (2022). What is decarbonization, and how do we make it happen? *Columbia Climate School.* https://news.climate.columbia.edu/2022/04/22/what-is-decarbonization-and-how-do-we-make-it-happen/

Conectas. (2021a). *Como as comunidades quilombolas enxergam os empreendimentos.* https://www.conectas.org/noticias/como-as-comunidades-quilombolas-enxergam-os-empreendimentos/

Conectas. (2021b). *O papel dos bancos de desenvolvimento.* https://www.conectas.org/noticias/o-papel-dos-bancos-de-desenvolvimento/

Griffith-Jones, S. (2015). *Financing global development: The BRICS New Development Bank.* Briefing Paper, No. 13. Deutsches Institut für Entwicklungspolitik (DIE).

Humphrey, C. (2016). *Time for a new approach to environmental and social protection at multilateral development banks.* Briefing paper – ODI.

Humphrey, C. (2020). *From drawing board to reality: The first four years of operations at the Asian Infrastructure Investment Bank and New Development Bank.* Working Paper. ETH Zurich Research Collection.

IRENA. (2021). *World energy transitions outlook.* International Renewable Energy Agency. https://www.irena.org/publications/2021/March/World-Energy-Transitions-Outlook

IRENA. (2022). *Energy transition.* https://www.irena.org/energytransition

Kweitel, J., & Krishnaswamy, S. (2016). O Banco do BRICS está apto a impulsionar o desenvolvimento sustentável? *Dialogo Chino.* https://dialogochino.net/pt-br/pt/7485-o-banco-dos-brics-esta-apto-a-impulsionar-o-desenvolvimento-sustentavel/

Kweitel, J., Toni, A., & Gordon, G. (2017). O Banco do BRICS precisa de uma estratégia sólida e participativa para o desenvolvimento sustentável. *Open Democracy.* https://www.opendemocracy.net/pt/o-banco-dos-brics-precisa-de-uma-estrat-gia/

Losekann, L., & Tavares, F. B. (2019). *Política Energética no BRICS: Desafios da Transição Energética*. Ipea.

Mineiro, A., Mello, F., & Jakobsen, K. (2018). *As Instituições Financeiras Internacionais com Participação do Brasil: seu papel atual*. INESC. https://www.inesc.org.br/wp-content/uploads/2018/09/IFI_E_O_PAPEL_DO_BRASIL_2018.pdf

Montenegro, R. H., Paiva, I., & Feitosa, L. M. (2020). O lugar das fontes renováveis no relacionamento do Brasil com os "RICS" na área de energia: uma anállise da agenda bilateral e das declarações de cúpula (1990-2018). *Conjuntura Austral*, *11*(53), 139–160.

Nelson, R. M. (2011). *Multilateral development banks: Overview and issues for congress*. Congressional Research Service.

New Development Bank – NDB. (2014, July). *Agreement on the New Development Bank*. Fortaleza.

New Development Bank – NDB. (2017). *General strategy (2017-2021)*. https://www.ndb.int/wp-content/uploads/2017/08/NDB-Strategy.pdf

New Development Bank – NDB. (2021). *NDB initiates membership expansion, extends global outreach*. https://www.ndb.int/press_release/ndb-initiates-membership-expansion-extends-global-outreach-development-bank-established-by-brics-welcomes-the-admission-of-uae-uruguay-and-bangladesh-as-new-members/

New Development Bank – NDB. (2022a). *General strategy (2022-2026)*. https://www.ndb.int/wp-content/uploads/2022/07/NDB_StrategyDocument_Eversion-1.pdf

New Development Bank – NDB. (2022b). *List of all projects*. https://www.ndb.int/projects/list-of-all-projects/

Oxfam. (2021). *Information disclosure and grievance mechanisms of the New Development Bank (NDB)*. Briefing Paper – Oxfam South Africa.

Papadis, E., & Tsatsaronis, G. (2020). Challenges in the decarbonization of the energy sector. *Energy*, *205*, 118025.

Paris Agreement. (2015). *Adoption of the Paris Agreement*. United Nations. https://unfccc.int/sites/default/files/english_paris_agreement.pdf

Ribeiro, R. A., & Abdenur, A. (2022). Como os Brics podem impulsionar a cooperação em energias renováveis. *Dialogo Chino*. https://dialogochino.net/pt-br/mudanca-climatica-e-energia-pt-br/55236-opiniao-como-os-brics-podem-impulsionar-a-cooperacao-em-energias-renovaveis/

Teixeira, G., & Pimentel, G. (2017). *Caminhos da Responsabilidade Socioambiental no BNDES: uma avaliação da evolução no Período de Junho/2016 a Junho/2017*. SITAWI.

Vazquez, K. C. (2020). Development impact, public-private partnerships and regional integration: Possible way-forward for the BRICS-led New Development Bank. *Revista Tempo do Mundo*, (22).

Volpon, F., & Ribeiro, M. R. d. S. (2018). Desafios da governança energética global e a participação do brics na construção de um novo paradigma energético. *Revista de Direito Internacional*, *15*(1), 199–220.

Zhu, J. (2020). Two approaches to institutionalizing the new development assistance: A comparative analysis of the operational institutions of NDB and AIIB. In Y. Jing, A. Mendez, & Y. Zheng (Eds.), *New development assistance: Emerging economies and the new landscape of development assistance. Governing China in the 21st century*. Palgrave Macmillan.

Chapter 8

Notes on the Performance of the New Development Bank[1]

Jonnas Esmeraldo Marques de Vasconcelos[a] *and Ana Elisa Saggioro Garcia*[b]

[a]Federal University of Bahia (FD-UFBA), Brazil
[b]Institute of International Relations at PUC-Rio, Brazil

Abstract

The New Development Bank (NDB) was established by BRICS to address the need for a new balance in the global financial order. It is primarily composed of developing economies and initially lacked Western presence. The NDB was envisioned as a bank *from and for the Global South*, promoting *green* initiatives and adopting a *noninterventionist* approach, which led to high expectations for its performance. However, after it began operations, our analysis revealed that the NDB has encountered operational limitations. Our evaluation followed three steps: discussing the creation and expectations of the NDB, analyzing its funding policies and performance, and presenting future challenges. The NDB was evaluated by considering its Articles of Agreement, General Strategy, Annual Reports, and a comparison with the Asian Infrastructure Investment Bank's performance.

Keywords: BRICS; New Development Bank; performance; funding policies; limitations

[1]This chapter is an updated and expanded version of the article published by the authors in 2023. https://revistas.unifacs.br/index.php/redu/article/view/8060

The Multilateralism of the New Development Bank on the Sustainable Economic Growth in BRICS Nations and Beyond, 125–142

Published under exclusive licence by Emerald Publishing Limited
doi:10.1108/978-1-83662-292-520251011

Introduction

Over its more than 15 years of activities, BRICS has undergone a process of institutional densification (Ramos et al., 2018).[2] It is in the financial arena that the group has stood out. Since its first official meeting in 2009, BRICS has demanded reforms in the institutional financial architecture derived from Bretton Woods' agreement (such as in the World Bank, in the International Monetary Fund and in the dominant role of the US currency in the international monetary relations). As a part of its "regulatory agenda towards the international monetary and financial system" (Vasconcelos, 2020), the group has also created its own multilateral institution: the New Development Bank (NDB), which became fully operational in mid-2016.

The purpose of this chapter is to discuss the capacity of the NDB in providing a new model of development finance. We raise the hypothesis that BRICS' capacity of providing an alternative has been limited due to its operational problems. Therefore, the NDB has showed little impact in BRICS' economies, diminishing its capacity to attend its own financial goals.

Our evaluation of the NDB consisted of three steps: (i) discussing the creation and expectations of the NDB, (ii) analyzing its funding policies and performance, and (iii) presenting challenges for its future. The financial institution created by BRICS was evaluated by considering NDB's Articles of Agreement (2015), NDB's General Strategy (2017a; 2022b), NDB's Annual Reports (2016a; 2017b; 2018; 2019; 2020; 2021; 2022a), and a comparison with the Asian Infrastructure Investment Bank's (AIIB's) performance.

Expectations and Innovations Toward the NDB

While demanding reforms in Bretton Woods institutions, BRICS created the NDB to finance infrastructure and sustainable energy projects in emerging economies and developing countries. One of the official reasons for BRICS to establish its own bank was their disappointment at the lack of progress in reforming Bretton Woods institutions. From the standpoint of the group, its own institution-building initiatives supposed to be crucial to share BRICS' vision of transforming the global financial architecture, allegedly "based on the principles of fairness and equity."[3]

After the idea of the BRICS bank was first made public at the third summit in Delhi in 2012, the agreement to establish it was signed two years later, in 2014, the

---

[2]Besides cooperation between government agencies in several sectors, BRICS must be seen as more than a group of States, as they have created civil society and business entities as well, namely the BRICS Business Council (which organizes the annual BRICS Business Forum), the Think Tanks Council and Academic Forum, and the "Civil BRICS." Social movements, NGOs, and grassroots organizations that are more critical toward BRICS have been organizing parallel "People's BRICS" summits since 2013.

[3]"45. *(...)* We believe that BRICS institution-building is critical to our shared vision of transforming the global financial architecture to one based on the principles of fairness and equity" (BRICS, 2016).

same year that the AIIB was also announced. Both banks began their financial operations in 2016.

With an initial authorized capital of US$ 100 billion with initial subscribed capital of US$ 50 billion and paid-in capital of US$ 10 billion, one innovative aspect of the NDB is that the internal governance statute has started with equal voting power for the bank's founding members.[4] As noted by Batista Jr (2022, p. 39): "None of the major international financial institutions display this feature."[5]

In the bank's narrative, it is precisely "new" because it is a 21st-century multilateral development bank (MDB) that builds on the experiences of existing institutions and reflects the growing role of BRICS countries in the world economy (NDB, 2017a, pp. 7–8).

This BRICS initiative was a high point to those who considered the group challengers of US economic supremacy.[6] The creation of a new multilateral financial institution composed primarily by "developing" economies, without the presence of the United States or other Western powers, at least initially, was seen as reflecting the need for a new equilibrium in the world order.[7]

The banks' narrative highlights two important issues that distinguish it from Bretton Woods institutions. The first is the emphasis on national sovereignty. According to the NDB's General Strategy 2017–2021, "the NDB's mandate does not

---

[4]The founding members are the five BRICS countries, but the NDB is open to other UN members. With headquarters in Shanghai, the bank opened its Africa Regional Centre in Johannesburg in 2017, its Eurasian Regional Centre in Moscow, and its Americas Regional Office in São Paulo, both in 2020. In 2022, NDB announced the launch of its Indian Regional Office in Gujarat International Finance Tec-City.

[5]According to Batista Jr's conjecture: "During the negotiations, China tried to have the lion's share of capital and votes, but the other countries managed to rebuff the aspiration. Perhaps because of this, I conjecture, China went ahead to create shortly thereafter the AIIB in Beijing. In the NDB, no country plays the leading role that the United States plays in the IMF and the World Bank. Or that China plays in the AIIB. In these organizations, the US or China have veto power over crucial decisions" (Batista Jr, 2022, p. 39).

[6]For example: Rhadika Desai, "The BRICS are building a challenge to western economic supremacy." *The Guardian*, April 2, 2013. https://www.theguardian.com/commentisfree/2013/apr/02/brics-challenge-western-supremacy; or Walden Bello, "The BRICS: Challengers to the global status-quo." *Foreign Policy in Focus*, August 29, 2014. https://fpif.org/brics-challengers-global-status-quo/

[7]"Banco dos BRICS muda equilíbrio mundial, diz economista." Interview with Deepak Nayyar in *Folha de Sao Paulo*, August 16, 2014. https://m.folha.uol.com.br/mercado/2014/08/1501027-banco-dos-brics-muda-equilibrio-mundial-diz-economista-leia-integra.shtml?cmpid=menupe. As Elmar Altvater wrote in a piece to the 70th anniversary of the Bretton Woods institutions (in 2014) the need for reform was on the top of the agenda, but decision-makers were still reluctant to lose power: "To lessen dependency on the IMF, the World Bank and Wall Street, and to increase their developmental leeway, similarly structured organizations of the Global South are being formed against the Monetary Fund and the Development Banks of the Global North. The 70th anniversary of the Bretton Woods System may be the date later historians will write that it is the birth of an autonomous political formation of the global South against the global North" (Altvater, 2014, our translation).

include prescribing policy, regulatory and institutional reforms to borrowing countries" (NDB, 2017a, p. 11). This approach means adhering to nationally defined laws and procedures for project implementation without compromising project quality. This reflects the bank's approach to a national country's system of environmental protection. The second intention is to use local currencies for its transactions.[8]

In sum, the NDB was intended to be an example of a new generation of MDB because it would: (i) be a bank *from and for the South* (addressing the needs of developing and emerging countries), (ii) be a *green* bank (focusing its major funding on infrastructure and sustainable projects), and (iii) be a *noninterventionist* bank (i.e., its operational decisions would be allegedly based on merit, and not on a hidden political agenda).[9]

The NDB's Limitations

Given these previous assumptions, the high expectations over NDB as a possible alternative to the existing Bretton Woods institution are understandable. Having started promisingly, the bank concluded its first loans in each member country as early as 2016. During that year, it successfully issued its inaugural green bonds denominated in Renminbi (3 billion RMB, equivalent to US$ 442 million at the time). From 2017 onward, it embarked on a strategy of establishing regional offices, beginning with South Africa, followed by Brazil in 2019, Russia in 2020, and India in 2022. Despite these achievements, the NDB has faced challenges that have impacted its performance in the early years, reducing its ability to meet those expectations.

The NDB's underperformance in critical areas has been a significant issue. When considering the operational principles outlined in the NDB's Articles of Agreement, the objectives stated in its initial General Strategy (2017–2021), the operational model of the AIIB (a similar and contemporary institution), and their respective Annual Reports, the BRICS institution has not delivered satisfactory results.

According to the NDB's General Strategy (2017–2021), the bank aimed to be fast and efficient, setting a goal to appraise, negotiate, and approve loans in less than six months on average. This six-month target was intended to provide a competitive advantage to the NDB. For comparison, the approval process at the World Bank typically takes 14–16 months (Humphrey, 2016).

In its first operational year of 2016, the NDB already achieved project approvals within this timeline, investing up to US$ 1.5 billion. Regarding the

---

[8]At the same time, this strategy aims to reduce financial transaction costs by addressing the risk of devaluation. It also aligns with BRICS' goal to weaken Dollar's hegemony in the international monetary system (Zoe Liu & Papa, 2022). According to NDB's current General Strategy (2022–2026), the bank aims to provide 30% of its total financing commitments in national currencies of member countries.

[9]As the Brazilian former NDB Vice President Paulo Nogueira Batista Jr (2016, p. 179, our translation) clearly stated: "NBD is not a political bank. The bank will be guided by technical criteria to approve projects. Our constitutional agreement makes this point clear. We want to avoid over-politicizing the decisions that are taking place in existing multilateral institutions."

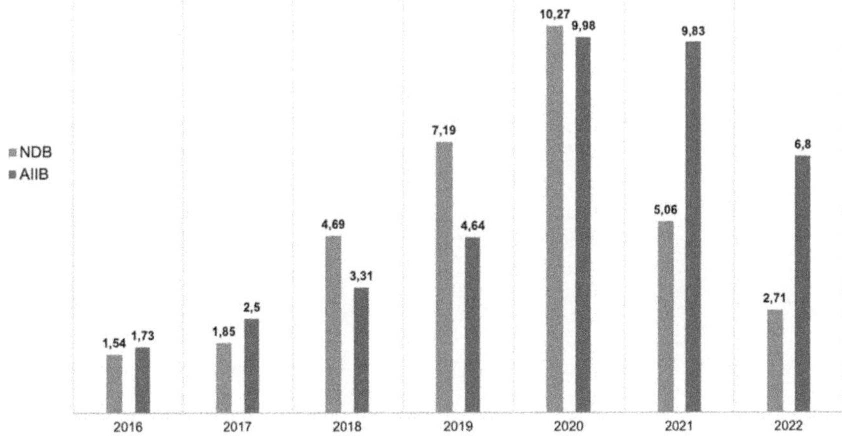

Fig. 8.1. Total Amount of Approved Loans per Year (US$ Billion).
Source: Elaborated by the authors based on data from NDB and AIIB Annual Reports.

annual investment amounts for approved projects, as shown in Fig. 8.1, the NDB has exhibited a pattern quite similar to that of the AIIB (even exceeding it before the outbreak of the pandemic crisis, the specific effects of which will be studied for both banks' performance subsequently).

Despite the BRICS' bank's ability to approve loans quickly, it has struggled to disburse funds as planned in its General Strategy. For instance, by the end of 2018, the NDB had a loan portfolio of US$ 8 billion, but awkwardly, it had disbursed less than US$ 650 million (less than half of its target). Before the onset of the COVID-19 pandemic, the NDB had approved more than 50 projects, committing up to US$ 15 billion in investments (in contrast, the AIIB had invested up to US$ 12 billion in 63 projects). However, during the same period, the NDB's cumulative loan disbursements only reached approximately US$ 1.5 billion (almost half of the AIIB's disbursements), which represents less than one-third of the amount expected according to the most conservative official forecast (at least US$ 4.6 billion by then).

As shown on Fig. 8.2, these data did not meet the NDB's own strategic goals for the period, as outlined in its first General Strategy (2017–2021), while also revealing its poor performance compared to the AIIB.

Such data suggest that the NDB has approved projects without the necessary maturity in regarding technical feasibility and financial viability analysis, thereby reinforcing the notion that the bank's speedy actions are a fiction in fact. Since the onset of the pandemic, the NDB's disbursement rates have changed considerably, even surpassing the optimist amount forecasted in its first General Strategy (*scenario 2*) in 2020. In 2021, the NDB disbursed up to US$ 7.6 billion – more than the total in all previous years combined. Nevertheless, considering the cumulative disbursements from 2020 to 2021, at least eight billion were fully allocated not to infrastructure projects but to meet the special needs of its member states due to the pandemic crisis.

In fact, the NDB established a "Fast Track COVID-19 Emergency Assistance Response Facility" of up to US$ 10 billion to support BRICS countries. With agility and flexibility as core principles, this Facility was designed to allocate up to US$ 5 billion for BRICS' most urgent needs, including health expenditures and social safety

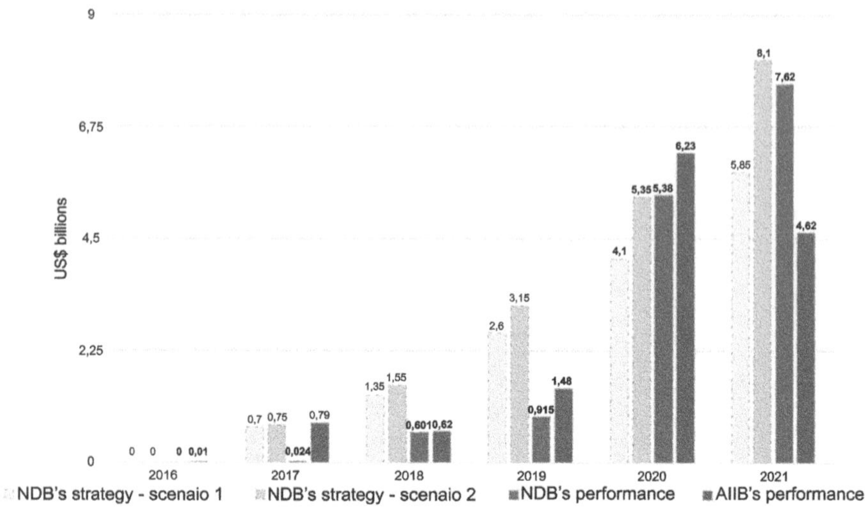

Fig. 8.2. Total Amount of Loan Disbursements per Year (US$ Billion). *Source:* Elaborated by the authors based on data from NDB General Strategy (2017–2021) and from NDB and AIIB Annual Reports.

nets, and an additional equal amount for economic recovery.[10] It's worth noting that the AIIB has also announced a similar program, known as the "COVID-19 Crisis Recovery Facility."[11] Therefore, one can't assume that these loans align with the NDB's or even AIIB's previous strategic plan. In reality, the exceptional circumstances created by the COVID-19 pandemic were the primary reasons for both banks' significant and rapid disbursements in 2020. If one takes COVID-19 emergency assistance out of the equation, the NDB's disbursements in 2020 were only US$ 2.3 billion and only 2.5 billion in 2021 (almost half of the conservative amount forecasted in its own General Strategy – *scenario 1* – for both years). Furthermore, according to the latest available Annual Report, the bank disbursed approximately US$ 1.16 billion in 2022, a sharp decline compared to previous years.[12]

Moreover, compare to the AIIB, the NDB faced significant difficulties in obtaining international credit rating. In its first two years, the BRICS' bank only had ratings from Chinese domestic credit agencies: triple A from *China Chengxin International Credit Rating* and from *China Lianhe Credit Rating*. During the same period, by contrast, the AIIB had already achieved the highest rates from major international credit rating agencies: a triple A from *Standard and Poor's* and from

[10]See: https://www.ndb.int/wp-content/uploads/2020/07/Policy-on-Fast-track-Emergency-Response-to-COVID-19.pdf

[11]AIIB's COVID-19 Crisis Recovery Facility has offered up to US$ 13 billion to support the bank's members and clients in alleviating and mitigating economic, financial and public health pressures arising from COVID-19. See: https://www.aiib.org/en/policies-strategies/COVID-19-Crisis-Recovery-Facility/index.html

[12]See https://www.ndb.int/wp-content/uploads/2023/12/NDB_AR_2022_complete-1.pdf

Fitch Ratings, as well as an "Aaa" score from *Moody's*. It was only in 2018 that the NDB obtained ratings from these well-known agencies: a "AA+" from *Standard and Poor's* and from *Fitch Ratings*.[13] One reason for this discrepancy between the NDB and the AIIB's ratings lies in the number and variety of their members (see Fig. 8.3).

While AIIB had approved 106 members, including several advanced countries as shareholders, NDB faced significant difficulties in expanding its membership, despite recognizing that expansion membership is crucial for achieving the BRICS' bank strategic goals.[14] As pointed by Batista Jr, the

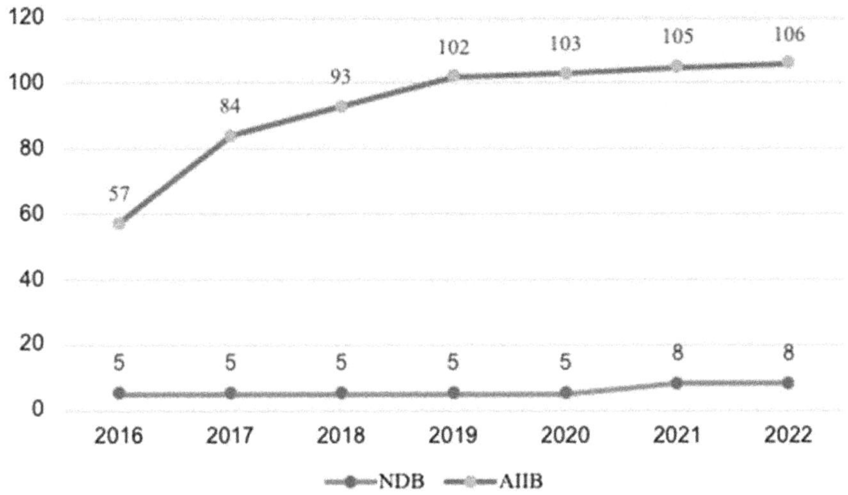

Fig. 8.3. Membership Expansion per Year. *Source:* Elaborated by the authors based on data from NDB and AIIB Annual Reports.

[13]In 2019, a "triple A" international rating was granted by *Japan Credit Rating Agency*. The following year, the NDB also received a triple A from a Russian institution called *Analytic Credit Rating Agency*. Cf: https://www.ndb.int/investor-relations/credit-ratings/. Due to the war in Ukraine, Fitch decided to downgrade NDB's to "AA" in July 2022. See: https://www.fitchratings.com/research/sovereigns/fitch-downgrades-new-development-bank-to-aa-outlook-negative-18-07-2022. By May 2023, Fitch's rating was revised from "negative" to "stable." See: https://www.fitchratings.com/research/sovereigns/fitch-revises-new-development-bank-outlook-to-stable-affirms-at-aa-16-05-2023

[14]According to NDB's first General Strategy: "The Bank also expects to influence the international financial architecture and global practices by being a fundamentally new kind of development institution based on mutual respect and reflecting the evolution of the world economy in recent decades. To achieve these goals, NDB must operate at scale, and that means bringing in new members beyond the founding five shareholder countries *(...)*. Expansion of membership will help raise the Bank's profile and international standing, diversify NDB's sphere of operations to more countries and reduce portfolio concentration, increase paid-in capital, and leverage the experience of other countries in project design and implementation" (NDB, 2017a, p. 26).

NDB's lack of leadership compared to AIIB's is one of the main reasons for that discrepancy:

> The contrast with President Jin Liqun of AIIB was embarrassing for us. Created shortly after the NDB, the AIIB has a dynamic and creative president, who led his institution to a prominent role from the very beginning, casting a deep shadow over our bank. In fact, despite its regional focus – the AIIB was intended as an Asian bank that would compete with the ADB where Japan and the United States have prominent positions – the bank headquartered in Beijing increasingly came to play the global role that was designed for the NDB. Early on the AIIB had managed to bring in a large number of countries, including from outside Asia and all major advanced countries with the exceptions of the US and Japan. Meanwhile, under Kamath's leadership (or lack thereof) the bank created by the BRICS languished. Five years after its operations began in July 2015, no new countries have joined the Bank and plans for expansion of membership have suffered repeated delays. Lack of initiative and leadership on the part of the Indian President was one major reason for this. (Batista Jr, 2022, p. 50)

It's worth noting that only in 2021, the NBD managed to secure agreements to incorporate Bangladesh, United Arab Emirates (the first nonborrowing member), Egypt, and Uruguay as new members, but the latter still need to finish its internal procedures to complete the membership. As anticipated, a bank with a limited number of shareholders, such as the NDB, faces a higher concentration of risk in its portfolio.[15] Furthermore, the lack of developed countries among its members detracts from the NDB's international credit rating.

[15]While working at the institution, Paulo Nogueira Batista Jr noted that the main force against NDB's expansion of memberships was the Russians. According to Batista Jr (2021), international embargos, along with their support by major advanced countries and the consequent difficulties in access international credit, explain the Russian reluctance to incorporate new members in BRICS' bank. About Russian's struggles, Batista Jr (2022, p. 54) also noted that: "Just as in older multilateral institutions, the Europeans had formed a block in AIIB and began to object against any operations of the institution with Russia. Now, they did not have sufficient votes to block operations, but President Jin Liquin – so I was told by Russian representatives to the NDB – indicated at one point that he would somehow accept this veto, even if not explicitly. Russian indignation with this was so strong that something uncommon occurred. During a BRICS ministerial meeting, in Shanghai, in June 2017, with as many as about 30 persons in the room, the Russian Finance Minister, Anton Siluanov, addressing directly the Chinese Finance Minister, Jin Renquing, complained emphatically about what was going on in the AIIB, adding that this only increased Russia's reluctance to agree with membership expansion in the NDB."

According to the NDB's articles of agreement, "the Bank shall not allow a disproportionate amount of its resources to be used for the benefit of any member. The Bank shall seek to maintain reasonable diversification in all of its investments." Nonetheless, during its first years, the NDB's portfolio was severely concentrated in the Asian region. For instance, until the end of 2019, the NDB had only approved six projects from Brazil, representing more or less 10% of its portfolio.

Considering the amount of funding approved by the NDB until the end of 2022, it is evident that India and China still concentrated almost half of the NDB's portfolio. Russia received the least resources from the BRICS institution. The image in Fig. 8.4 shows the amount of approvals by country until the end of 2022.

When considering the evolution of approvals by countries, the data indicate the NDB's difficulties in establishing an economic presence outside Asian region. One explanatory factor could be the underutilization of the regional offices (Chin, 2024, p. 377).[16] It's worth noting that by the end of 2020, the NDB approved six additional

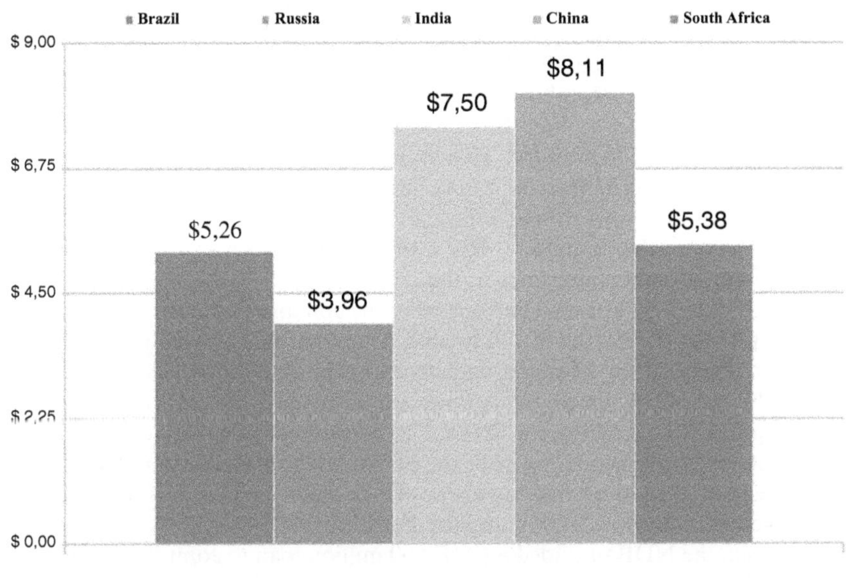

Fig. 8.4. Project Portfolio by Country (End of 2022). *Source:* Elaborated by the authors based on data from NDB Annual Reports.

[16]Regarding Brazil, it's worth noting that since at least 2015, the country has faced a severe political and economic crisis, exacerbated by the coup d'état against Dilma's presidency. Subsequent right-wing administrations (under both Temer and Bolsonaro) have shifted foreign policies, seeking closer alignments with traditional "Northern" countries, particularly the United States, thereby weakening Brazil's participation within BRICS structures (Berringer, 2022). The new administration under Lula appears poised to change this course.

projects in Brazil, amounting investments exceeding US$ 3,4 bi. At that time, Brazil represented approximately 20% of the NDB's portfolio. However, by 2022, Brazil's share of investments had decreased to less than 17% of the NDB's portfolio (US$ 5.2 billion out of the bank's total approved projects of US$ 30.2 billion). In terms of loan disbursements, Brazil received the smallest amount of funding from the bank, with just over US$ 1.38 billion disbursed, representing about 10% of the total. In contrast, China received the largest share, with US$ 4.15 billion disbursed, accounting for 32% of the bank's disbursements. Given that the majority of the investments in Brazil came from the COVID-19 Facility, the NDB still needs to make greater efforts to build a more diverse and less concentrated portfolio.

The NDB's Investments

Another crucial aspect to evaluate the NDB's performance is the quality of its investments. This involves examining the bank's operations within BRICS countries and assessing the economic sectors and types of projects it sponsors.

The NDB's initial operation in Brazil occurred in 2016 in collaboration with the Brazilian Development Bank (BNDES) for an amount of US$ 300 million (NDB, 2017b, p. 34). Notably, the 2019 annual report highlighted a US$ 300 million corporate loan to Vale S.A., the largest mining company and a major logistics operator in the country. This loan aimed to enhance the transportation system, particularly in railway and port infrastructure, to increase the company's cargo capacity and operational efficiency (NDB, 2019, p. 40). However, it's important to note that Vale S.A. has a significant history of human rights violations and environmental crimes in the country.[17]

In 2019, Vale S.A. was also implicated in the collapse of the Brumadinho dam, which resulted in the deaths of 270 people. This disaster occurred just three years after the collapse of the Mariana dam, both in the state of Minas Gerais.[18]

In 2020, the NDB approved its largest loan to date: a sovereign guaranteed loan of up to US$ 1.2 billion for BNDES to be used for sustainable infrastructure subprojects in Brazil, benefiting both the public and private sectors. Additionally, until the end of 2022, the bank had approved 18 other projects in Brazil, including a nonsovereign loan to the oil company Petrobras.

In Russia, the NDB provided a CHF 500 million loan to Joint Stock Company Russian Railways for its locomotive fleet renewal program, facilitating the acquisition of 3,576 new locomotives equipped with cutting-edge technologies, thereby modernizing Russia's railway system (NDB, 2019, p. 40). However, a US$ 300 million loan to the Russian petrochemical company SIBUR raised

---

[17]These violations have been documented by the international alliance of People Affected by Vale, for instance, in its "Vale Unsustantabiliy Reports". https://atingidosvale.com/relatorio/. Accessed on July 2022.

[18]See: https://www.bbc.com/news/world-latin-america-51220373

controversy due to allegations that it benefited oligarchs associated with Vladimir Putin's inner circle, including his former son-in-law.[19] Due to the Russia–Ukraine war, the NDB has put new transactions in Russian "on hold." It is important to note that one of the sensitive and strategic issues for the bank since then has been to shield the institution from potential sanctions from the West.

India's projects highlighted in the 2019 annual report focus on the state of Madhya Pradesh, receiving loans in transportation infrastructure – two loans of US$ 323 million each for road and bridge renovations – and urban development – a US$ 225 million loan for a new metro line (NDB, 2019, p. 44). Overall, until the end of 2022, the NDB has approved US$ 7.5 billion for projects in transportation, urban infrastructure, water, sanitation, and related sectors in India.

As mentioned before, the NDB issued its first "green" bonds in China, totaling 3 billion yuan (US$ 442 million) in 2016. By late 2017, the bank had approved four projects in renewable energy and water sanitation totaling US$ 895 million, with three projects financed directly in Chinese currency (NDB, 2017b, p. 37), supporting China's Renminbi internationalization strategy. The 2019 report highlights the Lanzhou New Area Regional Hub Multimodal Logistics and Transport Infrastructure Demonstration Project, providing RMB 2.5 billion to finance multimodal logistics options including rail, road, and air freight (NDB, 2019, p. 41). According to the 2022 Annual Report, the NDB had approved 21 Chinese projects in total, with US$ 8.1 billion in investments, representing more than 25% of the bank's portfolio.

In South Africa, the NDB approved two additional loans to Eskom Holdings SOC Ltd., a state-owned electricity utility providing about 95% of the country's electricity (NDB, 2019, p. 38). Another loan of US$ 200 million was granted to Transnet for expanding a container terminal at Durban Port, an operation criticized by D'Sa and Bond (2018) for lacking adequate consultation and analysis. The South Durban Community Environmental Alliance (SDCEA) has opposed the ultra-polluting port-petrochemical complex, citing environmental racism due to health issues and ecological degradation in the predominantly poor, black area (D'Sa & Bond, 2018, p. 180). Transnet previously received a loan from the China Development Bank in 2013 during the Durban BRICS summit, leading to subcontracting with a Chinese firm under questionable terms (D'Sa & Bond, 2018, pp. 181–182).

Following these data, one may question the NDB's ability to finance infrastructure projects while ensuring sustainability, environmental protection, and the rights of populations in project-affected territories. Altvater (2015, p. 242) aptly highlights the "limits of growth," asserting that "Capitalist dynamics are overshooting the limits of the living and the natural resources of Planet Earth." Major infrastructure projects such as roads, railways, ports, and hydroelectric plants across BRICS territories and their hinterlands often serve extractive industries and agribusinesses, facilitating the export of their products to international

[19]https://www.valor.com.br/international/news/5975457/ndb-approved-loan-sibur-despite-controversy-about-sanctions

markets. These infrastructure networks can sometimes create new channels for exploitation, establishing extensive logistical corridors that link territories and natural resources with global markets. The Nacala Development Corridor in Mozambique serves as a vivid example of this phenomenon (Garcia & Kato, 2020).[20]

Human Rights' Standards and Practices Within the NDB

The NDB elaborated a socio and environmental framework in 2016, only after releasing its first approvals. This framework is composed of two parts: the first being a series of overarching policies on the social and environmental management of the bank's operations, and the second, on the socio-environmental standards related to the environment protection, involuntary resettlement, and indigenous peoples (NDB, 2016b, p. 13). Among its objectives, there is the strengthening of national environmental and social systems, which would mean that, "Through its operations, NDB seeks to balance economic, social, and environmental interests while fostering ownership and accountability of member countries" (NDB, 2016b, p. 4).

According to the NDB, there were problems of the 1980s World Bank's environmental and social safeguards, concerning their restrict applicability (it would be applied exclusively to projects funded by the World Bank), imposition over national laws (raising questions of sovereignty), and the unrecognition of the variety of legal frameworks and enforcement capacities across developing countries (NDB, 2017a, p. 16). The BRICS bank asserts that the optimal approach to managing social, environmental, and procurement risks is to utilize and enhance existing country systems rather than circumventing them with external standards. According to its narrative, "instead of starting from externally-designed set of standards, the NDB will take a country's system as a starting point" and follow mandated local procedures with rigor and transparency. This would lead to the achievement of protection against misuse of project resources and strengthening of local frameworks and implementation capacities (NDB, 2017a, p. 16).

To be sure, the policy of strengthening national systems meets the principles of noninterference in internal affairs and preserves the scope of action of national states. However, there is a risk that these new multilateral banks could precipitate a widespread downgrading of standards, given the lack of environmental and social safeguards, which are a result of struggles already won at the level of the

[20]It illustrates, within the concrete context of African territories, the prominent role played by multinational corporations (like Brazilian Vale and Japanese Mitsui), funding agencies from the Global North (such as JICA), and multilateral financial institutions such as the World Bank and the African Development Bank. This underscores the convergence of actors and initiatives in the production chain of mineral and agricultural commodities, which are crucial for global capitalist accumulation. Therefore, the Nacala Corridor suggests that the aid and investment efforts of emerging economies within BRICS, such as Brazil, are complicit in the same processes of expropriation and exploitation of territories as major global players, rather than standing in opposition to them.

World Bank. This has been a topic of major discussion among civil society organizations.[21]

Notably, the NDB, the AIIB, and the World Bank launched their socio-environmental standards almost simultaneously in the same year 2016 (Esteves et al., 2016). The NDB and the AIIB prioritize utilizing national socio-environmental protection and risk management systems, whereas the World Bank has adjusted its socio-environmental safeguards policy to align with this approach.[22] According to Esteves (2018), the use of "country systems" brought together the World Bank, the AIIB, and the NDB, making them compete at the same level for infrastructure projects in peripheral areas. In order to meet "global development" goals and minimize risks for the private sector, regulation must be made more flexible, not only in terms of environment but also financial management procedures, procurement, taxation, and profit remittance (Esteves, 2018, p. 14).

It's worth noting that, whereas capital pushes for global investment and trade regulation regimes (which favors capital movements worldwide), regulations over labor, wages, and work safety conditions are set at the national level, forcing workers to compete for jobs in least favorable conditions. Here too, social and environmental standards are left for national institutions to decide, implement, and monitor, without multilateral financial institutions taking responsibility on questions of lack of transparency, public consultation, human rights violations, and environmental disasters. Consequently, national social-environmental standards may be put to global competition to attract investors. As Borges and Cortez (2018) have pointed out, although the Brazilian national environmental regulations and institutions are relatively strong, there are many vulnerabilities concerning indigenous and traditional communities in processes of decision-making and implementation of mega-projects such as hydroelectric plants, ports, railways, wind farms, that received huge amounts of credit from the BNDES, or from the World Bank through the BNDES (Borges & Cortez, 2018, p. 18).

The NDB has opened channels for participation of business entities, as well as nongovernmental organizations (NGOs), in its annual meetings. Some organizations have presented suggestions and demands for the bank in terms of human rights and environmental issues. Yet, the reorientation of BRICS institutions will depend upon the political and economic orientation of governments that compose BRICS.

[21]For example: Center for Financial Accountability. "The new development banks: Why AIIB and NDB should be monitored?" Briefing Paper, October 2016. https://www.cenfa.org/wp-content/uploads/2017/11/Briefing-paper-AIIB-NDB.pdf; Caio Borges and Julia Cortez. "Country Systems and Environmental and Social Safeguards in Development Finance Institutions: Assessment of the Brazilian System and Ways Forward for the New Development Bank." *Conectas Human Rights*, May 2018.

[22]According to Esteves, Zoccal and Torres (2016), there is no clarity on the mechanisms for strengthening national systems and on how the NDB and the AIIB intend to align them with their own parameters (Esteves et al., 2016).

Regarding other human rights aspects, the NDB has also failed to set a high standard. For instance, the bank's lack of gender diversity is critical, especially at its highest administration levels, which are only led by men.[23] Even though gender diversity is a real issue for the majority of international banks, the NDB isn't making a case for changing its current situation.[24]

Furthermore, the NDB needs to improve transparency significantly. Comparing it to the comprehensive information readily accessible on the AIIB's website, the NDB's transparency practices appear opaque. For example, while the NDB's website provides only generic data about its approved projects, the AIIB's website offers specific details and documents such as *Environmental and Social Due Diligence Reports*, *Project Implementation Monitoring Reports*, *Land Acquisition and Resettlement Plans*, *Stakeholder Engagement Plans,* etc.

As for labor rights, it's embarrassing that the NDB has yet to establish an impartial mechanism to settle disputes between the bank and its employees.[25] With the jurisdictional immunity adopted by the NDB's articles of agreement, if a labor dispute arises, the staff member is not able to appeal to a national court.[26] One should note that it is very common to concede jurisdiction immunities (labor-related, tax-related etc.) to international organizations, and as summarized by Berenson (2012, p. 133), there are two basic reasons to justify this practice:

> (i) Preventing any one state from gaining an unfair advantage in or crippling an international organization by way of its courts and/or administrative agencies with adjudicative authority; and (ii) Providing a guarantee that a member State, in disputes with those organizations, is not likely to become both judge and party thereby denying the organization a mechanism for the fair and independent adjudication of the dispute in accordance with due process.

Nevertheless, immunity isn't the same as impunity. When State members agree on not extending their national jurisdictions to an international organization, this means that they are to choose a different structure to perform the role of competent jurisdiction, in which the resolution of the international organization's disputes will occur. Therefore, in order to allow staff members to exercise their

---

[23]See: http://www.bricsfeministwatch.org/

[24]According to NDB's 2021 Annual Report, women accounted for 38% of the Bank's headcount. However, as for the qualitative aspect, positions of power within the bank have been occupied by men.

[25]By the end of 2021, NDB had 207 employees (1 President, 4 Vice Presidents, 188 full-time staff, and 14 short-term consultants and outsourced staff) (NDB, 2021, p. 52).

[26]As pointed out by Thévenot-Werner (2015, p. 112): "in the absence of an institution vested by the employing organisation with the power to settle such disputes, and recognised as an independent and impartial tribunal by the applicant, the staff member turns to the national judges. In this case, the organisation in question usually raises its immunity from jurisdiction as a total or partial protection from the action of national tribunals."

fundamental right to a fair trial, international organizations should have a dispute settlement mechanism.[27] Usually, there are two ways to do so: one is by creating its own tribunal, and the other is by adhering to the jurisdiction of an existing international court. To take a few examples, the World Bank has its own administrative tribunal, as well as the IMF. Others, such as the World Trade Organization and the ASEAN+3 Macroeconomic Research Office, have recognized the jurisdiction of the International Labour Organization Administrative Tribunal.

While the AIIB has established procedures and rules allowing its employees to appeal against decisions (albeit with room for improvement), the NDB cannot justify its lack of similar mechanisms based on its shorter operational history.[28] The absence of such procedures contributed to several human rights violations against the former Brazilian Vice President of the NDB, Paulo Nogueira Batista Jr. He was unlawfully dismissed through an internal process that not only violated the NDB's articles of agreement and its Code of Business Conduct and Ethics but also breached his own contract and international law. This incident exemplifies a case of lawfare, where the inherently political nature of his dismissal was inadequately masked as a breach of the bank's ethical code (Vasconcelos, 2023).

Final Remarks

In light of all the aforementioned aspects and data, it is challenging not to conclude that, despite BRICS' intentions to establish the NDB as an exemplar of a "global financial architecture based on the principles of fairness and equity," they have fallen short in its initial years. It is clear that much remains to be done by the NDB to meet BRICS' self-declared expectations. As our evaluation demonstrates, there are numerous critical issues undermining the BRICS bank's capacity to offer an efficient and robust alternative to the current international financial order.

Nevertheless, our evaluation doesn't argue that the NDB has not been an important initiative. For instance, even though it's not the major player in the international financial market, the NDB's existence diversifies options for funding infrastructures in developing countries. In a different dimension, the NDB also helps strengthening BRICS' cohesion and agenda. That particular role can be observed not only with the rise of internal frictions within BRICS in recent years (such as the geopolitical tensions between India and China regarding their borders and Pakistan or the conflicts between Bolsonaro's administration and the Chinese government, etc.) but also during the pandemic context (Garcia et al., 2020).

---

[27]According to Article 10 of the Universal Declaration of Human Rights adopted by the United Nations: "Everyone is entitled in full equality to a fair and public hearing by an independent and impartial tribunal, in the determination of its rights and obligations and of any criminal charge against him."

[28]See Staff Regulation and Staff Rules documents: https://www.aiib.org/en/about-aiib/basic-documents/staff-regulations/index.html and https://www.aiib.org/en/about-aiib/basic-documents/staff-rules/index.html

It is important to note that the change in bank presidency in mid-2020 did not resolve the chronic problems faced by the NDB. Marcos Troyjo's tenure at the NDB saw efforts to expand membership, but progress has been disappointingly slow. By the end of 2022, the NDB disbursed US$ 14.4 billion.[29] However, the majority of these disbursements were driven by exceptional circumstances created by the COVID-19 program, rather than the NDB successfully overcoming its historical difficulties in disbursing funds for its regular approved projects. While the bank increased its portfolio of investments, it remains heavily concentrated in the Asian region. Despite significant demands and financing opportunities in Brazil, the NDB has maintained a limited presence in the Brazilian economy.

In terms of currency diversification, the NDB also needs to increase the share of local currencies used in its projects. By the end of 2022, nearly 25% of its financial operations were already conducted not in US dollars or euros, which helps reduce transaction costs and currency risks. This is close to the official target of 30%. However, there is still much to progress on this agenda, as the majority of these transactions in national currencies were primarily conducted in Chinese yuan (approximately three-quarters of them).

In terms of currency diversification, the NDB also needs to increase the proportion of local currencies used in its projects. By the end of 2022, nearly 25% of its financial operations were already conducted not in US dollars or euros, which helps reduce transaction costs and currency risks. This is close to the official target of 30%. However, there is still significant progress needed on this agenda, as the majority of these transactions in national currencies were primarily conducted in Chinese yuan (approximately three-quarters of them).

While the NDB's initial years have fallen short of official expectations, it remains a relatively new organization with a less entrenched bureaucracy. This flexibility allows the bank to adjust strategies with lower political and administrative costs compared to traditional institutions like the World Bank, which face substantial challenges in adapting even minor rules and practices. However, achieving necessary transformations requires a conscientious and cohesive administration committed to advancing this ambitious BRICS project.

In this context, following the interruption of Marcos Troyjo's tenure and the appointment of former Brazilian President Dilma Rousseff as the new President of the NDB in early 2023, there is renewed optimism for enacting essential reforms within the bank. Effective leadership is crucial in addressing challenges of this magnitude, and Dilma Rousseff is well-prepared for this role. She understands the public's expectation for the NDB to exemplify a fair, inclusive, and equitable global financial framework, rather than merely functioning as another conventional bank.

---

[29] According to the first NDB's General Strategy *Scenario 1*, the Bank aimed to disburse at least US$ 5.85 billion, while *Scenario 2* had an optimistic forecast of up to US$ 8.1 billion (NDB, 2017a, pp. 18–19). By the end of 2021, the Bank had disbursed US$ 13.9 billion (NDB, 2021, p. 7), which was close to the *Scenario 1* target of US$ 14.6 billion but fell short of the *Scenario 2* target of US$ 18.9 billion.

References

Altvater, E. (2014). 70-Jahre Bretton-Woods. Die Geburtstunde von IWF und Weltbank. *Gegenblend*. https://gegenblende.dgb.de/artikel/++co++ddc52250-134b-11e4-a40f-52540066f352. Accessed on 07 24, 2014.

Altvater, E. (2015). BRICS at the brink of the fossil bonanza. In P. Bond & A. Garcia (Eds.), *BRICS, an anti-capitalist critique*. Jacana Press.

Asian Infrastructure Investment Bank – AIIB. *Annual reports*. https://www.aiib.org/en/news-events/annual-report/overview/index.html

Batista Jr, P. N. (2016). BRICS – Novo Banco de Desenvolvimento. *Estudos Avançados*, *30*(88), 179–184. https://www.revistas.usp.br/eav/article/view/124278

Batista Jr, P. N. (2021). *O Brasil não cabe no quintal de ninguém: bastidores da vida de um economista brasileiro no FMI e nos BRICS e outros textos sobre nacionalismo e nosso complexo de vira-lata*. Leya.

Batista Jr, P. N. (2022). *The BRICS and the financing mechanisms they created: Progress and shortcomings*. Anthem Press. (*Kindle*).

Berenson, W. M. (2012). Squaring the concept of immunity with the fundamental right to a fair trial: The case of the OAS. In H. Cissé, D. D. Bradlow, & B. Kingsbury (Eds.), *The World Bank legal review: International financial institutions and global legal governance* (Vol. 3). https://documents1.worldbank.org/curated/en/825721468333054677/pdf/653710PUB0EPI2061563B09780821388631.pdf

Berringer, T. (2022). *Brazilian bourgeoisie and foreign policy*. [Translated by Martin Charles Nicholl]. Brill.

Borges, C., & Cortez, J. (2018, May). *Country systems and environmental and social safeguards in development finance institutions: Assessment of the Brazilian system and ways forward for the New Development Bank*. Conectas Direitos Humanos. https://www.conectas.org/wp-content/uploads/2018/05/relatoriobrics_digital04.pdf

BRICS. (2016, October 16). *VIII Summit, Goa, India*. https://www.mea.gov.in/bilateral-documents.htm?dtl/27491/Goa+Declaration+at+8th+BRICS+Summit

Chin, G. (2024). Introduction – The evolution of New Development Bank (NDB): A decade plus in the making. *Global Policy*, *15*, 368–382. https://doi.org/10.1111/1758-5899.13399

D'Sa, D., & Bond, P. (2018). New Development Bank should have consulted before lending corrupt Transnet $200 million for Durban port. In *BRICS politricks:* New subimperial power plays (pp. 180–185). A BRICS-from-below reader for the Johannesburg Teach-In, July 23–24. https://legacy.ippmedia.com/en/features/sa-brics-bank-should-have-consulted-lending-corrupt-transnet

Esteves, P. (2018, May). Preface. In C. Borges & J. Cortez (Eds.), *Country systems and environmental and social safeguards in development finance institutions: Assessment of the Brazilian system and ways forward for the New Development Bank*. Conectas Human Rights. https://allafrica.com/stories/201806290453.html

Esteves, P., Zoccal, G., & Torres, G. (2016). Multilateral development banks and socio-environmental safeguards. *BPC Policy Brief*, *6*(3). https://bricspolicycenter.org/en/publicacoes/the-new-multilateral-development-banks-and-socio-environmental-safeguards-2/

Garcia, A., Curty, R., Aguiar, A. C., Rezende, L., & Dantas, M. V. (2020). Os BRICS frente à pandemia da COVID-19: uma análise preliminar sobrepolíticas comparadas. *Conjuntura Internacional*, *17*(2), 33–46. https://www.conectas.org/wp-content/uploads/2018/05/relatoriobrics_digital04.pdf

Garcia, A., & Kato, K. (2020). A road to development? The Nacala Corridor at the intersection between Brazilian and global investments. In V. Satgar (Ed.), *BRICS and the new American imperialism: Global rivalry and resistance*. Wits University Press.

Humphrey, C. (2016). The "hassle factor" of MDB lending and borrower demand in Latin America. In J. Strand & S. Park (Eds.), *Global economic governance and the development practices of the multilateral development banks*. Routledge.

New Development Bank – NDB. (2021). *Annual report 2021*. https://www.ndb.int/data-and-documents/annual-reports/

New Development Bank – NDB. (2015). *NDB articles of agreement*. https://www.ndb.int/wp-content/themes/ndb/pdf/Agreement-on-the-New-Development-Bank.pdf

New New Development Bank – NDB. (2016a). *Annual report 2016*. https://www.ndb.int/wp-content/uploads/2022/11/NDB-ANNUAL-REPORT-2016.pdf

New Development Bank – NDB. (2016b). *Environment and social framework*. https://www.ndb.int/wp-content/uploads/2017/02/ndb-environment-social-framework-20160330.pdf

New Development Bank – NDB. (2017a). *NDB general strategy 2017-2021*. Available on: https://www.ndb.int/wp-content/uploads/2017/07/NDB-Strategy-Final.pdf

New Development Bank – NDB. (2017b). *Development solutions for a sustainable future. Annual report 2017*. https://www.ndb.int/data-and-documents/annual-reports/

New Development Bank – NDB. (2018). *Annual report 2018*. https://www.ndb.int/data-and-documents/annual-reports/

New Development Bank – NDB. (2019). *Annual report 2019*. https://www.ndb.int/data-and-documents/annual-reports/

New Development Bank – NDB. (2020). *Annual report 2020*. https://www.ndb.int/data-and-documents/annual-reports/

New Development Bank – NDB. (2022a). *Annual report 2022*. https://www.ndb.int/data-and-documents/annual-reports/

New Development Bank – NDB. (2022b). *NDB general strategy 2022-2026*. https://www.ndb.int/about-ndb/general-strategy/

Ramos, L., Garcia, A., Pautasso, D., & Rodrigues, F. (2018). A decade of emergence: The BRICS institutional densification process. *Journal of China and International Relations*, *6*(1).

Thévenot-Werner, A. (2015). The right of staff members to a tribunal as a limit to the jurisdictional immunity of international organisations in Europe. In A. Peters, M. Devers, A. Thévenot-Werner, & P. Zbinden (Eds.), *Les Acteurs dans l'Ère du Constitutionnalisme Global/Actors in the age of global constitutionalism* (pp. 11–139). https://rm.coe.int/the-right-of-staff-members-to-a-tribunal-as-a-limit-to-the-jurisdictio/16808b3ac9

Vasconcelos, J. (2020). *A agenda regulatória dos BRICS*. Dialética.

Vasconcelos, J. (2023, September). Lawfare no Banco dos BRICS. *Cátedra Celso Furtado*, (2). https://revistas.unifacs.br/index.php/redu/article/view/8266

Zoe Liu, Z., & Papa, M. (2022). *Can BRICS de-dollarize the global financial system?* Cambridge University Press. https://doi.org/10.1017/9781009029544

Chapter 9

The Role of BRICS Business Council and the New Development Bank in Environmental, Social, and Governance (ESG) Agenda

Rafaela Mello Rodrigues de Sá

McMaster University, Canada

Abstract

With great relevance of climate change, energy transition, and sustainable development in the global scenario, companies and financial institutions have increased their concern with environmental, social, and governance (ESG) aspects. As a result of which, this agenda has gained more importance, being at the center of the international debate. While there are ESG efforts from BRICS countries' companies and institutions, this agenda needs to be addressed collectively within the group. The BRICS Business Council (BBC) and the New Development Bank (NDB) seem to be positioned as actors that could catalyze these issues in this sphere. The Council brings together companies from the five countries, being an appropriate place for discussions on corporate ESG practices. And the Bank operates with a focus on sustainable infrastructure, demonstrating the importance of ESG aspects for the institution's performance. In this sense, the research objective is to understand: in which ways can BBC and NDB expand and strengthen the ESG agenda within the BRICS grouping, particularly with regard to the activities of BRICS companies and the governance of the group's main financial institution? To this end, a detailed mapping of the aspects involving the ESG agenda in both BRICS initiatives will be carried out in order to identify – in the institutional documents and reports – the role of these two mechanisms in ESG aspects.

The Multilateralism of the New Development Bank on the Sustainable Economic Growth in BRICS Nations and Beyond, 143–156

Published under exclusive licence by Emerald Publishing Limited
doi:10.1108/978-1-83662-292-520251012

Keywords: Environmental, social, and governance (ESG) agenda; BRICS Business Council; governance practices; New Development Bank; sustainable infrastructure

Introduction

Environmental, social, and governance (ESG) aspects have been gaining space in international discussions, considering that major global processes such as climate change, energy transition, and efforts toward sustainable development have been receiving increasing attention from a wide range of players.

In this sense, the concern with the environment is added to the social and governance responsibilities in the decisions of companies and financial institutions with the emergence of the ESG agenda, which represents a set of standards for an institution's behavior. In this sense, organizations seek to adopt principles that will guide not only the preservation of natural resources but also reductions to social inequalities and to governance that is free of corruption, discrimination, and harassment.

While there are ESG efforts from BRICS countries' companies and institutions individually, this agenda needs to be addressed collectively within the grouping, in order to elaborate mechanisms that can function as a standard among the five countries, improving the strategic position of their companies and institutions and facilitating trade, investment, and business exchanges among them.

Considering the initiatives created within the BRICS grouping, there are two mechanisms that could advance the ESG agenda in their discussions, enabling more concrete actions in this direction.

On the one hand, the BRICS Business Council brings together companies from the five countries, being an appropriate place for discussions on corporate ESG practices. On the other hand, the New Development Bank (NDB) operates with a focus on sustainable infrastructure, demonstrating the importance of ESG aspects for the institution's performance. In this regard, both initiatives seem to be positioned as actors that could catalyze ESG issues in this sphere.

In this sense, the objective of this research is to understand: in which ways can the BRICS Business Council and the NDB expand and strengthen the ESG agenda within the BRICS grouping, particularly with regard to the activities of BRICS companies and the governance of the group's main financial institution?

To this end, a detailed mapping of the aspects involving the ESG agenda in both BRICS initiatives will be carried out in order to identify – in the institutional documents and reports – the contribution and the role of these two mechanisms in ESG aspects.

Thus, the research is composed of three sections, besides the introduction and the final remarks. The first section will present a literature review on the concept of ESG, demonstrating the emergence of these aspects, their main characteristics and metrics, and highlighting the impact on companies and financial institutions around the world. The second section seeks to understand the role of the BRICS Business Council in the ESG agenda, highlighting the history and core objectives of the council in order to assess how it can make a concrete contribution to the issue. Finally, the third section aims to understand how the NDB implements ESG aspects in its institutional governance, with the capacity to drive this agenda in more concrete dynamics within the BRICS grouping.

Defining and Contextualizing ESG Indicators

In the last two decades, several trends have encouraged the promotion of greater social responsibility by companies and an expansion of responsible investments by financial institutions. Thus, it is possible to point out that "social and environmental responsibility is now an integral part of financial market activities" (Leins, 2020, p. 01).

In this sense, several indicators are now being used as tools for evaluating companies and economic assets. One of the main indicators currently focuses on the ESG agenda, which is an "investment strategy that considers environmental (E), social (S) and governance (G) issues when valuing company stocks" (Leins, 2020, p. 02).

One of the reasons for this conjuncture is related to the 2008 financial crisis. Stefan Leins argues that "after the outbreak of the financial crisis in 2008, ESG became a technique for harmonizing the ethical order of the market with the ethical order of society" (Leins, 2020, pp. 03–04). In other words, ESG indicators have assumed a decisive role for financial actors, taking on the new ethical form of valuation. In this way, this higher level of responsibility in investments can be understood as a response to the faulty management that was being carried out before the crisis, demonstrating the growing relevance of more responsible activities.

Another element that can be associated with the mainstream ESG movement in the financial market are the environmental disasters caused by companies' investments and activities. Several examples can be cited, such as the cases of Exxon Valdez (United States), Bhopal (India), Vale in Mariana, and Brumadinho (Brazil). The negative perception of financial actors about the companies that caused these socio-environmental damages led to an increase in the directing of capital toward responsible business.

On the one hand, the financial crisis led to instability and lack of confidence in investments; on the other hand, the companies' disasters damaged the reputation of the companies. For that matter, actors were encouraged to connect financial development with sustainable development and "to integrate ESG information into investment strategies to restore social legitimacy" (Sciarelli et al., 2021, p. 41).

For this reason, the concern with the environment in corporate strategies has increased, connected with broader processes aimed at incentives for sustainable development and the search for transition to a low-carbon economy, considering the adoption of the Paris Agreement and the commitment to climate goals of zero carbon emissions (Arun et al., 2021, p. 03).

In this scenario, "companies in ecologically sensitive industries, including the oil and gas sector, carefully monitor their ESG performance in connection to climate change" (Popescu et al., 2022, p. 06). These greater demands by financial institutions "provide greater openness and local population trust in these companies' operations" (Popescu et al., 2022, p. 06).

To understand the main characteristics of ESG indicators and their applications in the corporate and financial sphere, it is important to evaluate the history of metrics used by companies and financial institutions over the years, considering the evolution and inclusion of new variables to influence the behavior of these actors.

This issue is primarily embedded in the literature on socially responsible investments (SRIs), which reflects the increased social awareness of institutions and the growth of public interest in corporate responsibility related to positive and negative impacts. SRIs are also understood as a process that "integrates ethical values, environmental protection, improved social conditions and good governance into traditional investment decision-making, [. . .] (establishing a relation) between SRI diffusion and a more sustainable economy" (Sciarelli et al., 2021, p. 40).

This research agenda goes back to the period to the 1980s, when large multinational companies expanded with the phenomenon of globalization, increasing the relevance of maintaining quality corporate governance to ensure the financial performance of these companies. This debate is related to the public debate about the "costs of ecologically harmful private behavior (that) has led to increased regulations and penalties" (Gerard, 2019, pp. 01–02).

From this issue, several instruments have been launched to direct companies' approaches, such as Principles for Responsible Investment, developed by the United Nations, a tool that works as guidelines that can help ensure levels of social responsibility. These mechanisms can increase corporate governance of companies, so that: "reduces agency problems, improves the alignment of manager and shareholders objectives, and thus enhances the long-term prospects and the value of the firm" (Gerard, 2019, p. 02).

This literature includes two central concepts: Corporate social responsibility (CSR) and ESG. If on the one hand, CSR encompasses the first two elements of ESG, the environmental and the social conduct of the firm; on the other hand, ESG combines the environmental and social impact of the firm, with its governance performance (Gerard, 2019, p. 02). The more recent relevance of the term ESG in actors' practice is associated with the introduction of these governance variables, which represent key elements for firms' performance, since "firms with better governance suffer smaller negative firm-value responses to adverse ESG events and positive rather than negative responses to positive ESG events" (Gerard, 2019, p. 18).

In order to assess the specific details of these indicators, it is essential to examine the elements that represent the variables, which are based on nonfinancial criteria per se, i.e., they indicate nonfinancial data on the commitment of companies at the ESG level (Leins, 2020, p. 02), thus directing investor decision-making toward more sustainably responsible corporations. Thus, the motivations of corporate actors to act voluntarily on ESG indicators may be associated with a growing pressure to "do good" to conduct themselves for more than financial gain, considering the profit-seeking nature of firms (Huang, 2021, p. 336).

The actions directed toward ESG can promote legitimacy and credibility, increasing its reputation and favoring competitive advantages. Since ESG activities could help a company for "reinforcing its authority and reputation by representing competing desires of its stakeholders as well as operating profitability. As a result, a firm has opportunity to perceive as a part of its community; also, its function would be authorized" (Bahadori, 2019, p. 10). On this path, it is possible that the company can "create more desirable communication with its stakeholders, generate worker loyalty, decrease their turnover, get better attention of workers talent, generate buyers' loyalty" (Bahadori, 2019, p. 10).

In this sense, the organizations seek to adopt principles that will guide not only the preservation of natural resources but also reductions to social inequalities and to governance that is free of corruption, discrimination, and harassment, aiming for financial gains and seeking to strengthen the positive impacts of externalities and reduce negative risks in their practical operation.

In the environment sphere, it may include issues like corporate climate policies, uses of renewable energy sources, reduction of waste and pollution, natural resource conservation, and treatment of animals, in order to "measures a company's impact on the natural ecosystem, which comprises its emissions, the efficient use of natural resources in the production process, pollution and waste, and innovation efforts to eco design its products" (Matos, 2020, p. 06). ESG considerations can also help evaluate any environmental risks a company might face and how the company is managing those risks. In this sense, we can remember the cases of Mariana and Brumadinho and on how the Brazilian company Vale had to deal with the risks and impacts caused by the environmental disaster.

About the social aspects, it represents elements related to company's relationships with internal and external stakeholders, understanding how it manages relationships with employees, suppliers, customers, and the communities where it operates, including: "efforts to maintain loyal workers (employment quality, health and safety), satisfy customers (producing quality goods and services), and being a good citizen in the communities" (Matos, 2020, pp. 06–07). In a manner that companies could promote ethical and socially conscious operations including diversity, inclusion, community-focus, social justice, and corporate ethics, in addition to fighting against racial, gender, and sexual discrimination.

Finally, on governance standards, this dimension captures the systems in place for management to act in the best interests of its long-term shareholders. Thus, the company is encouraged to use accurate and transparent accounting methods, pursues integrity and embraces diversity on board of directors, and is accountable to shareholders, including safeguarding shareholder rights, having a functioning board, maintaining well-designed executive compensation policies, and avoiding illegal practices (Matos, 2020, p. 07).

For investors, ESG considerations are a growing priority, defining criteria that drive financial market investments, so these criteria become a major guideline for investors and consumers alike, thus increasing their relevance in both the financial sector and the companies' social responsibility. For this reason, multiple players are taking ESG issues into consideration, such as companies, banks, and financial institutions.

If on the one hand, the incentive for practices based on ESG criteria can improve the reputation and image of companies in the BRICS countries, increasing their economic gains while helping to reduce the possibility of socio-environmental risks and negative externalities, on the other hand, ESG indicators can also contribute to improve the positioning of BRICS institutions in the financial system.

However, for this to be possible, the creation and consolidation of regulatory standards and guidelines at the collective level within the BRICS grouping is necessary to increase their effectiveness and favor the contribution of ESG indicators to the development of their economies.

There are two spheres of action that can serve as a space for dialogue, encouraging these discussions collectively. At the level of companies, the BRICS Business Council can be analyzed as a mechanism capable of harmonizing the demands and the key elements for the implementation of the ESG agenda, since it brings together the major corporations from the five countries, from the most varied sectors of activity. Regarding financial and investment institutions, the NDB, being the first institution founded by the BRICS countries, can develop the application of ESG criteria in its operation, and it may encourage the use of metrics and indicators by the various actors involved, given the relevance of the bank in the scope of the grouping.

Considering these two spheres of action in the BRICS, it is possible to interpret that both have potential for the expansion and effectuation of the ESG agenda, being well positioned to carry out the discussion and build concrete initiatives on the subject. For this reason, it is necessary to understand the history of these two initiatives in order to evaluate how the ESG issue is inserted. In this sense, it is relevant to understand the position of two BRICS initiatives in the sphere of ESG issues, which will be central themes in the next two sections.

BRICS Business Council and the ESG Agenda

With regard to the scope of the BRICS grouping and the various initiatives that resulted from the cooperation mechanisms between the five countries, it is important to mention that initially, the approximation efforts were formed primarily by heads of state and government, but since a process of deepening and expansion, various spheres of civil society have also entered this dialogue arena and established permanent channels of interaction, such as universities, nongovernmental organizations (NGOs), technical institutions, among others.

The BRICS structure that brings companies together is mainly characterized by the BRICS Business Council. This sphere can be interpreted as an enabling mechanism for initiatives to standardize the behavior of companies in ESG aspects, increasing productivity and improving the image of companies from BRICS countries in the world.

However, in order to evaluate the incentives and concrete actions that are already in process in this direction, it is important to understand the main characteristics of the council's activities and the trajectory of creation and consolidation of this interaction channel among the main BRICS companies.

The formation of the BRICS Business Council can be understood as a strengthening of the BRICS business forum that has been taking place annually since 2010. On March 26 and 27, 2013, in the city of Durban, South Africa, the fourth meeting of the business forum took place, and it was on this occasion that the BRICS Business Council was launched (Foro de São Paulo, 2013). In this sense, it is important to highlight that the council was officially founded only in 2013, but the meetings of the forum among businessmen had already been taking place since the first dialogues between the BRICS in 2010 (Garcia, 2017, p. 383).

With its formation, the scope of action of the council became clear, which will constitute a platform that will:

> strengthen and promote economic, trade, business and investment ties among the business communities of the five BRICS countries, as well as ensure that there is regular dialogue between these communities of BRICS nations and the governments of BRICS countries. (BRICS Business Council, 2013, p. 01)

In this way, the council allows the construction of a space for dialogue between the BRICS countries' business groups, enabling the coordination of joint interests and cooperation in various sectors, as it brings together business associations from each of the BRICS countries in order to promote frequent engagement between the business communities (Stuenkel, 2017, p. 135).

The council can be understood as a consultative mechanism of the heads of state and government that discusses and points out private sector priorities to strengthen and promote trade and investment relations, identifying challenges and opportunities. In this way, the council allows the construction of a space for dialogue between the BRICS countries' business groups, enabling the coordination of common interests and cooperation in various sectors and allowing the development of an agenda of common demands.

The demands described by the businessmen over the years can be divided into three groups:

(1) Instruments that facilitate trade: The Expedition of Business Visas, the BRICS Information Sharing and Exchanging Platform, and the harmonization of technical standards.
(2) Mechanisms that promote investment: Infrastructures for payment in local currencies of BRICS countries, creation of a BRICS Development Bank, cooperation in the development of infrastructures and connectivity.
(3) More recently, demands have been more focused on solutions and mechanisms to mitigate the effects of the pandemic, seeking postpandemic recovery under the Sustainable Development Agenda.

Regarding the organizational structure, the council is organized into five national sections. Each section has five principal CEOs, an elected chair, a secretariat, and a number of members, including companies and business organizations. The presidency of the council rotates on an annual basis, according to the host country of the BRICS grouping meetings. The chairs and members from each country meet to discuss general agendas but are also divided into thematic working groups (BRICS Business Council, 2019, p. 13).

The working groups discuss and select policies and technical recommendations on their sectors and express the areas that require the most investment. With this, annual reports are produced and the recommendations are addressed to the government spheres of the BRICS countries. The sectors that are covered by these working groups are: infrastructure, manufacturing, skills development, energy and green economy, aviation, digital economy, financial services, agribusiness, and deregulation.

The members of these groups discuss and select more specific and technical policies and recommendations on their sectors and address them to governments. During the year, the working groups carry out research and analysis on the sector's situation and prepare specific recommendations and propose projects and initiatives that are presented to the council, then passed on to the governments.

Considering these characteristics, the council brings together companies from the five BRICS countries and can be interpreted as an appropriate venue for discussions on ESG to take place within the group. During the meetings and reports, it is possible to find potential for dialogue and cooperation on the topic of ESG criteria, both in the search for more sustainable investments and also in improving the internal practices of companies in the BRICS countries. With the popularization of the ESG agenda, concrete initiatives on ESG-related aspects have been developed and presented within the BRICS Business Council.

The first initiative worth mentioning was introduced in the 2020 annual report, with the idea of establishing the BRICS ESG Association, which had the main objective of improving transparency and increasing the ESG scores of BRICS companies.

One of the arguments for establishing this initiative considers the context of:

> growing role played globally by responsible financing makes BRICS countries vulnerable to both low ESG scores from international assessors, which are given using methodologies that do not fully address the realities that exist in BRICS countries, and underinvestment as a consequence of those artificially low scores. (BRICS Business Council, 2020, p. 62)

For this reason, the idea of the council is to establish a unification for the approaches adopted by the BRICS countries toward the ESG. In this regard, there is a need for: (a) better unification of approaches for ESG assessment, (b) better disclosure methodologies for ESG certification, (c) ESG certification for goods and services be provided by BRICS countries in order to improve competitiveness considering environmental protectionism, (d) additional services to support the verification of ESG and green finance ratings, and (e) clarity of definitions of each country's carbon credit trading systems for the creation of fair parameters for the future BRICS carbon trading system (BRICS Business Council, 2020, p. 63).

Thus, greater transparency of ESG ratings would help increase capital inflows into BRICS economies, and better ESG ratings for goods and services from BRICS companies would provide better export opportunities, allowing them to counter developed countries' environmental protectionism.

In the 2021 annual report, a proposal to create the BRICS ESG Association was further elaborated and consolidated. The council further detailed the features of the BRICS ESG Association, which was formalized in 2021 with the aim of promoting an improved, efficient, and transparent ESG space that would help increase capital inflows between and to BRICS economies.

The idea is to improve experience sharing of ESG metrics and taxonomy to increase ESG adoption across BRICS nations and increase data comparability, as well as create an ESG index by BRICS nations followed by index benchmarking to measure relative performance. This is important especially "for rapidly developing BRICS countries that face higher macroeconomic risks than their developed counterparts" (BRICS Business Council, 2021, p. 60).

In this way, adherence to ESG standards will improve companies' green ratings and strengthen their value chains, positioning BRICS nations as a clear choice for other countries to facilitate international trade and global partnerships with them. In addition, the development of a common ESG index will encourage companies across BRICS to assess their ESG performance, attract private and institutional investors, identify best practices, and assess common risks and opportunities (BRICS Business Council, 2021, p. 61).

In addition to the ESG Association, the BRICS Business Council also presented in the 2021 report initiatives focused on green infrastructure development from the promotion of ESG best practices to attract sustainable infrastructure investments. From this, they conceive ESG as: "a set of criteria adopted by investors to assess a company's interaction with the environment and society, and the observance of high standards of corporate governance" (BRICS Business Council, 2021, p. 66).

Considering an increasing relevance of good business practices and social and environmental responsibility, the ESG principles drive the adoption of good environmental, social, and corporate governance practices. In this sense, the idea of the council is to promote ESG best practices to attract sustainable infrastructure investments in a way that can address issues related to climate change and natural disasters, reduce greenhouse gas emissions and contamination, manage natural capital, and increase resource efficiency (BRICS Business Council, 2021, p. 66).

Therefore, from the analysis of these initiatives presented and executed by the BRICS Business Council, it is possible to understand it as a favorable instrument for discussions on the ESG agenda within the grouping, especially regarding the performance of companies and their relations with the search for investments. However, there is another relevant actor in the BRICS scope that could carry out a more concrete discussion on the importance of sustainable investments in line with ESG principles, namely the NDB.

ESG Principles in NDB Practices

The BRICS bank, as it is also known, was established in 2014 through the signing of an agreement at the BRICS Annual Summit in Fortaleza, where the countries agreed to establish a bank that would strengthen cooperation among them. With the founding of the NBD, the institution became the first multilateral development bank that aims to have global reach that was set up exclusively by emerging economies, without the participation of developed countries in the initial stage of construction (Batista Jr., 2019, p. 249; Zhu, 2020, p. 94). In addition, the BRICS bank stands out for its operational focus on projects directed at sustainable infrastructure.

Considering the NDB's position as the main institution that has resulted in years of cooperation and dialogue among the five countries, in addition to the bank's sustainability-oriented characteristic, it is important to reflect on whether this governance structure would also be an appropriate space to discuss ESG principles during the financing and implementation of large BRICS infrastructure projects, making them more sustainable and socially and environmentally responsible.

As for the ESG agenda in the bank's activities, the theme is inserted mainly in its relationship with Country Systems, so that "the projects are implemented using country systems for environmental, social, governance (ESG) and procurement practices, without imposing policy prescriptions or conditionalities to the operations" (NDB, 2022).

The NDB Country Systems approach uses the borrower country legislation, instead of using international safeguards, which would prioritize national systems and could encourage bank staff to dig deeper into national laws and regulations and could suggest changes and indicate weaknesses (Humphrey, 2016, pp. 03–07).

However, despite the advantages of adopting this approach, there are also challenges that are presented, since, in these cases, it could lead to a transfer of responsibility from the multilateral institution, which disburses the resources and should be responsible for possible impacts of the project, to national entities. Moreover, in cases of weak mechanisms and gaps in local norms and laws, it is essential to define minimum standards to mitigate potential risks (Teixeira & Pimentel, 2017, p. 46).

In order to avoid failures in social and environmental protection and lack of effective monitoring of human rights violations in the national system, the NDB launched an instrument to manage the socio-environmental risks of its projects, based on categories and recommendations. The NDB's Environment and Social Framework is important to manage potential socio-environmental risks in the design and implementation phase of projects and to encourage good practices, being NDB's main instrument directed at the socio-environmental issues of its projects.

This socio-environmental framework presents some guiding principles, such as: (1) inclusive and sustainable development, (2) use and strengthening of national systems, (3) integration of environmental and social sustainability principles, (4) mitigation and adaptation to address climate change, (5) conservation of natural resources, (6) gender equality, (7) preventive approach, and (8) cooperation and knowledge dissemination with other multilateral financial institutions (NDB, 2016, pp. 03–04).

On the bank's part, the institution is responsible for elaborating a screening of each project to assign it a category, which can be: (a) Category A, when the project has significant environmental and social impacts that are irreversible, diverse, or unprecedented; (b) Category B, when the impacts are less adverse than those of category A; and (c) Category C, when the project has minimal or no environmental impact. Based on this, it will be possible to take appropriate measures to prevent and manage socio-environmental risks.

However, there are limitations in the bank's transparency. Although the website makes available the documents and the data about projects, there are still difficulties in accessing information about the implementation process, not disclosing details about what happens after approval. This makes it difficult for civil society groups to monitor and defend the rights of local communities. In this sense, NBD still needs to consolidate and enhance a dialogue channel with civil society and with the populations affected by financing projects, in addition to making available the projects and management plans developed by clients that aim to minimize or avoid socio-environmental impacts.

Another limitation worth mentioning is that despite the bank's targeting of sustainable infrastructure projects – with the goal of dedicating 2/3 of the financing to this sector – the NDB does not present a clear definition, with details and specific criteria, about the concept of sustainable infrastructure. This broad understanding ends up allowing the financing of projects that may question the bank's sustainable commitment, since the institution ends up financing projects that may generate negative socio-environmental impacts, which ultimately will not contribute to sustainable development.

One of the examples that can be cited to illustrate this issue is the fact that even in cases of financing directed to clean energy, negative socio-environmental impacts end up occurring. One of the cases that deserves evidence is the construction of wind farms that make up the Araripe 3 Wind Complex. If, on the one hand, the venture was related to positive gains for local populations – with job generation, energy supply for homes in the region, on the other hand, some negative impacts began to be reported by the local population, such as the impacts of the operation of the propellers in their routine, with loud noises, generating difficulties for people to sleep, besides generating effects on environmental issues, causing death of animals and a higher incidence of lightning in the region (Conectas, 2021a, 2021b).

Thus, despite the insertion of ESG principles characteristics, such as the concern with socio-environmental risk management through the Country Systems approach or through the appropriate institutional instrument – NDB's Environment and Social Framework – the BRICS bank still needs to consolidate its practices toward an improvement of its performance during the project design and implementation phases, seeking to take ESG indicators more and more seriously.

From this, the financial actors and even the companies involved with the bank will be able to increasingly implement and introduce indicators on ESG issues, so that the bank can be considered, if it improves its practices, as an instrument for promoting ESG indicators inside BRICS sphere.

Final Remarks

According to the current scenario, ESG aspects are increasingly being introduced in the daily life of companies and in the practices of international financial institutions. Taking into account major global processes such as climate change, energy transition, and efforts toward sustainable development, the ESG agenda has been gaining more and more space in international discussions, increasing the attention of a wide range of stakeholders.

Based on this, it is of great relevance to assess the presence of these elements in the performance of the cooperation mechanisms of the BRICS grouping. To this end, a detailed mapping of the aspects involving the ESG agenda was conducted in order to identify – in institutional documents and reports – the contribution and role of ESG aspects in the BRICS Business Council and in the NDB.

Considering the characteristics presented about the two arrangements within the BRICS grouping and their potentialities in the effort to discuss and implement the ESG agenda, it is possible to understand that both the BRICS Business Council and the NDB can be interpreted as instruments that seek to help the actors involved in the BRICS grouping to put into practice the ESG aspects, both in relation to companies and to financial mechanisms for investments in large infrastructure projects.

The BRICS Business Council could be analyzed as one of the appropriate places for ESG discussions within the BRICS group, as it brings together the main business leaders of the five countries, providing potential for dialogue and cooperation on the topic, with the elaboration of concrete initiatives on the subject.

From the NDB's innovative characteristics, seeking to introduce new practices, it can be evaluated that the institution still needs to advance in its socio-environmental risk management mechanisms. The NDB's socio-environmental approach ultimately shows gaps, with low transparency in the processes of designing and implementing financing and the absence of mechanisms that allow for the participation of affected communities, demonstrating elements that the bank still needs to consolidate and improve certain elements, which may affect the institution's approach to ESG issues, which is so relevant in the operation of institutions in the current scenario.

References

Arun, T., Girardone, C., & Piserà, S. (2021). *ESG issues in emerging markets and the role of banks*. Essex Finance Centre, Working Paper Series No 73: 08.

Bahadori, N. (2019). *The impact of ESG factors on financial performance in BRICS*. Thesis – Master of Business Administration, Eastern Mediterranean University.

Batista Jr., N. P. (2019). *O Brasil não cabe no quintal de ninguém: Bastidores a vida de um economista brasileiro no FMI e nos BRICS e outros textos sobre nacionalismo e nosso complexo de vira-lata*. Editora Casa da Palavra/LeYa.

BRICS Business Council. (2013). *Joint statement of the BRICS Business Council meeting*. Sandton Convention Centre, Johannesburg, South Africa.

BRICS Business Council. (2019). *Economic growth for an innovative future – BRICS Business Council annual report 2019*. Brasilia, Brazil.

BRICS Business Council. (2020). *The BRICS partnership for global stability, universal security and innovative growth – BRICS Business Council annual report*. Russia.

BRICS Business Council. (2021). *Intra-BRICS cooperation for continuity, consolidation and consensus – BRICS Business Council annual report*. India.

Conectas. (2021a). *Como as comunidades quilombolas enxergam os empreendimentos*. https://www.conectas.org/noticias/como-as-comunidades-quilombolas-enxergam-os-empreendimentos/

Conectas. (2021b). *O papel dos bancos de desenvolvimento*. https://www.conectas.org/noticias/o-papel-dos-bancos-de-desenvolvimento/

Foro de São Paulo. (2013). *V Cúpula do BRICS – Informações – Durban, 27 de março de 2013*. https://forodesaopaulo.org/aviso-as-redacoes-v-cupula-do-brics-informacoes-durban-27-de-marco-de-2013/

Garcia, A. E. S. (2017). BRICS: um balanço crítico. *Cadernos do CEAS, Salvador/Recife*, (241), 374–391. mai./ago.

Gerard, B. (2019). ESG and socially responsible investment: A critical review. *Beta*, *33*(01), 61–83.

Huang, D. Z. X. (2021, March). Environmental, social and governance (ESG) activity and firm performance: A review and consolidation. *Accounting and Finance*, *61*(1), 335–360.

Humphrey, C. (2016). *Time for a new approach to environmental and social protection at multilateral development banks*. Briefing paper – ODI.

Leins, S. (2020). 'Responsible investment': ESG and the post-crisis ethical order. *Economy and Society*, 71–91.

Matos, P. (2020). *ESG and responsible institutional investing around the world: A critical review*. CFA Institute Research Foundation – Literature Review.

New Development Bank (NDB). (2016). *New Development Bank environment and social framework*. https://www.ndb.int/wp-content/uploads/2017/02/ndb-environment-social-framework-20160330.pdf

New Development Bank (NDB). (2022). *NDB at 7: New Development Bank celebrates seven years of accomplishments*. https://www.ndb.int/press_release/ndb-at-7-new-development-bank-celebrates-seven-years-of-accomplishments/

Popescu, C., Hysa, E., Kruja, A., & Mansi, E. (2022). Social innovation, circularity and energy transition for environmental, social and governance (ESG) practices—A comprehensive review. *Energies*, *15*, 9028.

Sciarelli, M., Cosimato, S., Landi, G., & Iandolo, F. (2021). Socially responsible investment strategies for the transition towards sustainable development: The importance of integrating and communicating ESG. Socially responsible investment strategies. *The TQM Journal*, *33*(7), 39–56. Emerald Publishing Limited.

Stuenkel, O. (2017). *BRICS: o futuro da ordem global* (1st ed.). Paz e Terra.

Teixeira, G., & Pimentel, G. (2017). *Caminhos da Responsabilidade Socioambiental no BNDES: uma avaliação da evolução no Período de junho/2016 a junho/2017*. SITAWI.

Zhu, J. (2020). Two approaches to institutionalizing the new development assistance: A comparative analysis of the operational institutions of NDB and AIIB. In Y. Jing, A. Mendez, & Y. Zheng (Eds.), *New development assistance: Emerging economies and the new landscape of development assistance. Governing China in the 21st century*. Palgrave Macmillan.

Chapter 10

Development Effectiveness: The Role of Multilateral Development Banks and Their Evaluation: Reference and Insights for New Development Bank

Xiaochen Hou

Fudan University, China

Abstract

Multilateral development banks (MDBs) are essential players in international development, and various parties are now questioning their role. While providing global public goods, MDBs are affected by their governance structures, lending countries, and borrowing countries. This chapter analyzes the role of MDBs from the perspective of development effectiveness, compares and contrasts the evaluation mechanisms of MDBs, and points out that MDBs should closely integrate their development objectives with their policy frameworks to develop corresponding evaluation indicators. Through evaluation, MDBs can control the project process and gradually achieve development goals, thus playing a more significant role in international development. It is suggested that the New Development Bank should design a sound evaluation system with flexibility and also need close cooperation with the existing MDBs. It will be an excellent way to improve the evaluation work efficiently and effectively if the objective country's relevant data and background materials can be shared among these MDBs.

Keywords: Multilateral development banks; development effectiveness; evaluation mechanism; New Development Bank; data sharing

The Multilateralism of the New Development Bank on the Sustainable Economic Growth in BRICS Nations and Beyond, 157–175

doi:10.1108/978-1-83662-292-520251013

The Role of Multilateral Development Banks (MDBs) in International Development

The issue of development is a common problem that the world needs to face today. For example, poverty in developing countries, driven by economic globalization since the 1990s, has not been curbed globally. The gap between rich and poor has further widened among countries worldwide, with an increasing trend. Although middle-income countries have made significant progress in economic growth, employment, and infrastructure in the past decades, they still face development challenges: unequal income distribution, private sector financing is still weak, the market economy has yet to be perfected, and infrastructure needs continuous investment.

Solving global development problems requires international cooperation and, more importantly, international development financing, through international cooperation and collective action, to achieve the joint development of the world economy and society. Due to the lack of capital, technology, management experience, and other factors, developing countries can hardly eliminate the poverty trap by relying on their resources alone and must rely on international financial assistance; for some middle-income countries, national public expenditure is limited by the sustainability of debt and fiscal deficit, which is insufficient to support the construction needs in areas such as infrastructure and shows a pro-cyclical character, which has a delay in responding to the economic crisis and promoting economic recovery. There is an unavoidable delay in responding to the economic crisis and promoting economic recovery. In this situation, domestic development financing mechanisms cannot meet the enormous financial needs of poverty eradication issues and require the mutual complementarity of bilateral, regional, and global cooperation.

As an essential part of the international development financing mechanism, MDBs are international financial institutions aiming to reduce poverty and promote sustainable regional economic development and achieve development and poverty reduction goals by providing development financing for developing countries, helping specific regions achieve regional economic integration, and providing professional consultation for their economic and social development. Since the establishment of the World Bank (WB) in 1945, the international development financing system consisting of MDBs has been gradually established and improved, forming a global MDB led by WB and several regional MDBs, such as Asian Development Bank (ADB), African Development Bank (AfDB), European Bank for Reconstruction and Development (EBRD), European Investment Bank (EIB), Inter-American Development Bank (IDB), Andean Development Bank (CAF), etc.

The concept of international development financing is gradually changing. Since the financial crisis, global economic growth has been slow, developed countries have encountered significant problems in their economic development, the strength and enthusiasm of international aid have been relatively weakened, and the supply of funds from MDBs is insufficient. There is a massive gap between supply and demand for global infrastructure construction. Nobel laureate Stiglitz once pointed out that "the global demand for infrastructure construction is huge". In the energy sector alone, $33 trillion in investment will be needed over the next 25 years, with 64% of this projected investment requirement coming from emerging and developing economies. The existing multilateral financing system cannot meet the current financial needs because the relatively old operating mechanism has many problems.

China, Brazil, and other emerging economies are gradually assuming more and more responsibilities in the international financing system. The traditional international development financing system focuses more on "handouts" from developed to developing countries, and traditional MDBs are mostly "North-South banks." In recent years, the establishment of new MDBs such as the Asian Infrastructure Investment Bank (AIIB) and the New Development Bank (NDB) has opened up a new form of "South-South banks."

Mechanism Design and Influencing Factors of MDBs

Culpeper (1997) was the first to systematically discuss the origins and evolution of MDBs and to assess their effectiveness in poverty reduction and their role in debt crises. The authors argue that MDBs are no longer the strong gods of development finance with the development of financial markets. Still, with their unique advantages of evolving with the times, they will become the upholders of a more humane international order. Dirk W. t. Velde and Michael Warner analyse the transfer payments made by development finance institutions to the private sector in developing countries in the infrastructure sector and summarise the aid programmes of 10 multilateral, regional and global development banks in 2015. Prada, F. analyzes the operations and future potential of MDBs along three dimensions: division of labor and comparative advantage, the balance between fiscal strength, low borrowing costs, and development effectiveness, and distribution of net revenues among member countries, using the Latin American and Caribbean region as an example (Prada, 2012). Ravallion affirms that despite facing competition from the private sector and regional MDBs, the WB still plays an irreplaceable role in providing global public goods to promote development. In addition, the authors suggest three directions for WB reform. In its Financing for Development Post-2015 report, the Bank maps out a post-2015 framework for development finance that clarifies the respective roles of domestic resource flows, emerging market donors, private development finance, financial innovation, and MDBs.

Regarding the institutional design of international multilateral banks, foreign literature is more on the analysis of the Bank's system; for example, for the evaluation mechanism, foreign scholars are more through regression analysis based on the Bank's case data to derive which influencing factors are more dominant. Ika et al. (2012), through the study, tried to identify the critical aspects of the Bank's project success and the relationship between its project success. The study found five essential factors of success: control, coordination, design, training, and institutional environment. Regression analysis found that each element had a significant relationship with project success. The most salient of these for project supervisors were design and control. Denizer et al. (2013) analyzed data by examining more than 6,000 projects evaluated by the Bank from 1983 to 2011 to analyze macro and micro-level correlations in the outcomes of funded development projects and found that country-level performance was more influential in aid effectiveness. He also found that the success of specific projects within the same country varied more than that of projects in different countries. Project-level "micro" factors include project size, duration, and effort into project preparation and supervision.

Specifically on the comparison of international development bank mechanisms, Ren and Zhang (2015) compare and analyze the operating rules and characteristics of eight international organizations in terms of the degree of internationalization, use of local currency, positioning, operational background, model, lending capacity and conditions, etc. In analyzing the shortcomings of existing international financial organizations, it is pointed out that NDBs should learn from the experience of other banks, avoid deficiencies and open up their unique development paths, such as through institutional innovation in loan mechanisms and capital supply. The literature on the evaluation mechanism of international organizations is mainly focused on the analysis of the WB. There are also some concerns about the ADB and the United Nations Industrial Development Organisation but not yet about the NDB.

International organizations are in the midst of power politics and changing interests. Gutner and Thompson (2010) analyze the political logic in the design and performance of international organizations, noting that for most international organizations, the performance of international organizations is an effective way to gain legitimacy, but performance and effectiveness are different. Effectiveness refers to the ability or way to achieve specific goals with more emphasis on results, while performance is more complex, including both process and results.

Developmental Effectiveness: Concepts and Their Evaluation Methods

In March 2003, the United Nations convened the World Summit on Financing for Development in Monterrey, Mexico, and reached the Monterrey Consensus. In September 2015, the UN Sustainable Development Summit adopted the sustainable development goals (SDGs), a set of goals to help developing countries eradicate poverty and achieve sustainable development. In September 2015, the UN Sustainable Development Summit adopted the SDGs, which revised and extended the Millennium Development Goals (MDGs), increasing them to 17. Achieving the overall goals of the SDGs is complex, and the main challenge is to raise sufficient funds and channel them in an orderly manner to developing countries that are short of funds and need assistance.

Development effectiveness stems from the concept of development assistance. Official development assistance (ODA) has been recognized as an essential tool to help promote socioeconomic development in developing and least-developed countries. Since 1960, significant amounts of aid have flowed from rich to developing countries through bilateral and international multilateral institutions, but aid effectiveness has not been satisfactory. The OECD Development Assistance Committee has held four high-level meetings on aid effectiveness. In the Paris Declaration reached at the second high-level meeting in 2005, five principles were proposed to improve aid effectiveness: the "Ownership Principle" (Ownership), which means that recipient countries must formulate their development strategies, improve institutions and punish corruption, and assume responsibility for development; the "Alignment Principle" Alignment, which means that aid must be linked to the recipient's development strategy and prioritize the latter; Harmonization, which means that aid programs and actions should be coordinated among donors to avoid duplication and waste of resources; "Management for Results, where both recipient and donor countries focus on measuring and managing aid effectiveness and results; Mutual Accountability" (Mutual Accountability), which means that both recipient and donor countries should be accountable to their citizens and governments and for development results. The Seoul Consensus of the fourth high-level meeting of the OECD Development Assistance Committee (DAC) in 2011 promoted a shift in international development assistance from "aid effectiveness" focusing on "inputs" to "development effectiveness" focusing on "results" (He, 2011).

In 2017, the evaluation departments of the MDBs came together to discuss "Are multilateral development banks still relevant today?" The balance between being a bank, which is accountable to its shareholders, and being a development institution, which needs to achieve development goals, is the focus of the MDBs' development and external attention to the MDBs.

The development effectiveness policies of the MDBs are mainly related to the priority destination of funding allocations and their development effectiveness, lending policies, debt sustainability evaluations, and project evaluations. More closely and directly related to development objectives is primarily the evaluation of projects and their impact. Evaluation mechanisms are essential for multilateral development banks to carry out their tasks. Project appraisal is required for any project to aid decision-making and improve management. Preappraisal evaluates a project's economic, technical, environmental, and social aspects to ensure scientific decision-making and the feasibility and effectiveness of project implementation. Postevaluation considers the overall performance of the project to assess whether the project has achieved the expected objectives, whether the project implementation process complies with relevant policies and standards, and what social benefits and impacts have been generated, helps improve project management and is an essential basis for subsequent project review and scientific decision-making.

Suppose a MDB achieves its development goals through specific projects. How can project assessments design corresponding indicators to better evaluate whether development goals have been achieved? It is mainly through the project's

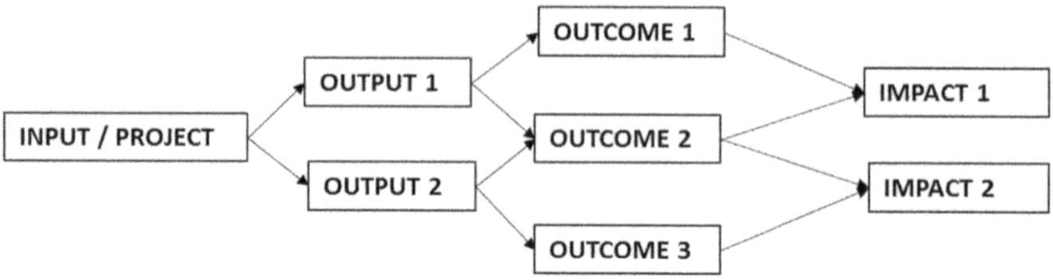

Fig. 10.1. The Logic of Project Evaluation. *Source:* NDB workshop documents.

output, the results generated, and the consequent impact on a larger scale? The logic is shown in Fig. 10.1.

This chapter compares the existing evaluation mechanisms of the World Bank (hereinafter referred to as "WB"), the Asian Development Bank (hereinafter referred to as "ADB"), and the Asian Infrastructure Investment Bank (hereinafter referred to as "AIIB") and summarizes their characteristics and experiences. It provides insights into the design of the evaluation mechanism of the New Development Bank established by BRICS countries (hereinafter referred to as "NDB"). The primary considerations for choosing these three banks for comparison are: first, they are typical representatives of multilateral development banks, the WB is the world's first and currently the most significant international development bank and the ADB is a model of regional multilateral development banks, so they are very representative; second, the WB and the ADB are relatively mature and have well-designed systems, so they are beneficial for reference. Once again, WB and ADB are more relevant to the NDB in terms of business and geography, and the business scope of the NDB is to radiate to the world with the region where the five BRICS countries are located. The AIIB and the NDB are both newly established multilateral development banks. In their institutional design, both draw on the experiences of existing, well-established organizations, while also making adjustments based on their own positioning and goals, offering a degree of flexibility. The AIIB and the NDB are both multilateral development banks promoted by China and established under the leadership of developing countries; in this sense, the comparative role of the AIIB is also critical.

Comparison of International Development Bank Evaluation Mechanisms

Since NDB and AIIB mainly focus on infrastructure and sustainable development, WB and ADB are involved in more areas and project categories. For this reason, this chapter selects projects with a common theme among the four organizations for comparison: green energy projects.

Project Introduction

Table 10.1 introduces the selected green energy projects of three organizations based on the background and evaluation results.

Table 10.1. Background of Green Energy Projects Selected by WB, ADB, and AIIB.

Organization Name	**World Bank**	**ADB**	**AIIB**
Project name	New Energy Projects in Rural Areas of Sri Lanka	New Energy Project in the Outer Islands of the Kingdom of Tonga	Tarbela Hydroelectric Power Station Expansion Project, Pakistan
Background	The project was funded by the Bank and approved in 2002, with a total investment of \$2.54 billion, exceeding projections by about 10%. The project was closed in 2011, three years behind schedule. Two adjustments were made during this period, the first lowering the expected project target and the second extending the project deadline to allow for the completion of the previous investment.	The project is financed by the Royal Government of Tonga and jointly implemented by the Ministry of National Planning and Finance and Tonga Electricity Corporation. The project plans to promote solar photovoltaic power generation projects on nine outer islands in the Kingdom of Tonga, promoting the use of new energy sources and reducing Tonga's dependence on fossil fuel imports through new photovoltaic plants and integration with the existing grid. The project is funded by a loan	The project is jointly sponsored by AIIB and WB, with a total investment of more than \$8.2 billion, guaranteed by the Sovereign Guarantee Fund and underwritten by the Pakistan Water and Power Development Authority (WAPDA Water and Power Development Authority).

(Continued)

Table 10.1. *(Continued)*

Organization Name	World Bank	ADB	AIIB
		and grant from ADB, the European Union, the Australian government, and the Danish Second Joint Fund for Remote Renewable Energy and Energy Efficiency (SDCFREEERA). The Tongan government will support the project with subsidies and land at an estimated cost of US$188.3 billion.	
Evaluation results	IEG evaluation includes four items, which are: 1. Project results: Satisfactory. 2. Risk: Negligible. 3. Bank performance: More satisfactory. 4. Debit performance: Satisfactory.	The project risk is rated as medium, and the financial evaluation for the Government of Tonga and Tonga Power is relatively positive.	The project risk is classified as high, but in the line, AIIB expressed satisfaction (Satisfactory) with the current preparation of the Pakistani side and considered the project ready to enter the implementation period.

Data source: Based on project reports (Asian Development Bank, 2015; Asian Infrastructure Investment Bank, 2016b; Independent Evaluation Group World Bank, 2014).

Evaluation Mechanism

The evaluation of multilateral development banks is mainly divided into pre-evaluation and post-evaluation. Pre-evaluations are used to review projects to decide whether to approve them and issue loans. Postevaluation is used to evaluate a project's process, results, and impact after it is completed to improve management and provide a basis for subsequent scientific decisions.

World Bank

The WB's evaluation agency is the Independent Evaluation Group (IEG), an evaluation agency independent of the WB. Each project has a Task Manager, a Sector Director, and a Country Director during the evaluation phase, separate from the project implementation staff. The IEG emphasizes the evaluation's independence to ensure the transparency of the Bank's operations and to draw lessons from previous projects.

Due to many Bank projects, IEG only evaluates 20–25% of the Bank's project operations through field work each year. The criteria for selecting projects are (1) innovative, large, or complex projects; (2) projects related to upcoming study or country evaluation; (3) projects evaluated at the request of the Administrator or the Bank; and (4) projects that may yield important lessons.

The Project Performance Evaluation Report (PPAR) process consists of four steps: (1) IEG staff review the project and other documents and travel to the lending country to discuss the modus operandi of the evaluation with the government and other domestic stakeholders; (2) Interviews with Bank and other funding agency headquarters (or branches) staff. Each report is in three steps within the IEG: Peer Review, Panel Review, and Management Approval. (3) Once finalized within the IEG, the message is sent to the Bank department responsible for the project for review. At this stage, the report is also sent to the lending country, and the IEG integrates the Bank's and the lending country's comments as appropriate and appends the lending country's words to the report. (4) After these steps are completed, the evaluation report is submitted to the Bank's Board of Executive Directors, and the information is then made available to the public.

Asian Development Bank

The Project Management Consultant (PMC) is responsible for post-evaluation in ADB. The PMC assists the lending government and the executing agency in implementing the project plan, coordinating the project process, preparing financial and audit documents and annual reports, managing the security aspects of the project and the impact on the local community, and participating in all aspects of the project. After the project is completed, the project results are monitored and evaluated. The management consultant will continue to provide local advice and support for five years after project completion. For the Tonga project, ADB's project manager is a supervisor in the Transportation, Energy, and Natural Resources Division of the Ministry of the Pacific.

The Project Management Unit (PMU) assesses and regulates the social and environmental aspects. The PMU comprises staff from Tonga Power and Tonga's

Ministry of Energy, assisted by a PMU from ADB. The ADB has also set up a Project Steering Committee to oversee the overall project, including financial and environmental aspects and social impacts. The committee is chaired and composed of members from the Tongan government's Ministry of Energy and other project implementation agencies in the country. ADB and other funders attend as observers (Asian Development Bank, 2015).

Asian Infrastructure Investment Bank

As shown in the current organization chart of AIIB, the most relevant project evaluation is the International Advisory Panel (IAP). There is no independent evaluation body like the WB and AIIB. The AIIB's current documents, such as the "Operational Policy on Financing," clearly list nine criteria to be considered in the prior evaluation of projects. The themes of the approved projects announced so far are sustainable development and infrastructure development. The AIIB's project process consists of six steps: strategic planning, project identification, project preparation, board approval, project implementation, project completion, and evaluation. The AIIB clearly states in the project process document that the AIIB's focus is on the efficiency and quality of the projects (Asian Infrastructure Investment Bank, 2016a).

Pre-evaluation

World Bank

IEG's pre-evaluation focuses on combining four aspects: the macro-environment (economic and political) of the borrowing country, the structure of the industries involved in the project, the market supply and demand situation of the sectors, and the Bank's previous cooperation and experience with the country. The pre-evaluation was mainly based on project documents and interviews with relevant personnel by IEG. The pre-evaluation of the project in Sri Lanka concluded that energy is of great importance to the country's economic development, and the current energy structure of Sri Lanka is not adequate in terms of new energy supply. Remote areas have severe energy shortages, making it more challenging to enjoy the benefits of new energy. Therefore, this project is significant and feasible. From the data on Sri Lanka's macro economy and Sri Lanka's energy industry in the evaluation report, we can see that IEG paid more attention to the macro economy and industry of the target country in the pre-evaluation.

Asian Development Bank

ADB's pre-evaluation of the project was divided into four main areas: financial management, risk, environmental and social impact, and gender impact. The ADB assessed the financial management status of the project implementer, Tonga Power, through its own developed financial management evaluation questionnaire and interviews with relevant personnel, including six indicators: financial flow management, staff, accounting procurement, internal and external audit, reporting supervision, and information systems. In the second block of risk evaluation, ADB's evaluation still focuses on financial and human risks. Three of the four risks presented in the report are related to finance (overspending, slow allocation of funds, foreign exchange risk, and lack of capacity of Tonga Power's staff, including finance staff). In the third block of environmental and social impact evaluation, ADB does not list specific data and materials, and the report mentions that it has assessed the project's impact on the report notes that the impact of the project on climate change has been evaluated and will be taken by PMU during construction. The project will not result in involuntary relocation and will not impact indigenous peoples. The last gender impact is not so much an pre-evaluation as it is an ex ante plan. Through the project, ADB hopes to promote local women's employment and increase women's participation in all phases of the project, providing a conducive environment for women's work and priority in hiring and job selection. This component will also be implemented by PMU, with advisory support from ADB's gender expert, PMC.

Asian Infrastructure Investment Bank

AIIB first assessed the macroeconomic situation of Pakistan and the status of the industries where the loan projects are located. The macroeconomic situation of Pakistan was briefly described in terms of GDP growth rate, fiscal deficit, inflation, foreign exchange reserves, and foreign direct investment (FDI). It is concluded that although Pakistan's growth in the current fiscal year is relatively optimistic, there are still risks, including natural disasters, energy shortage, lower-than-expected remittances, FDI, and tax revenue. It is worth noting that the AIIB has also considered the project performance of other international organizations in the country in its evaluation. As for the status of the industry in which the project is located, AIIB has made an outlook mainly from the perspective of subsidies received by the industry and social and environmental sustainability, concluding that the uncertainty faced by the industry remains high.

The remaining two evaluations are routine, i.e., expected project effects and feasibility. The figures for project effects are not indicated as sources. They are presumed to be the evaluations of the relevant AIIB working groups. At the same time, in terms of feasibility, AIIB adopts a cooperative approach with the governments of the project applicant countries, i.e., the governments of the project host countries first organize experts to assess the projects, prepare relevant documents, and then submit them to AIIB for further review. The following sections were examined for this project evaluation, including technical, economic, and financial analysis, fiduciary evaluation, environmental and social impact, and risk and mitigation measures. The evaluation section is the critical element regarding environmental and social impacts. Since the project is an expansion of a dam project previously financed by the Bank, AIIB has emphasized the need to maintain consistency with the Bank's evaluation criteria and to learn from the experience accumulated by the Bank's projects in all phases of the project and will continue the institutions already in place at the Bank in three areas: land acquisition dispute adjustment, maintenance of project employees' rights and interests, and the project's only complaint handling institution. The project's main conclusion is that it will have some adverse environmental impacts, but they will be temporary and reversible, and these impacts will be addressed locally. In general, the new project will not require much recent land acquisition and will contribute to employment in the local communities. Other issues that may arise during construction have been assigned to WAPDA and National Transmission and Dispatch Company (NTDC) agencies for monitoring. The risks of this project are mainly divided into technical and political aspects. The complexity of large projects poses a challenge to WAPDA, and AIIB believes that WAPDA's experience in previous hydropower projects will help carry out the project. The political risks, including an inadequate legal framework, ineffective public authorities, and reluctant posturing to accept proposals, are not issues that can be resolved quickly. The measures proposed by AIIB are to maintain timely communication with the Pakistani side and to hedge against possible political risks by communicating with sovereign countries promptly by the Bank's disclosure requirements.

Post-evaluation

World Bank

IEG has a well-established scoring system that ensures rigor through multiple appraisal methods but with a degree of flexibility to accommodate different lending instruments, program designs, or industry characteristics. All appraisers adopt the same underlying methodology to achieve the appraisal. As mentioned earlier, the IEG evaluation consists of four dimensions, the first of which is the program outcome (Outcome), which is the achievement of the goals expected to be met that are most relevant to the program and is assessed in three main dimensions: Relevance, Efficacy, and Efficiency. Relevance is mainly the relevance of objects and design relevance. Relevance of things, i.e., whether the project is consistent with the country's current development priorities/overall strategic objectives of the country-level and industry-level assistance provided by the Bank. Relevance of design: The extent to which the project design is consistent with the project's objectives. Effectiveness is the extent to which the project objectives are achieved or predicted to be achieved. Multiple goals are balanced according to their importance. Efficiency is an evaluation of the time to which the project is implemented or estimated to be implemented and whether a higher return can be achieved relative to other options. The second is Risk to Development Outcome, which is the extent to which the project's results (or expected results) will not be maintained (or achieved) at the time of the evaluation. The third item, Bank Performance, refers to the extent to which the bank provided supportive services and adequate supervision during the start-up phase and subsequent project implementation. (Supervision includes providing transitional arrangements for project development outcomes after loan closing.) The fourth item is the performance of the lender (including the host government and the project implementing agency), i.e., the extent to which the lender has ensured the quality of project preparation and implementation and has followed relevant contracts and agreements. The evaluation is divided into two parts, government performance and project implementing agency performance. The evaluation results are categorized as highly satisfactory, more satisfactory, satisfactory, less satisfactory, unsatisfactory, and highly imperfect.

In addition to combing through relevant documents, IEG's post-evaluation conducts field surveys in the project countries. It collects data through interviews with residents, small and medium enterprises (SMEs), and public organizations in the project implementation areas (1,500 households were interviewed in the Sri Lanka project). In the case of Sri Lanka, the IEG team interviewed staff from the Bank's offices in Washington and Colombo, project developers, commercial banks, think tanks, independent consultants, residents, and the ADB, and conducted field surveys of new energy supply stations and households in remote areas where new energy supply facilities were installed.

The project results are assessed as "satisfactory" overall, as the project has improved social and economic welfare in remote areas of Sri Lanka, private sector activity in the new energy sector has increased, and the sustainable benefits of the project are substantial. Development risks are classified as negligible because the private sector in Sri Lanka has started to take ownership of activities in the new energy sector, and the installation and use of solar facilities continue. Bank performance: more than satisfactory because the Bank has demonstrated good adaptability to the project, the market, and the host country. Borrower Performance: Satisfactory because the Sri Lankan government has firmly fulfilled its responsibility to advance the project.

Asian Development Bank

The ADB report does not list specific evaluation criteria but mainly describes the appropriate institutional arrangements. The gender and social evaluation were carried out by gender specialists in the PMU, using methods such as literature review, field visits, consultations, and meetings with affected parties. For potential project social and environmental impacts, ADB has put in place a Stakeholder Communication Strategy and an Accountability Mechanism to safeguard the interests of local communities, mainly through the provision of workshops by ADB staff and the receipt of complaints. The ADB has put in place a Stakeholder Communication Strategy and an Accountability Mechanism to safeguard the interests of local communities, mainly through the provision of forums by ADB staff and receiving complaints.

The ADB has more detailed evaluation requirements for project progress and audits. Project Performance Monitoring (PMU) is the responsibility of the PMU, assisted by the PMC, which is required to submit quarterly project performance monitoring reports to ADB, including an evaluation of environmental and social impacts. Another monitoring aspect is whether the lender has met its commitments (Compliance Monitoring) and complied with ADB's requirements. The

ADB requires lenders to submit quarterly reports on project progress and biennial financial audits of loans and disbursements. International and Tongan experts will conduct environmental and social evaluations in the PMU, and the results will be included in the quarterly reports. With the assistance of PMU, ADB will also perform two annual assessments and a mid-term evaluation of the loan/grant during project implementation, including the quality of project outputs, implementation schedule, implementation progress, and expenditures. The PMU is required to submit to ADB (1) quarterly project progress reports; (2) annual reports including the following items (current progress against forecasted targets; major implementation issues and solutions, updated procurement program, implementation program for the next 12 months, and a project implementation report within three months of completion of project implementation.) Finally, ADB, through its representatives, will conduct random and targeted inspections of project funding flows, in-process work, and subproject implementation, as a way to prevent corruption (Asian Development Bank, 2015).

Asian Infrastructure Investment Bank

The Pakistan hydropower project is expected to be completed around 2022, so the project does not yet have an post-evaluation component. Still, the criteria for its post-evaluation can be inferred from the AIIB's description of the project implementation. In the core compact, AIIB states that project implementation must comply with WB regulations on anti-corruption, social and environmental protection, procurement, and disbursement. It can be inferred that this should be one of the criteria for post-evaluation. In the part of project implementation arrangements, AIIB has adopted the practice of reviewing the relevant WB and organization regulations in advance and consolidating them to improve the efficiency of project operations. The WB criteria are mainly corruption prevention, while the AIIB criteria include environmental and involuntary relocation aspects, i.e., environmental and social sustainability.

Comparison Summary

The three evaluation systems and criteria are generally similar but different, as shown in Table 10.2.

The three evaluation systems have some similarities: first, they all focus on the social and environmental impacts of the projects; second, they all pay attention to enhancing the autonomy of the lenders and provide support in the form of advice and observers in the hope that the local community can develop a sustainable operating system instead of relying only on external support. In addition, apart from cooperation with the government, they all attach importance to communication and collaboration with local communities and guarantee communication in the system and institutional setting.

Each organization's evaluation system has its characteristics and strengths. The Bank's evaluation system is more mature and emphasizes the importance of

Table 10.2. Comparison of the Evaluation System and Criteria of WB, ADB, and AIIB.

Organization Name	Preevaluation	Postevaluation	Feature
WB	Macro-environment (economic and political) in lending countries, Structure of the project involving industry, The market supply and demand situation of the industry, The Bank's previous cooperation with the country and its experience.	Project results, Development risk, Bank performance, Debit and credit performance.	1. Strong focus on project sustainability 2. Take into account multiple dimensions
ADB	Financial management, Risks, Environmental and social impact, Gender impact.	Financial aspects, Environment, Social impact, Gender impact, Anti-corruption.	1. Pay attention to the time point 2. Pay great attention to financial aspects 3. Emphasis on professionalism 4. Gender impact is its unique evaluation criterion
AIIB	Benefits (economic, environmental, social), Risks (economic, environmental, social, political), Feasibility (existing systems and other resources, experience and capacity of project contractors, establishment and operation of the consulting and supervision system, etc.).	Anti-corruption, Information transparency, Environmental impact, Social impact.	Collaboration with established international development agencies, such as integration with WB regulations
Similarities	Evaluate mainly from economic and financial aspects, environmental aspects, and social aspects		

Data source: Based on its project evaluation report and related information (Asian Development Bank, 2015; Asian Infrastructure Investment Bank, 2016b; Independent Evaluation Group World Bank, 2014).

local involvement (Local Involvement) to the project's success. Combined with one of the criteria for postevaluation, development risk, the Bank's evaluation of projects places a strong emphasis on sustainability in terms of economic and social development and in terms of sustaining the operation of the project itself. Another distinctive feature of the Bank's evaluation is that it takes into account the performance or feedback of participants at multiple levels (e.g., central, local, and industry-specific institutions in the host country), which to some extent ensures the impartiality of the Bank's evaluation and is more relevant for future projects.

ADB's evaluation system has distinctive features. First, it focuses on prior planning and timing, with many progress schedules in the project reports detailing the expected and actual processes. The information required from the off-takers is divided into quarterly, annual, and biennial. Second, great attention is paid to the management of financial aspects. While the Bank's pre-evaluation analyzes the macroeconomic performance of the lender, ADB's reports look at the lender's and implementer's financial discipline, and the risk evaluation also focuses on financial aspects. Third, emphasis is placed on professionalism, but this is achieved not by requiring the lender but by having a professional consulting group. Most consultants are from the energy, infrastructure, and finance sectors, and even a smaller number of consultants from the social sector are required to have extensive experience. Last, the promotion of gender equality and women's participation in social impact are listed separately, with apparent indicators of the involvement of women in recruitment and seminars, which are unique to ADB.

The AIIB's evaluation system is characterized by integrating its projects with the Bank's regulations and evaluations to enhance evaluation efficiency. The Pakistan Hydropower Project is a project that has taken over from the Bank's projects. The pre- and post-evaluations show that environmental and social sustainability is essential to the AIIB. The pre-evaluation is divided into benefits (economic, environmental, social), risks (economic, environmental, social, political), and feasibility (existing systems and other resources, experience and capacity of the project contractor, the establishment and operation of the advisory and regulatory system and other factors). At the same time, the post-evaluation seems to focus on four aspects: anti-corruption, information transparency, environmental impact, and social impact.

AIIB evaluates during the project period in collaboration with the Bank's working group and local government agencies and local enterprises (NTDC) within the framework of the Bank's disclosure requirements to guarantee the sovereign's right to information and to provide access to information (website, regular meetings) and remedies (arbitration committees, etc.) to the local community. The AIIB's collaboration with established international development institutions is of interest. The AIIB has adopted a more flexible stance in applying some of the Bank's project criteria and institutional systems, and its macroeconomic evaluation of Pakistan is based mainly on IMF data, all of which have improved the efficiency of project operations and saved operational costs.

Conclusion

The comparative analysis of the evaluation mechanisms of WB, ADB, and AIIB shows that the evaluation systems of multilateral development banks are similar. They all pay much attention to environmental and social impacts based on economic and financial feasibility. Still, they have their characteristics, mainly in combination with their positioning and focus. The author believes that NDB can refer to the system design of mature institutions in the setting of evaluation mechanisms and suggests that based on a perfect and flexible evaluation system, communication with existing multilateral development banks should be maintained, especially in sharing relevant data information and background information when allowed, to facilitate the efficient implementation of the evaluation work.

First, an institutional framework for project performance evaluation should be constructed. It includes evaluation agencies, evaluation methods, and evaluation standards. Pre-evaluation can be based on project departments of internal assessment. As for postevaluation, we should learn from the existing multilateral development banks and establish an independent evaluation agency to ensure the evaluation's scientific validity and be able to be directly accountable to the project investment subject.

Second, about the setting of evaluation criteria. Depending on the type of project, different groups of evaluation criteria should be set, i.e., various specific indicators. However, the main aspects of the evaluation examination should be similar so that analogies of projects can be made and different projects in the same country can be integrated to facilitate an understanding of the local situation. At the same time, the evaluation criteria should be flexible enough to be adjusted to the recipient country's situation.

Third, pre- and post-evaluation should be combined with ex ante and ex post assessment criteria. Performance appraisal should be carried out throughout the project implementation process for better monitoring and evaluation of the project. It is suggested that the project should be result-oriented, and the project can be assessed regularly according to the evaluation criteria at the beginning of the project implementation, which is conducive to the supervision of the project. The project evaluation should be carried out throughout the implementation process to be able to decide whether the next installment or the remaining amount can be released based on the implementation status and to be able to provide knowledge and technical support. At the same time, the evaluation intensity should be determined by the situation of the target country, i.e., its carrying capacity and willingness to reform. Recipient countries should be encouraged to strengthen their accountability mechanisms and monitoring systems.

Fourth, ensure that the views fully inform the evaluation of different groups, including citizen groups and nongovernmental organizations. Taking into account participants at multiple levels (e.g., central, local, industry-specific related institutions in the host country) and incorporating their performance or feedback into the evaluation system can, to a certain extent, ensure the fairness of the evaluation and be more informative for future projects.

Fifth, it is recommended to form a shared database among MDBs. Based on the cooperation with WB, ADB, and AIIB, the NDB can share background information on projects and borrowing countries to form a more credible database so that more background information on countries and similar projects can be obtained when evaluating projects to save evaluation time and improve evaluation quality.

The evaluation mechanism is essential for scientific decision-making, management improvement, and project implementation. NDB should integrate the evaluation mechanism throughout the project to improve the quality of project implementation and provide a solid basis for better scientific decision-making in the future. More importantly, the project evaluation's policy framework and indicator set should be closely integrated with the development objectives. The specific evaluation indicators should be gradually subdivided from the development objectives; the project process should be controlled through evaluation to achieve the development objectives gradually.

References

Asian Development Bank. (2015). *Proposed loan, grants and administration of grants for additional financing Kingdom of Tonga: Outer island renewable energy project administration manual.* https://www.adb.org/sites/default/files/project-document/217131/43452-024-pam.pdf

Asian Infrastructure Investment Bank. (2016a). *From due diligence to loan negotiations, AIIB's focus remains on the efficiency and quality of each task for fast delivery of the project.* https://www.aiib.org/en/projects/process/index.html

Asian Infrastructure Investment Bank. (2016b). *Project document of the Asian Infrastructure Investment Bank, Islamic Republic of Pakistan Tarbell 5 Hydropower Extension Project.* https://www.aiib.org/en/projects/approved/2016/_download/pakistan-tarbela-5/approved_project_document_tarbela_5_hydropower_extension.pdf

Culpeper, R. (1997). *Titans or behemoths?* (Vol. 5). Lynne Rienner Publishers.

Denizer, C., Kaufmann, D., & Kraay, A. (2013). Good countries or good projects? Macro and micro correlates of World Bank project performance. *Journal of Development Economics, 105*, 288–302.

Gutner, T., & Thompson, A. (2010). The politics of IO performance: A framework. *Review of International Organizations, 5*, 227–248.

He, W. (2011). From "aid effectiveness" to "development effectiveness": The evolution of aid concepts and the role of China's experience. *West Asia and Africa, 9*, 120–135.

Ika, L. A., Diallo, A., & Thuillier, D. (2012). Critical success factors for World Bank projects: An empirical investigation. *International Journal of Project Management, 30*(1), 105–116.

Independent Evaluation Group World Bank. (2014). *Project performance assessment report Democratic Socialist Republic of Sri Lanka renewable energy for rural economic development project.* https://ieg.worldbankgroup.org/sites/default/files/Data/reports/Sri_Lanka_RenewableEnergyRuralEcon_PPAR_885470PPAR0P070C0disclosed060260140.pdf

Prada, F. (2012). *World Bank, Inter-American Development Bank and subregional development banks in Latin America: Dynamics of a system of multilateral development banks. Asian Development Bank Working Paper*, 35 p. (No. 380).
Ren, Z., & Zhang, H. (2015). Comparative analysis of operating rules of international organizations and inspiration for the operation of BRICS Bank. *Shanghai Finance*, *12*, 52–57.

Part III

Case Studies

Chapter 11

Export Sophistication and Industrial Upgrading: A Study of Energy Vehicles in BRICS

Xuwen Cao[a] *and Rajah Rasiah*[b]

[a]Changzhou Vocational Institute of Textile and Garment, China
[b]University of Malaya, Malaysia

Abstract

The automobile industry is widely recognized as a key sector with strong industrial linkages that significantly contribute to economic growth. This chapter focuses on the export of energy vehicles in BRICS countries from 2015 to 2021, evaluating export sophistication using panel data. Given that industrial upgrading is a long-term and dynamic economic process, the study employs a dynamic panel model to analyze the relationship between energy vehicle export sophistication and industrial upgrading. The findings reveal a significant positive correlation between the export sophistication of energy vehicles and industrial upgrading in BRICS countries from an economic perspective. Export sophistication emerges as a critical internal factor in advancing the technological structure of export trade. Conversely, external factors such as research and development, foreign direct investment, and GDP growth show comparatively less influence. Therefore, the exportation of energy vehicles presents a valuable opportunity for driving industrial upgrading in BRICS countries.

Keywords: Energy vehicle; export sophistication; industry upgrading; *BRICS*; *automobile industry*

Introduction

With the deepening of the global energy crisis, the increasing air pollution, and the increasing harm of global temperature, the impact of a large number of cars

The Multilateralism of the New Development Bank on the Sustainable Economic Growth in BRICS Nations and Beyond, 179–196

Published under exclusive licence by Emerald Publishing Limited
doi:10.1108/978-1-83662-292-520251015

around the world is sharply prominent (Celik, 2020). Under the tremendous pressure of the energy environment, the automobile industry needs to make revolutionary changes to meet the challenge of the environmental energy system (Colmenar-Santos et al., 2019). Governments of all countries and automobile enterprises generally realize that energy saving and emission reduction is the main direction of the future development of automobile technology (He et al., 2021). At the same time, governments have introduced a timetable to ban the sale of traditional fuel cars (Barkenbus, 2020). On the one hand, to seek a breakthrough in the corresponding critical conventional car technology optimization (Wen et al., 2018). On the other hand, they are vigorously developing the energy vehicles industry. The latter is undoubtedly an effective way to alleviate the problem of energy conservation and emission reduction (Mahi et al., 2021).

The BRICS countries, comprising Brazil, Russia, India, South Africa, and China, are not only an essential engine of world economic growth but also a significant force in promoting green energy development. Renewable energy is one of the major areas of cooperation among BRICS countries, and the BRICS countries' increasing share of global renewable energy has demonstrated their determination to develop renewable energy (Kudryashova & Shashkova, 2020).

The automobile industry is an integral part of the economic development of BRICS countries. As an essential part of the automobile industry, new energy is the main direction of the green transformation and upgrading of the global automobile industry (Mikhno et al., 2021). Although BRICS countries are all developing countries, the future market for energy vehicles is no less than developed countries. The gross domestic product (GDP) of BRICS countries and the need for energy vehicles are expanding simultaneously.

By 2021, China's production and sales of energy vehicles have ranked first in the world for seven consecutive years, becoming the world's largest country of energy vehicles (Li et al., 2021). China's further energy vehicle market penetration is entering the fast lane of high growth (Wang et al., 2020). Since 2021, energy vehicles have wholly entered the market-driven stage, with an annual market penetration of 13.4%. According to China's current policy objectives and the space of the automobile consumption market, it is estimated that by 2035, China's energy vehicle sales will have six to eight times the growth space, and the "golden 15 years" of China's energy vehicle market is coming.

Brazil is a vital automobile production and sales country in South America. The government attaches great importance to developing and utilizing new energy products and supports the development of the new energy automobile industry (Velandia Vargas et al., 2020). Russia's automobile industry is a little backward. Nevertheless, science and technology are still high, and energy vehicle technology research and development are also increasing in recent years. The Russian government attaches great importance to the development of domestic cars too. The government strongly supports domestic automobile brands; In addition, the per capita ownership of Russian vehicles is low, so the market prospect has enormous potential (Klyuev, 2019). The Indian automobile industry attaches great importance to independent research and development. India has become a global automobile production and market power, with a specific ability of trade competitiveness (Miglani, 2019). South Africa is the second largest economy in Africa, with a developed transportation industry, which provides a good development environment for the automotive industry. South Africa's automobile production and sales are small, the per capita car ownership is relatively low, and the market potential is enormous (Barnes et al., 2018).

At present, the international automobile market competition is fierce. Compared with developed countries with global auto giants, BRICS countries should strengthen cooperation in the energy vehicle industry, leverage the comparative advantages of each country, carry out diversified cooperation, and improve the competitiveness of the energy vehicle industry.

This study focuses on the relationship between the export sophistication and industry upgrading first, then add other factors which are also relevant with industry upgrading. Considering energy vehicles in different product cycle stages, the economic impact is not the same. This study conducted a dynamic long-term survey to detect the long-term implications of energy vehicles on the economy and evaluate whether it is worth promoting energy vehicles in the long term.

Literature Review

BRICS Energy Vehicle Development Status

Brazil Energy Vehicle Development Status

Energy vehicles have yet to find their way in Brazil, and energy vehicle manufacturing has yet to take shape. Brazil has only a handful of imported models and lacks the legal framework and infrastructure to develop energy vehicles. Charging piles, for example, are barely visible in cities, and government support for energy vehicles is scarcely perceptible. However, the Brazilian market is not yet saturated with energy vehicles, and Brazilian consumers strongly demand cost-effective energy vehicles. According to the National Association of Automobile Industries, 34,990 energy vehicles were sold in Brazil in 2021, up to 77% yearly. Of these, 4,545 energy vehicles were sold in December, the highest since 2012. Although Brazil's infrastructure and market system for energy vehicles remain underdeveloped, and consumer acceptance is hindered by high costs (Posada & Façanha, 2015). The government has recognized that the energy vehicle market will create more green jobs, promote local manufacturing and assembly in the auto industry, and promote renewable energy development.

The Brazilian government encourages the development of new energy. In 2019, the Rota 2030 act was passed, providing about 387 million dollars to the automobile manufacturing industry every year. It will give incentives to energy vehicles in terms of tariffs, consumption taxes, and other taxes, which will continue to promote the growth of the energy vehicle market in the future.

Russia Energy Vehicle Development Status

Energy vehicles in Russia are affected by the cold climate, and the market size is limited. The sales scale of electric vehicles in Russia is limited and mainly stays at the level of displaying new products and promoting innovative ideas for environmental protection. By 2020, the number of electric vehicles in Russia was about 6,300, with a penetration rate of 0.01%. At the same time, the infrastructure construction of energy vehicles in Russia is still in its infancy. The capital of Moscow, as the "pioneer of electric cars," only plans to increase the number of charging piles in the city by five times to 600 in 2023, while designing parking spaces for electric cars (Pagliaro, 2021).

In terms of policy, the Russian government has increased policy support for developing energy vehicles. According to the National Plan of Russian energy development, Russia plans to increase the consumption of natural gas for vehicles to 2.7 billion square meters by 2024, increase the number of filling stations to 1,273, and produce 7,960 sets of natural gas vehicles every year. The Russian government plans to allocate 65 billion rubles (about $1 billion) a year to develop autonomous driving, hybrid, and electric technologies. Initial results have been achieved in independent research and development. Russia Lada Has launched Ellada, a local electric vehicle brand, and St Petersburg University of Technology has successfully developed Kama 1, an urban electric SUV, and Zetta, a compact electric vehicle platform. At the same time, subsidies will be increased. For example, Russia gives a fixed subsidy to purchase natural gas vehicles. Taking "Lada" brand natural gas cars as an example, the subsidy scale accounts for about 10% of the purchase amount. Loan subsidies for the purchase of environment-friendly cars, including electric vehicles, can reach up to 25%.

India Energy Vehicle Development Status

India is the world's third largest auto market after China and the United States. However, it has been criticized by the international community for its reliance on fossil fuels such as gasoline for 70% of transportation energy needs. The Indian government, which has been passive in the supply of environmentally friendly vehicles, announced alternative fuels and electric vehicles, and plans to expand the collection of hybrid vehicles, pure electric vehicles, hydrogen fuel cell vehicles, and bioethanol have attracted industry attention. The Indian government is strengthening emission standards to facilitate the supply of clean fuel vehicles, including electric vehicles, to meet greenhouse gas reduction targets (Vidhi & Shrivastava, 2018). Many Indian automakers, including India's largest automaker Maruti Suzuki, have been working hard to delay stricter emissions regulations to implement more stringent emissions regulations. The Indian government plans to increase the share of electric vehicles in total passenger vehicle sales to 30% by 2030 and the percentage of electric two-wheelers to 40%. At the same time, they are also pushing for mandatory sales of flexible fuel vehicles (FFVs) that use both gasoline and ethanol. The government aims to replace 20% of gasoline-powered vehicles with FFVs by 2025. As part of the Paris climate agreement, this will reduce carbon emissions by 33–35% by 2030. At the same time, the Indian government wants developed countries to set up climate funds to provide incentives for developing countries.

China Energy Vehicle Development Status

The Chinese government has issued several policies to support the development of domestic energy vehicles, including pure electric vehicles and plug-in hybrid vehicles. At present, China is the world's largest energy vehicle market. In 2021, the sales of energy vehicles reached 3.334 million, accounting for nearly half of the global sales of energy vehicles. New energy, intelligent control system, and telematics are the development direction of the global automotive industry. So far, the global energy vehicle market has increased significantly, and China's energy vehicle market will continue to maintain rapid growth. Relevant data showed that the global sales of energy vehicles maintained steady growth, from 1.1621 million in 2017 to 6.0212 million in 2021. It is estimated that the global sales of energy vehicles will reach 9.5856 million in 2022.

In the development goal of energy vehicle, China is relatively active and stable. The long-term development plan for China's energy vehicles is mainly based on the energy vehicle industry development plan (2021–2035) by the general office of the State Council in 2020, which defines the key points of China's long-term development plan for energy vehicles. According to the official disclosure of countries, the proportion of energy vehicles in the sales of vehicles, China has adopted the strategy of gradual improvement according to the "energy saving and energy vehicle technology roadmap 2.0," which will be 20% by 2025, 40% by 2030, and 50% by 2035. According to the top 20th data of global energy vehicle brand sales in 2021 published on the website, shown in Fig. 11.1, China's energy vehicles brands: BYD, SAIC Group, Shanghai passenger car, Great Wall Euler, GAC, Chery group, Xiaopeng automobile, and Chang'an automobile are all on the list. Hence, China's market plays an important role in global energy vehicles market.

Fig. 11.2 shows that since 2016, Chinese energy vehicle stocks have held half of the worldwide market share. Despite the impact of the COVID-19 pandemic, sales of energy vehicles increased 47% in 2020 compared to the previous year, the highest annual growth rate since 2012. The energy vehicles market is expected to reach 6.5 million units in 2021, with a market share of 9%. The growth rate of pure electric vehicles differs significantly from that of plug-in hybrid vehicles, with 320,810 pure electric vehicles sold compared to 272,935 DM plug-in hybrid vehicles sold. Pure electric and plug-in hybrid vehicle sales increased by 69% and 31%, respectively, while hybrid vehicle sales increased by 9%.

South Africa Energy Vehicle Development Status

Known as "Africa's Detroit" due to the developed automobile industry, South Africa is the only country in Africa with energy vehicles currently. It is considered the most significant energy vehicle market in Africa. However, South Africa has

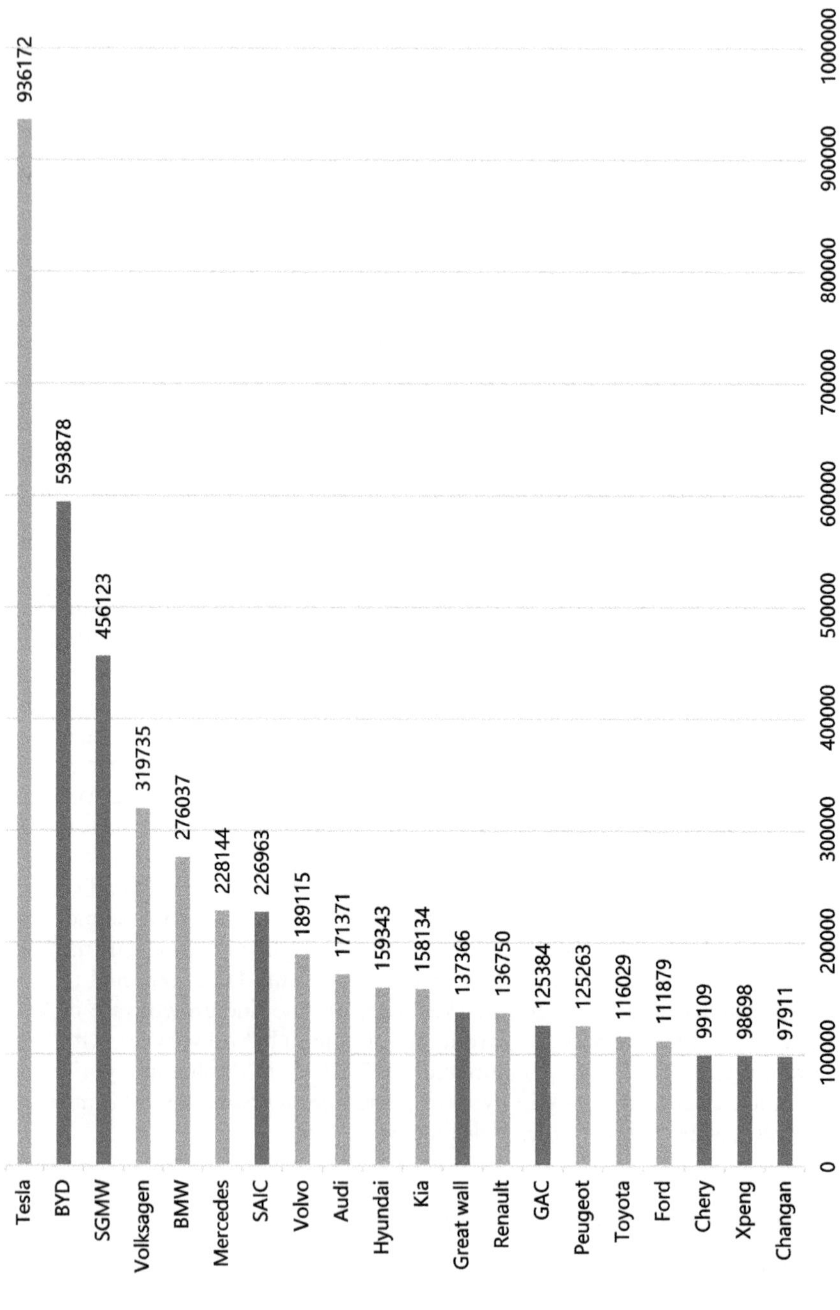

Fig. 11.1. Top 20th Energy Vehicle Brands in 2021. *Sources:* China Association of Automobile Manufacturers' EV Volumes. Units: car.

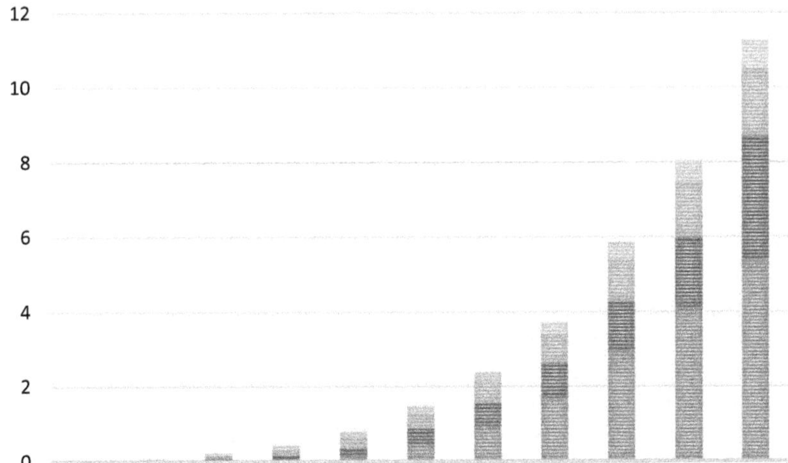

	2010	2011	2012	2013	2014	2015	2016	2017	2018	2019	2020
Other	0	0.02	0.05	0.09	0.14	0.18	0.22	0.32	0.45	0.6	0.78
United States	0	0.02	0.08	0.17	0.29	0.41	0.57	0.77	1.13	1.46	1.79
Europe	0.01	0.02	0.06	0.12	0.23	0.42	0.64	0.93	1.33	1.86	3.32
China	0	0.01	0.03	0.05	0.13	0.46	0.94	1.69	2.94	4.12	5.37

Fig. 11.2. Global Energy Vehicles Stock by Region, 2010–2020. *Source:* IEA, Global electric vehicle stock by region, 2010–2020. Units: million.

experienced a severe power crisis since 2008, and developing energy vehicles has encountered serious obstacles. Energy vehicles are still in their infancy in South Africa. In South Africa, only 1,000 energy vehicles are in proportion to 12 million automobiles. In 2020, 324 energy vehicles were sold in South Africa, accounting for 0.07% of the fuel vehicle sales. The ratio of energy vehicles can be negligible. Sales of energy vehicles in South Africa nearly double in 2021 compared to 2020. Still, high import tariffs and limited local manufacturing have left South African consumers with few options other than high-end brands.

In 2019, the South African Government called on the nation's automobile manufacturers to contribute to the development of a global roadmap for energy vehicle production. South Africa has issued a draft of the "National Commitment Contribution" (NDC), which states that from 2031 to 2040, South Africa will focus on green transportation and vigorously develop green vehicles such as energy vehicles. Through the long-term national strategy, it hopes South Africa will be at the forefront of advanced automobile and auto parts manufacturers. The Green Paper plans to reduce AD Valorem taxes and eliminate tariffs on energy vehicle components, as well as incentivize innovation in the local energy vehicle manufacturing industry and reward the use of local raw materials, including lithium, nickel, and cobalt for energy vehicles, to chart a road map for energy vehicle development in South Africa (Collett et al., 2021).

The Impact of Export Sophistication on Industrial Upgrading

Export Sophistication is an integrated concept of exports' technology content and productivity, extending a new horizon on international trade research. This study presents the competitiveness of countries. Commodities exported by rich countries (controlling for overall economic size) get ranked more highly than commodities exported by poorer countries. Classical trade, neoclassical, and technical gap theories believe that a country's export level of technology and structure should genuinely reflect the factor endowment. Studying and analyzing the export sophistication and influencing factors of energy vehicles trade should be based on the above international trade theory, which has important theoretical significance to improve the export sophistication, the optimization and upgrading of China's export structure (Hausmann & Rodrik, 2003). This formal model shows that some traded products are associated with higher productivity levels than other countries. Countries latch on higher productivity goods (through the cost discovery process described) will perform better. Therefore, the key novelty is a quantitative index that ranks traded goods in terms of their implied productivity. Usually, high per capita income means high skills, and high technology brings high wages. This measure takes a weighted average of the per capita GDP of the countries exporting a product, where the weights reflect the comparative advantage of each country in that product. This model proposes a way of classifying traded products, which does not require detailed industry data but infers product characteristics from the exporter, rather than from parent industry data on factor content or research and development (R&D) activity.

The concept of industrial upgrading is from the theory of industrial economics. The research on industrial upgrading is ongoing and has produced considerable results. Industrial upgrading is the step-wise development of manufacturing skills from simple to more complicated tasks and can be a highly effective approach for late entrants. Industrial upgrading is based on the step-by-step strategy for developing more complex industry-established methods (Azadegan & Wagner, 2011). Whether technological progress plays a significant role in promoting the upgrading of industrial structure, or even whether it has a hindering effect on the upgrading of industrial design, is affected by many factors, such as the structure of technological progress, the change of the relative rate of technological advancement in the industry, and the effect of industrialization of achievements. The system of technological progress refers to the industry in which technological progress occurs; that is, different industries in which technological progress occurs will bring other effects on upgrading industrial structure. If technological progress occurs in the high-end technology manufacturing industry, or the rate of technological advancement in the high-end manufacturing industry is relatively high, suppose the technological progress occurs in the high-end technology manufacturing industry, or the speed of technological advancement in the high-end manufacturing industry is relatively high, in that case, it will promote the growth of the high-end technology industry and the upgrading of the industrial structure of the manufacturing industry. However, if the technological progress occurs in the middle or even low-end technology manufacturing industry, or the technical progress rate of the middle and low-end manufacturing industry is relatively high, it is not conducive to upgrading the industrial structure of the manufacturing industry. This study uses Petty-Clark theory to measure the economic development of a country and the increase of per capital national income. In this theory, with the development of economy and society, the relative proportion of the national income and labor force in the primary industry (agriculture) will gradually decrease, while that in the secondary industry (industry) will gradually increase. With the further development of the economy, the tertiary industry (services) national income and the relative proportion of labor force also began to rise.

Hausmann proposed that under the same factors endowment, a country would obtain more significant benefits in international trade if it exported products with a higher technological level or government focused on developing the ability to produce and export products with a higher technical level (Hausmann et al., 2007). Many scholars have proposed that increasing the impact of export sophistication on the industrial technology level can promote the transformation and upgrading of industrial structures. The elimination of inferior industries and the development of superior industries are the functional path to realizing the industrial upgrading of a country or a region through the improvement of export technology (Lucchese et al., 2016). Based on the theoretical and empirical analysis of some European countries, it is concluded that the technological difference caused by technological innovation in various industries is an important reason for industrial upgrading (Pianta et al., 2020).

This chapter focused on the impact of export sophistication as an internal influencing factor on industrial upgrading. However, it is rare to check export sophistication as a new indicator reflecting industrial upgrading. This chapter researched the impact of export technical complexity on industrial development. In theory, industrial structure and foreign trade are determined by their production structure, and their relationship is mutual influence and mutual promotion. Due to other uncertain variables such as financial, government policies, and other factors, industrial structure development and foreign trade will sometimes deviate from the actual economic environment. Therefore, it is reasonable to assume in this study that raising the export sophistication of BRICS energy vehicles might improve BRICS transformation of their foreign trade model and accelerate BRICS industrial upgrading.

Measurement Model and Data Processing

There are many researches on the export sophistication, but most of them are carried out at the international level and the industrial level. The export sophistication is a composite index, including the change in trade structure, the progress of production technology, and the upgrade of product quality. The influencing factors of export sophistication are complex and diverse. As an essential characteristic of the change of trade structure, what is the impact of the optimization and upgrading of the industrial design determined by production on the export sophistication? Presently, research on export sophistication and industrial design are generally conducted in parallel, and few scholars have studied the relationship between them. The study of the impact of industrial structure upgrading on the complexity of export technology has both a theoretical basis and specific feasibility.

This study is based on the Hausmann's per capita income EXPY index calculation approach to measure export sophistication (Hausmann et al., 2007).

First, calculate the technical complexity of the commodity which called PRODY. PRODY is an index from the perspective of income level associated with products, EXPY_i is the export sophistication index of energy vehicle exports in a country, weighted average of the per capita GDP of countries exporting a given product. Then, the productivity level associated with product j, EXPY_i, is as follows:

$$X_j = \textstyle\sum_j X_{ij} \tag{1}$$

$$\text{PRODY}_i = \sum_j \frac{(X_{ij}/X_i)}{\sum_i (X_{ij}/X_i)} Y_i \tag{2}$$

$$\text{EXPY}_i = \sum_i \frac{X_{ij}}{X_i} \text{PRODY}_i \tag{3}$$

In Eqs. (1), (2), and (3), X_{ij} represents the export value of each product j in country i; X_i represents the total export value of energy vehicle commerce of country i; and the per capita GDP of country i is denoted as Y_i.

When calculating the export sophistication of a country's energy vehicles, the actual value for each year is used, which better reflects the dynamic trends in the evolution of the country's energy vehicle exports toward greater sophistication.

Second, construct another part to measure the relation between export sophistication and industrial upgrading according to Petty-Clark theory (ISR), industrial upgrading as the explanatory variable (Li et al., 2017). In order to facilitate the introduction of all explanatory variables into the model, and combination with relevant research results, the alternative variables of all factors are selected as Table 11.1.

In Eq. (4), in order to avoid the influence of differences in data units on the stability of the model, all data except per capita GDP growth rates require logarithmic processing, then introduce data into the model. i denotes country, t denotes time, $\epsilon_{i,t}$ is the error term.

$$\text{UP}_{i,t} = \text{EXPY}_{i,t} + \text{GDP growth}_{i,t} + \text{R\&D}_{i,t} + \text{FDI}_{i,t} + \text{Patent}_{i,t} + \epsilon_{i,t} \tag{4}$$

Table 11.1. Variable Measurement.

Variable	Explain
UP	The ratio of the sum of secondary industry plus tertiary industry to GDP
R&D	Research and development expenditure (% of GDP)
FDI	Foreign direct investment
GDP growth	Growth rate of country
Patent	The number of country's patents

The nature of this study is quantitative research which uses STATA 16.0, analyzing the primary data collected by authority for achieving the research objectives. Considering energy vehicles had drastic increase from 2015, so this study chooses data from 2015 to 2021. The categories, key parts products of energy vehicles, and their Harmonization System Code 6 (HS-Code6) are 870220, 870230, 870240, 870340, 870350, 870360, 870370, 870380, 870911, 871160, 850650, and 850760. All data are sourced from the Organization for Economic Cooperation and Development (OECD) statistics and UN Comtrade (International Energy Agency, 2020).

Empirical and Results

The unit root test is the stationarity test of the sequence. First, the unit root test is conducted to see whether the variable line is stationary. Then, classical models such as regression models can be constructed if unit root test is static. The results in Table 11.2 show that all the first levels are significant, so the regression model is reliable.

We constantly choose the fixed effect to test the process of continually introducing variables for regression. The effect coefficient in Table 11.2 means export sophistication on industrial upgrading is between 8.63% and 1%, presents the impact range scope at the highest level and the lowest level, also suggests that each one percentage point growth in energy vehicles' export specialization provides more than one percentage point to industrial upgrading. Also, the results show that the effect of the export sophistication is positive at 0.0863 when adding all variables by turn. The influence of these control variables R&D and the patent on industrial upgrading is significantly less than the effect of export sophistication, and the coefficients of variables R&D and patent are all positive. However, not all variables positively affect industrial upgrading; GDP growth and foreign direct investment (FDI) variables negatively impact industry upgrading, unlike these variables which usually have a positive impact on industrial upgrading.

Table 11.2. Unit Root Tests Results.

Variables	PP
UP	11.2235***
	(0.0000)
R&D	14.4821***
	(0.0000)
GDP growth	8.4445***
	(0.0000)
PATENT	3.8432***
	(0.0001)
EXPY	16.7475***
	(0.0000)
FDI	7.8856***
	(0.0000)

Note: Significance ***$p < 0.01$, **$p < 0.05$, and *$p < 0.1$.

We can judge whether there is multicollinearity in the multiple linear regression model by checking the magnitude of the variance inflation factor (VIF). Generally, we take 10 as the threshold. When VIF < 10, there is no multicollinearity. When $10 \leq$ VIF < 100, there is strong multicollinearity. When VIF ≥ 100, the model has severe multicollinearity. All VIF results in Table 11.3 are less than 10, so there is no multicollinearity in this regression model.

Note Table 11.4 above. Two-stage least squares (TSLS) regression involves two regressions. In the first regression, endogenous variables are regressed on instrumental and exogenous variables, and the predicted values from this regression are obtained. In the second regression, the dependent variable is regressed on the predicted values and the exogenous variables to get the final model result. In reality, industrial upgrading is not a static process but a dynamic one that changes over time and involves long-term development. This study uses export sophistication as an instrumental variable to measure the long-term relationship between energy vehicles and industrial upgrading. Table 11.5 shows the final results of TSLS (second-order lag), with $R^2 = 0.405$ indicating that the explanatory power of the endogenous and exogenous variables for wage is 40.5%. Specifically, in the first-order lag, export sophistication negatively impacts industrial upgrading, but over time, export sophistication has a positive impact on industrial upgrading.

Table 11.3. Analysis of Results on Fixed Effect Analysis.

Variables	(1) Model 1 Up	(2) Model 2 Up	(3) Model 3 Up	(4) Model 4 Up	(5) Model 5 Up
EXPY	0.0101*	0.0100*	0.0860	0.0693***	0.0863*
	(1.7365)	(1.8343)	(1.5675)	(4.0948)	(1.6592)
FDI		−0.0012	−0.0221	−0.0074	−0.0098
		(−0.1534)	(−0.8265)	(−0.5375)	(−0.7479)
R&D			0.0545	0.0741***	0.0470
			(0.9445)	(3.3106)	(0.6913)
GDP growth				−0.0135***	−0.0154***
				(−7.3210)	(−3.1419)
PATENT					0.0091
					(0.4596)
	(−0.1332)	(−0.0699)	(−0.6376)	(0.5346)	(0.6240)
Constant	0.8187***	0.8260***	0.2215	0.2721**	0.0756
	(10.7093)	(19.6109)	(0.4257)	(2.1378)	(0.1358)
R^2	0.2087	0.0947	0.4975	0.4975	0.5012
Observations	35	35	35	35	35
Number of country	5	5	5	5	5

Note: Robust z-statistics in parentheses, $^{***}p < 0.01$, $^{**}p < 0.05$, $^{*}p < 0.1$.

Table 11.4. Multicollinearity VIF Test.

VAR	VIF	1/VIF
EXPY	1.27	0.7863
R&D	7.32	0.1367
PAPENT	8.85	0.1130
FDI	1.95	0.5131
GDP growth	1.52	0.6583

Table 11.5. TSLS Results.

	(1) Up	(2) Up
EXPY	−0.008	−0.015
	(0.009)	(0.014)
R&D	0.013	0.004
	(0.013)	(0.019)
GDP growth	−0.001	−0.001
	(0.001)	(0.001)
PATENT	−0.000	0.033
	(0.015)	(0.023)
FDI	0.002	0.000
	(0.004)	(0.005)
L.EXPY		0.036*
		(0.016)
_cons	0.957***	0.560*
	(0.151)	(0.260)
N	27.000	23.000
r^2	0.194	0.405

Note: Standard errors in parentheses, $*p < 0.1$, $**p < 0.05$, $***p < 0.01$.

Conclusions and Recommendations

This chapter first measures the export complexity of energy vehicles in BRICS countries from 2015 to 2021. Secondly, based on the panel data of these seven years and the calculation results of export complexity, it empirically tests the theoretical analysis. It dynamically examines the long-term impact of export technological complexity on the industry, enriching the theoretical basis for how the technical complexity of energy vehicles can promote industrial upgrading. Overall, this study combines theoretical analysis, export complexity measurement, and empirical test results. The research conclusions are significant for understanding and mastering the current state of BRICS' export sophistication and its accurate correlation with industrial upgrading. Therefore, based on the research conclusions, this chapter mainly puts forward the following four suggestions.

Optimize the Trade Environment, Actively Embed the International Market and the International Division of Labor System

BRICS' energy vehicles have different export technology complexity levels. China's export technology complexity is relatively high, while India's is relatively low. Higher export complexity means a higher position in the global value chain and a strong competitiveness of export products. Its driving effect on the overall technological complexity of the manufacturing industry and the upgrading of the industrial structure of the manufacturing industry are also more significant.

Therefore, BRICS export enterprises, especially processing trade enterprises, should fully use the international trade environment and foreign partners. To advance technology, encourage independent research development and innovation, enhance the domestic added value of BRICS exports, promote the transfer of BRICS export enterprises to the high-end link of the global value chain, and obtain a higher level of export technology, which have great significance to improve the technological complexity of BRICS manufacturing industry and upgrade the industrial structure of manufacturing industry.

Encourage Investment in Technological Innovation and Improve the Ability to Absorb Technological Spillovers

An insufficient innovation environment will weaken the export sophistication, increase the technological sophistication of the manufacturing industry, and further promote the effect of industrial upgrading structure of the manufacturing industry. Therefore, while vigorously developing international trade, benefiting from the international division of labor, and actively improving export complexity, BRICS should pay attention to the investment in technological innovation in BRICS manufacturing industry, including the accumulation of technological capital, human capital, material capital, and other advanced production factors. In addition, we should create a technical and market environment that encourages independent innovation and technological progress, promoting the smooth transformation from the increase of export complexity to the rise in domestic manufacturing technological sophistication.

In addition, under the dynamic test, the empirical results show that the export technology complexity of BRICS significantly affects industrial technology upgrading in the long term. Still, it is not substantial in the short time. Therefore, this chapter believes that if BRICS would like to take advantage of the increase of export sophistication, radiate the increase of single industry export complexity to the whole manufacturing industry, and realize the industrial upgrading of the whole country, it needs to pay more attention to the input of advanced production factors, the enhancement of the industry's absorption capacity and learning ability for advanced technology, and establish a perfect research development environment and other supporting institutional environment; these are more conducive to stimulating technological innovation.

Strengthen Inter-industry Technical Contacts and Optimize the Technology Diffusion Environment

On the one hand, the increase in export technical complexity can occur among industries through extensive and close technical linkages between sectors. Vertical technology spillover drives industrial upgrading. On the other hand, the technological progress occurring in a single core enterprise can also spread to the whole manufacturing industry through inter-industry technical linkages, further promoting the industrial structure upgrading of the manufacturing industry. Therefore, BRICS should strengthen the technological connections between upstream and downstream industries, including upstream and downstream sectors' direct technical demand and supply.

The advanced flow of human capital, physical capital, and other production factors fosters indirect connections between industries, creating mechanisms for technology diffusion and innovation. This process enhances individual initiatives, promotes technological progress in technology-related industries, and strengthens collaboration among enterprises. Together, these efforts improve the overall technological complexity of manufacturing and contribute to the upgrading of the industrial structure.

Promote the Marketization of the Economy and Promote the Upgrading of the Industrial Structure of the Manufacturing Industry

Industrial structure upgrading is not only driven by technological progress but also affected by demand changes. By increasing export sophistication through growing domestic and foreign demand for products in high-complexity industries, we can further attract investment from producers in high-end technology industries.

To play a role in increasing export complexity and promoting industrial structure upgrades, it is essential to focus on enhancing economic marketization. This involves improving market self-regulation, enabling the market to adjust in real time according to changes in demand. By reshaping the demand structure, export complexity can drive the upgrading of the manufacturing industry's structure.

References

Azadegan, A., & Wagner, S. M. (2011). Industrial upgrading, exploitative innovations and explorative innovations. *International Journal of Production Economics*, *130*(1), 54–65.

Barkenbus, J. N. (2020). Prospects for electric vehicles. *Sustainability*, *12*(14), 5813.

Barnes, J., Black, A., & Monaco, L. (2018, July). State–business bargaining, localisation and supply chain development in the South African auto industry. In *4th annual competlition and economic development (ACER) conference Johannesburg, South Africa* (pp. 19–20). https://static1.squarespace.com/static/52246331e4b0a46e5f1b8ce5/t/5b90fb434d7a9c5d79b8691f/1536228170573/Barnes%2C+Black+%26+Monaco_State+business+bargaining.pdf

Celik, S. (2020). The effects of climate change on human behaviors. In S. Fahad, M. Hasanuzzaman, M. Alam, H. Ullah, M. Saeed, I. Ali Khan, & M. Adnan (Eds.), *Environment, climate, plant and vegetation growth* (pp. 577–589). Springer.

Collett, K. A., Hirmer, S. A., Dalkmann, H., Crozier, C., Mulugetta, Y., & McCulloch, M. D. (2021). Can electric vehicles be good for Sub-Saharan Africa? *Energy Strategy Reviews*, *38*, 100722.

Colmenar-Santos, A., Muñoz-Gómez, A. M., Rosales-Asensio, E., & López-Rey, Á. (2019). Electric vehicle charging strategy to support renewable energy sources in Europe 2050 low-carbon scenario. *Energy*, *183*, 61–74.

Hausmann, R., Hwang, J., & Rodrik, D. (2007). What you export matters. *Journal of Economic Growth*, *12*(1), 1–25.

Hausmann, R., & Rodrik, D. (2003). Economic development as self-discovery. *Journal of Development Economics*, *72*(2), 603–633.

He, Z., Zhou, Y., Wang, J., Li, C., Wang, M., & Li, W. (2021). The impact of motivation, intention, and contextual factors on green purchasing behavior: New energy vehicles as an example. *Business Strategy and the Environment*, *30*(2), 1249–1269.

International Energy Agency. (2020). *Global EV outlook 2020: Towards cross-modal electrification*. IEA.

Klyuev, N. N. (2019). New industrial and transport construction in Russia: Economic and geographical aspects. *Herald of the Russian Academy of Sciences*, *89*(4), 333–341.

Kudryashova, E., & Shashkova, A. (2020). Tax incentives issue for innovations in sustainable energy within the BRICS strategic partnership framework. In *E3S web of conferences* (Vol. 220, p. 01007). EDP Sciences.

Li, J., Jiao, J., Xu, Y., & Chen, C. (2021). Impact of the latent topics of policy documents on the promotion of new energy vehicles: Empirical evidence from Chinese cities. *Sustainable Production and Consumption*, *28*, 637–647.

Li, W., Wang, W., Wang, Y., & Qin, Y. (2017). Industrial structure, technological progress and CO2 emissions in China: Analysis based on the STIRPAT framework. *Natural Hazards*, *88*(3), 1545–1564.

Lucchese, M., Nascia, L., & Pianta, M. (2016). Industrial policy and technology in Italy. *Economia e Politica Industriale*, *43*(3), 233–260.

Mahi, M., Ismail, I., Phoong, S. W., & Isa, C. R. (2021). Mapping trends and knowledge structure of energy efficiency research: What we know and where we are going. *Environmental Science and Pollution Research*, *28*(27), 35327–35345.

Miglani, S. (2019). The growth of the Indian automobile industry: Analysis of the roles of government policy and other enabling factors. In K. C. Liu & U. S. Racherla (Eds.), *Innovation, economic development, and intellectual property in India and China* (pp. 439–463). Springer.

Mikhno, I., Koval, V., Shvets, G., Garmatiuk, O., & Tamošiūnienė, R. (2021). Green economy in sustainable development and improvement of resource efficiency. *Central European Business Review*, *10*(1), 99–113.

Pagliaro, M. (2021). Renewable energy in Russia: A critical perspective. *Energy Science & Engineering*, *9*(7), 950–957.

Pianta, M., Lucchese, M., & Nascia, L. (2020). The policy space for a novel industrial policy in Europe. *Industrial and Corporate Change*, *29*(3), 779–795.

Posada, F., & Façanha, C. (2015). *Brazil passenger vehicle market statistics: International comparative assessment of technology adoption and energy consumption.* https://theicct.org/wp-content/uploads/2021/06/Brazil-PV-Market-Statistics-Report.pdf

Velandia Vargas, J. E., Seabra, J. E., Cavaliero, C. K., Walter, A. C., Souza, S. P., & Falco, D. G. (2020). The new neighbor across the street: An outlook for battery electric vehicles adoption in Brazil. *World Electric Vehicle Journal*, *11*(3), 60.

Vidhi, R., & Shrivastava, P. (2018). A review of electric vehicle lifecycle emissions and policy recommendations to increase EV penetration in India. *Energies*, *11*(3), 483.

Wang, L., Fu, Z. L., Guo, W., Liang, R. Y., & Shao, H. Y. (2020). What influences sales market of new energy vehicles in China? Empirical study based on survey of consumers' purchase reasons. *Energy Policy*, *142*, 111484.

Wen, J., Chen, Y. X., Nassir, N., & Zhao, J. (2018). Transit-oriented autonomous vehicle operation with integrated demand-supply interaction. *Transportation Research Part C: Emerging Technologies*, *97*, 216–234.

Chapter 12

New Development Bank in India: Growth, Development, and Futuristic Prospects

Zakia Tasmin Rahman[a], *Ruhi Lal*[b] *and Ravinder Rena*[c]

[a]Amity University, India
[b]Manav Rachana International Institute of Research and Studies, India
[c]Durban University of Technology, South Africa

Abstract

The New Development Bank (NDB) is assisting the development of India's financial system. India's financial needs are met by NDB. It can contribute to the BRIC countries' economic and social development and helps in the sustainability of the country's growth and development. The study is focused on the role of NDB in India, the growth and development of NDB, and to explore the future prospects of NDB in India. The plans and strategies of NDB are studied thoroughly, and positive conclusions can be drawn on India and other member nations of NDB. The research study is qualitative, exploratory research. It is based on secondary data. Government reports, records, published research papers, websites, related documents, etc. are taken into consideration. Content analysis is done of the secondary data. The NDB strategies are designed in such a pattern that the member nations and emerging nations of the world can get the advantage of infrastructural development, sustainable growth, and development. Investment and employment generation can lead the nations. The research study has found out that NDB accelerates development in a flexible and effective way. Also, it was found out that various infrastructural developmental projects were undertaken. Initiatives like financial support for adopting various developmental technologies and strategies should be from medium- to long-term priority.

Keywords: India; New Development Bank; financial architecture; growth; development; economic and social growth

The Multilateralism of the New Development Bank on the Sustainable Economic Growth in BRICS Nations and Beyond, 197–224

doi:10.1108/978-1-83662-292-520251016

Introduction

In July 2015, the governments of Brazil, Russia, India, the People's Republic of China, and South Africa established the New Development Bank (NDB) (BRICS) (Morozkina, 2015). Shanghai, People's Republic of China, houses the corporate headquarters of NDB (Tadas, 2020). NDB claims that the main goals of its operations are to support economic growth, promote member country development, increase competitiveness, make job creation easier, and offer a platform for knowledge exchange among developing nations. The NDB's main operational areas include transportation of infrastructure, clean energy, irrigation, sanitation, resource management for water, urban development, that is, sustainable urban development, and economic blending between associated nations (Ganguly & Roy, 2021).

NDB cofinanced a project in 2019 to improve urban mobility in India by enhancing and extending its railway network (NDB, 2019). NDB, a multidimensional progressive bank, was founded by the BRICS countries in conjunction with 2014's sixth BRICS Summit took place in Fortaleza, Brazil (Sudarvizhi, 2014).

It was created with the aim of accelerating growth through novelty and modern methods of technology to help with the development of sustainable infrastructure in the BRICS and other underdeveloped emerging economies (Morozkina, 2015). NDB received observer status at the United Nations General Assembly (UNGA) in 2018, laying the foundation for a committed and successful partnership with the UN (NDB, 2021a, 2021b; Regarding the New Development Bank, Agreement, 2015). In order to further its goals, the Bank finances public or private projects through loans, guarantees, equity involvement, and various means.

In its first five years, roughly two-thirds of the Bank's financing commitments were made, and it involved in the creation of environment-friendly infrastructure, which is at the center of the operational plan for NDB from 2017 to 2021 (NDB's General Strategy, 2017). Faster and more inclusive economic growth depends on physical infrastructure, and sustainability standards are needed to guarantee that this infrastructure protects the social and physical environment for current and future generations (Vazquez et al., 2017). Due to lack of funding and technical know-how for developing sustainable infrastructure despite rising demand, NDB is assisting in bridging a significant gap in the global development finance architecture (NDB's General Strategy, 2017). NDB is still free to support traditional infrastructure and sustainable development initiatives that are consistent with the borrowing nation's overarching development goals ("New Development Bank," 2021). In addition to long-term loans, the NDB also uses a range of other financing techniques, such as guarantees, syndicated loans with private investors, equity investments, project bonds, and cofinancing agreements with domestic and foreign development finance institutions (Masamba, 2022). Because it reduces risks for borrowers and fosters the growth of member countries' capital markets, local currency financing is a crucial part of the NDB's value proposition (NDB's Human Capital, Annual Report, 2017).

To fulfill its mission, NDB needs a strong financial position, financial robustness, and equitable access to the capital markets (General Strategy of the

NDB, 2017; Morozkina, 2015). Strong systems and policies for financial and risk management are being implemented by the Bank. For NDB to become a reputable multilateral development finance institution, it must possess solid liquidity buffers, a diversified, high-performing portfolio, conservative leverage, a low loan-to-equity ratio, and prudent leveraging (Modak, 2021). According to the "List of All Projects," the Bank can frequently issue bonds in member nations and on international capital markets, including local currencies. As part of its dedication to sustainability, NDB plans to finance its business operations using the booming green bond market (BS Reporter, 2022).

The research study's objectives are to:

- To explore the function of NDB in India.
- To analyze the growth and development of NDB.
- To examine the futuristic prospects of NDB in India.

Need of the Study

The study will help the nations with financial assistance for infrastructural, sustainable growth, and development. Welfare activities can be given to the needy and financially downtrodden. The study will be of great help to the citizens of India, member nations of NDB, and other emerging nations which need support for economic growth and development. Agriculture, tertiary sector, education, welfare activities, development of the youth, help and assistance to senior citizens, and various other activities of nation building can become possible. The study will help all the citizens of India, NDB's member nations, and other emerging nations of the world. It will highlight the strategies and plans of NDB. The study will give right direction toward a bright future to India and other emerging nations of the world. The study will help in global food security and give solutions to various problems faced by the countries of the world economically and socially.

Literature Review

India proposed that the NDB's mandate be expanded to strengthen social infrastructure in addition to promoting industry during a recent BRICS country's meeting (Suneja, 2021).

- Buildings that house and provide social services like housing, healthcare, and education are referred to as social infrastructure (Business Line Bureau, 2021).
- India served as the BRICS grouping's chair in 2021 (ANI, 2021).

Commercial banks and development banks differ from one another

The establishment of *commercial banks* enables us to offer standard banking services like accepting deposits, lending money, etc. (Nanda, 2022). A *development bank*, however, is a financial organization with several goals that are established to aid in development by funding the industrial and agricultural sectors (Surbhi, 2020).

Banks are crucial to the functioning of the financial system in every country (Njogu, 2019). If the financing system in the nation is successful, it will aid in the growth of the country's economy (Yadav, 2022). Every social group makes use of various bank services for a variety of purposes (Prasad, 2020).

The three categories of banks are cooperative banks, commercial banks, and development banks (Smirti, 2021). Table 12.1 lists the distinctions between commercial banks and development banks (Surbhi, 2020).

Table 12.1. Comparison of Banks for Commercial Purpose and Banks for Developmental Purpose.

S/ No.	Source of Comparison	Commercial Purpose Bank	Developmental Purpose Bank
1.	Connotation	The basic banking and financial services that are provided to both individuals and businesses are provided by commercial banks.	Development banks are financial organizations established to fund the construction of infrastructure and the economy.
2.	Nature	Active.	Enterprising.
3.	Set up	Under the Companies Act, established as Banking Companies.	Founded under the Specialized Act.
4.	Source of funds	Obtain funding by taking public deposits.	Borrowing, granting, and securities sales.
5.	Loans provided	Loans with short and medium terms.	Long- and medium-term loans.
6.	Orientation	Driven by profit.	Dedicated to development.
7.	Purpose	To gain money by making loans with high interest rates.	To generate social profit by contributing money to projects that promote development.
8.	Services offered	For a set fee, legal, business, and credit investigation services are offered.	Advisory and counseling services are offered to aid in the development and marketing of the business.
9.	Clients	Individuals and corporate entities.	Administration.

Source: The Authors' Own Compilation.

Table 12.2. List of Public Sector Banks and Private Sector Banks of India.

S/No.	Public Banks	Private Banks
1.	State Bank of India	Axis Bank
2.	UCO Bank	Bandhan Bank
3.	Union Bank of India	CSB Bank
4.	Punjab and Sind Bank	City Union Banks
5.	Punjab National Bank	Dhanlaxmi Bank
6.	Indian Overseas Bank	Federal Bank
7.	Indian Bank	HDFC Bank
8.	Central Bank of India	ICICI Bank
9.	Canara Bank	IDBI Bank
10.	Bank of India	IndusInd Bank
11.	Bank of Baroda	Kotak Mahindra Bank
12.	Bank of Maharashtra	Yes Bank

Source: The Authors' Own Compilation.

Some of the popular public sector and private sector banks of India are stated in Table 12.2.

Indian banking structure consists of commercial as well as development banks. The commercial banks help in various kinds of transactions that happen between the common account holders and the bank. On the other hand, the Development Bank takes care of financing welfare and infrastructural activities in the nation.

Banks for Commercial Purpose

Founded to accept public deposits, provide current account services, make loans, and offer a range of financial products to individuals and businesses, for-profit financial institution is Commercial Bank.

The banks act as a go-between for depositors and borrowers (Functions of Commercial Banks, 2020). Depending on the level of risk involved, it either lends money to borrowers at a high rate of interest or pays depositors interest on the money deposited at a low rate of interest. This is how the commercial bank generates revenue ("Commercial Bank, Bankers," 2022).

The borrowing rate is the rate at which interest is paid to depositors, whereas the bank's lending rate is the rate at which it issues loans ("What are Commercial Banks," 2021). Profit is the spread, which is the distinction between lending and borrowing rates (Singh, 2019). Deposits from the public increase their responsibility to provide liquidity and safety, which limits their ability to use the money they provide ("What Is Commercial Bank," 2022).

Development Banks

The development of the industrial and agricultural sectors is supported by a brand-new, specialized financial institution known as the development bank, which provides medium- and long-term loans and infrastructure facilities (Khandelwal, 2021).

It also provides business entities with additional services like share underwriting, investment and guarantee operations, and marketing initiatives (Gutierrez et al., 2011). Development banks' main duty is to finance capital-intensive projects with low rates of return that are typically long term in nature (Musacchio et al., 2017).

NABARD, National Bank of Agricultural and Rural Development, was initiated on July 12, 1982. NABARD helps in the growth and development of agriculture, handicrafts, small-scale and cottage industries. Indian economy needed such kind of a bank for a long time, and finally, NABARD came into existence.

Goals of the Development Bank (Romero, 2017):

- To promote industrial development.
- To open up job opportunities.
- To heal sick units.
- To promote projects involving self-employment.
- To eliminate regional inequality.
- To advance underdeveloped areas.
- To expand the housing industry.
- To support small-scale industries financially.
- To assist in the growth and development of significant industries.

Key Differences Between Commercial Banks and Development Banks

Following reasons make it easy to distinguish between commercial and developmental purpose banks (Surbhi, 2020):

- The primary objective of commercial banks is to provide the public with the most fundamental banking services. On the other hand, development banks are financial organizations created to finance new businesses and initiatives related to industrial, agricultural, and economic development.
- To establish the commercial bank, a joint-stock company called a banking company is formed in India. Development banks, on the other hand, are set up in accordance with a specific act that the parliament has approved.
- A development bank is proactive by nature because it actively promotes projects and helps to nurture start-up businesses. Contrarily, commercial banks are receptive to business opportunities because they need bankability before they will consider an idea once the entrepreneur has decided.

- Commercial banks raise money by taking deposits from the public. Development banks, on the other hand, raise money through borrowing, government grants, and the sale of securities.
- Development banks offer loans of medium and long term, whereas commercial financial institutions only provide short- and medium-term loans.
- Business banks are for-profit corporations. Development banks, on the other hand, are set up to promote development.
- Commercial banks aim to turn a profit by charging high interest on loans. In contrast, by funding capital-intensive projects, development banks seek to generate social profit.
- Commercial banks offer credit, legal counsel, and business advice. A set fee for investigation services is offered. On the other hand, a development bank offers counseling and advisory services for the growth and promotion of the business.
- Commercial banks work with the general public and businesses, whereas development banks collaborate with the government.

The NDB's Primary Concern is The Development of Resources in Emerging and Developing Economies

On May 19, 2022, the Board of Governors of the NDB approved the bank's general strategies from the years 2022–2026 under the theme "Scaling Up Development Finance for a Sustainable Future" (Njogu, 2019). As per the general strategies, NDB outlines the steps it will take to become a top provider of infrastructure and sustainable development for the progress of emerging market economies (NDB/Press Release, 2022).

The General Strategy seeks to elevate NDB to a higher standard of operational excellence and strengthen the Bank's developmental impacts ("NDB's General Strategy," 2017). The General Strategy targets enhancements in the Bank's capacities to mobilize resources at a higher scale, finance various types of projects, employ sophisticated instruments, maximize impact, and continue building a robust institutional profile ("New Development Bank," 2021).

NDB's primary aspirations for the 2022–2026 period are reflected through the General Strategy. It includes the following main targets for the Bank (ndb.int/Press Release, 2022):

Over the period 2022–2026, a total volume of approved financing of USD 30 billion was provided. Extension of 30% of total financing over the period 2022–2026 in local currencies. Allocation of 30% of all financing to nonsovereign operations between 2022 and 2026. Cofinancing of 20% of projects (measured in project numbers) from 2022 to 2026 with MDB partners.

From the year 2022 to 2026, 40% of all approvals to initiate the support to climate change adaptation and mitigation was done; and increasing female representation upto 40% of professional and managerial staff by 2026.

Additionally, NDB will give developing and emerging nations a stronger voice in the system for financing international development.

In Gujarat International Finance Tec-City, NDB opened a regional office for India, and on June 21, 2022, the director general of the office was appointed.

The Gujarat International Finance Tec-City location of the NDB publicized Dr DJ Pandian's appointment as the Director General in charge of the Indian Regional Office (IRO) Bank on June 20, 2022 (GIFT City) (Srnivas & Hofman, 2022).

The NDB has approved 20 projects totaling about 7.2 billion USD in India. In order to achieve the desired project outcomes, the IRO will closely collaborate with Project Implementation Agencies and encourage the timely and effective completion of these projects. IRO will be crucial in developing new projects, helping government organizations build their capacities, and offering technical support, according to Dr DJ Pandian.

The opening of the IRO marks a pivotal moment for the Bank because it carries out the founders' pledge to do so in each of the bank's other four founding countries: South Africa, Brazil, Russia, and India.

In order to identify projects that have a significant impact on development and are in line with the priorities for national development, the IRO closely collaborate with the government, organizations of the government and industry sectors, and other relevant stakeholders in the Indian subcontinent.

By avoiding pointless red tape in the project approval and execution processes, NDB seeks to be quick and efficient without sacrificing quality.

In-country missions, document length, internal review, formal approval "gates," and internal review times will all be reduced by managements in order to ensure project quality and lower risks (NDB's General Strategy, 2017). Project readiness received special consideration prior to approval in recognition that doing so lessens implementation and disbursement challenges throughout the project lifecycle (Malik, 2017). NDB hopes to appraise, negotiate, and approve loans in its first five years on average in less than six months (Singh et al., 2017). To shorten lead times and alert management of problematic projects that might prevent timely payment, technical solutions are being developed (Massdorp, 2019).

Research Methodology

The research study is a qualitative research based on the role played by NDB in India and other emerging nations. Content analysis is done based on secondary data like government records and reports, published research papers, websites, and other relevant documents.

The study is qualitative to know the success of the strategies of NDB and support got by India and other emerging nations. The research approach is qualitative, exploratory – descriptive, and contextual as the researcher aims to understand the plans, strategies, guidelines of NDB, and extent of success in various sectors like sustainable development, infrastructural development in India and various member countries.

Research Phase

In three phases, the study was completed involving the conceptual phase, the narrative phase, and the interpretative phase.

Conceptual Phase – At this stage of the conceptual phase, formulation of research questions, objectives, and the review of the literature was done to familiarize with the concept, content, and preconceived idea about the research to understand the contribution of NDB and success of the NDB's strategies in the member nation, India, and other emerging nations.

Narrative Phase – The planning of research design was based on the plans and strategies implemented by NDB and its influence in India and other member nations. India and member nation's impact of the various plans, policies, and strategies was part of the narrative phase. The impacts are stated in reports, records, newspapers, press releases, and mass media.

Interpretative phase – The data collection phase was qualitative information gathering, analysis, and interpretation.

Context – The study is India based. In qualitative research, the context is significant. The participants in this research are from India, and various member nations of NDB are part of the study. Newspapers, magazines, research papers, government documents, reports, and records which were published in the context of growth and development in various sectors in India, and other member nations' perspectives are taken into consideration. Social media and internet calling also helped in gathering requisite information for the research study.

Reflexivity of the research – In the research study, the researcher self-monitored the preconceived values, notions, feelings, assumptions, and conflicts to increase objectivity and to prevent biasness while selecting the stakeholders of the plans and strategies of NDB and data for the credibility of the research.

Intuiting of the Study

In the study, the researchers tried to understand the concerned stakeholders by totally immersing them in the study. The researcher's main attention was only on the phenomenon described by India and member nations about NDB. The challenge was to collect the correct information from various sources. The contents were reviewed and analyzed.

The research study is qualitative and explorative in nature. Primary and Secondary data were used.

Sample Size is 30.

Sample Units – Bank employees, government employees, corporate employees, entrepreneurs, political leaders, and senior citizens.

Secondary data – Government reports, records, surveys, financial institution's information, web sites, research papers, newspapers, journals, and magazines.

Sample Area – Delhi/NCR.

A semi-structured open-ended questionnaire was given to the respondents. The responses of the respondents were analyzed by using a coding and tabulation method.

Method – A focus group interview was conducted though a self-administered questionnaire with a semi-structured open-ended questionnaire for interview. The research process was conducted in three phases including conceptual, narrative, and interpretative.

The time frame for the research study was three months from March to May 2022.

The interview data coding was done by using deductive technique. The qualitative data were collected by probing verbally and nonverbally. The data collection followed several steps including exploring, silence, prompting, and summarizing.

Comprehending, synthesizing, and theorizing were done during the analysis of qualitative data. The data analysis plan was objective oriented. The data types were transcription and observational notes collected during the interview process. Data coding approach was concept driven, and the technique used was content analysis of focus group interview.

The data analysis process started with data cleaning leading to immersion of primary data. After data immersion, memoing and data chunking were conducted. Data clusters were created to interpret and present findings and the results. See Table 12.3.

Table 12.3. Functions, Growth, Development, and Futuristic Prospects of NDB in India.

Open Code	Axial Code	Selective Code
Multilateral development	Functions	Functions, growth, development, and futuristic prospects
Finance infrastructure		
Sustainable developments		
Assist developing nations		
Socioeconomic activities		
Funding projects	Growth	
Rural employment		
Lending in local currencies		
Social standards		
Environmental standards	Development	
AA+ credit rating		
Green bonds		
Healthcare capabilities	Futuristic prospects	
National readiness		
Climate change		
Utilizing renewable energies		
Long-term financial success		

Source: The Authors' Own Compilation.

Findings and Analysis

The NDB is a multilateral development bank (MDB) which was founded by the BRICS nations. It comprises of Brazil, Russia, India, China, and South Africa. It helped to finance infrastructure and sustainable development projects in the BRICS countries itself and other developing and emerging economies ("Building Sustainable Future," 2022). For further details, see Table 12.4. The NDB complements multilateral and regional financial institutions' efforts to support global growth and development ("Corporate Culture," 2022).

Table 12.4. Role of NDB in India.

S/No.	New Development Bank's Function
1.	A multilateral development bank is NDB (MDB).
2.	NDB's goal is to finance infrastructure and sustainable development initiatives.
3.	NDB seeks to assist developing nations and emerging economies.
4.	The work of NDB complements that of regional and multilateral financial institutions.
5.	The goal of NDB's work is to maximize development's effects in a quick, adaptable, and effective way.
6.	NDB is eager to speak with, learn from, and work alongside other MDBs, governments, financial institutions, and nonprofits organizations.
7.	The NDB backs both public and private projects.
8.	NDB provides assistance to the nations through loans, guarantees, equity participation, and other forms of financing.
9.	NDB engages in information, cultural, and personnel exchanges while also providing technical assistance for projects.
10.	NDB wants to help make environmental and social sustainability a reality.
11.	The development of NDB is based on global, sustainable growth.
12.	The objectives and guiding principles of the United Nations are consistent with NDB's socioeconomic activities.
13.	NDB laying the groundwork for an active and fruitful partnership with the UN.
14.	The following are the key areas of operation where NDB-funded projects are located: i. Clean Energy ii. Transport Infrastructure iii. Multi-theme

(Continued)

Table 12.4. *(Continued)*

S/No.	New Development Bank's Function
	iv. Urban Development
	v. Irrigation, Water Resource Management, and Sanitation
	vi. Digital Infrastructure
	vii. Environmental Efficiency
	viii. Social Infrastructure
	ix. COVID-19 Emergency Assistance

Source: The Authors' Own Compilation.

NDB aims to maximize developmental effects in a prompt, flexible, and efficient manner (BS Reporter, 2022). NDB is consistently eager to work with other governments, MDBs, social organizations, and financial institutions to support the type of development they envision ("India wants BRICS NDB," 2021).

In order to further its goals, the Bank finances private and public projects by way of finances, equity participation, guarantees, and other techniques (Ganguly & Roy, 2021).

The Bank participates in project's technical assistance, information, cultural, and personnel exchanges to support the achievement of environmental and social sustainability (Gutierrez et al., 2011).

Being a new and vivacious MDB, the NDB is competently positioned to launch a fresh type of progressive based on wholesome and sustainable growth for the world (Khandelwal, 2021).

The initiatives of the NDB are in line with the socioeconomic goals and tenets of the United Nations, a global organization that supports sustainable development (Sudarvizhi, 2014). The NDB was granted observer status by the UN General Assembly in 2018, laying the foundation for an active and fruitful partnership with the UN (Sunil, 2022).

NDB-Funded Major Projects in India

Important infrastructure projects in India, such as the Regional Rapid Transit System between Delhi and Ghaziabad and Meerut, have received funding from this source, the Mumbai Metro Rail, and numerous Renewable Energy projects ("List of All Projects," 2022). See Table 12.5.

Up to this point, 14 Indian projects totaling nearly USD 4.2 billion have received approval from the NDB ("New Development Bank," 2021). India announced a USD 1 billion loan agreement with NDB in 2020 to increase infrastructure and employment in rural areas ("New Development Bank (NDB)," 2021).

Table 12.5. Growth and Development of NDB.

S/No.	Growth and Development of NDB
1.	Funding of infrastructure projects of India.
2.	Rural employment.
3.	Lending in local currencies to shield borrowing nations from an increase in the value of the dollar.
4.	The bank accepts guidelines created by borrowers in accordance with their own policies for adherence to social and environmental standards.
5.	Collaborations with a range of banks and financial institutions.
6.	The NDB has an AA+ credit rating.
7.	The bank has issued several bonds, including "green bonds," with success.
8.	NDB under its Emergency Assistance Facility provides loans to the member countries.
9.	70 projects for sustainable development and infrastructure totaling USD 25.07 billion have already received NDB approval.
10.	NDB provides funding for projects in a variety of sectors, including smart cities, irrigation, agriculture, water and sanitation, social safety, public health, and education, as well as sustainable infrastructure and clean energy.

Source: The Authors' Own Compilation.

Achievements and Innovations

Lending in local currencies to shield borrowing countries from an increase in the value of the dollar was one of the NDB's founding principles ("New Development Bank Celebrates," 2022). Another novel practice is that while respecting its members' own policies, the bank accepts guidelines for adherence to social and environmental standards created by borrowers ("New Development Bank (NDB) – BRICS," 2021).

Collaboration with Additional Developmental Financial Institutions

The World Bank Organization, the China-led Asian Infrastructure Investment Bank (AIIB), and the regional development bank CAF for Latin America are notable development banks with which it has worked together ("New Development Bank," 2021). See Table 12.6.

Table 12.6. Credit Rating Agencies of India.

S/No.	Various Credit Rating Agencies of India
1.	Credit Rating Information Services of India Limited (CRISIL)
2.	Investment Information and Credit Rating Agency of India Limited (ICRA)
3.	Credit Analysis and Research (CARE)
4.	Onida Individual Credit Rating Agency of India (ONICRA)
5.	Fitch India
6.	Brickwork Ratings (BWR)
7.	SME Rating Agency of India Limited (SMERA)

Source: The Authors' Own Compilation.

Credit Rating of AA+

("New Development Bank" aspirations, 2021) The NDB has an AA+ credit rating, one notch below the AIIB's highest rating, despite the difficult domestic economic conditions faced by many of its members, particularly Brazil and South Africa ("New Development Bank" byjus, 2021).

Emission of Different Bonds

Forty-two projects in member nations totaling more than USD 12 billion have been approved by the bank, compared to the AIIB's approximately USD 8 billion portfolio. In 2016, the bank issued several bonds, including "green bonds," with success ("Investor Relations," 2022). A special kind of fixed-income investment known as a "green bond" was developed to finance specific environmental or climate-related projects. Green bond issues are backed by NDB ("New Development Bank Sustainable Financing," 2020).

Various Issues of NDB

Less Loan Money is Dispersed

Although the bank has approved loans totaling more than USD 12 billion, it has only so far disbursed USD 1 billion, which is a very low amount ("Overview. Our Vision Our Mission," 2022).

Political Unrest

China and India's relations deteriorated, lending to Russian businesses was difficult due to the sanctions imposed on that country, and South Africa and Brazil both experienced political unrest and economic crises (Modak, 2021). It proved to be a challenging task, one at which member countries don't seem to have excelled, to continue advancing the interests of the developing world in a volatile political environment (Pardesi, 2022).

Sustainability Problem

Despite recently approving loans for renewable energy projects in India and Brazil as well as for reducing climate change and preparing for it in Brazil, the NDB has designated several environmentally dubious projects as sustainable without outlining the criteria it employs ("Environment and Social Sustainability," 2021). The Trans-Amazonian highway in Brazil is one of its environmentally friendly initiatives, which many environmentalists accuse of hastening the destruction of the world's largest tropical rainforest ("Goals for Sustainable Development Awarded RMB 5 billion by NDB," 2021).

Relationship Between NDB and Other Institutions

As per the bank's Agreement Articles, the NDB was founded to complement the current endeavor of multidimensional and local monetary institutions for worldwide expansion and development ("Regarding New Development Bank, agreement," 2015). In addition, the NDB's founders authorized it to collaborate with other international organizations and national organizations (public or private) in the context of its mandate, particularly with national development banks and global financial institutions ("Agreement on the New Development Bank," 2015). See Table 12.7.

Table 12.7. Relation of NDB With Other Institutions.

S/No.	**Relation of NDB With Various Institutions**
I.	*Institutions of International Finance*
1.	Global Financial Institution
2.	Worldwide Monetary Fund (IMF)
3.	Financial Institution for Asian Development
4.	Asian Infrastructure Investment Bank
II.	*Banks for Multidimensional Growth*
1.	Inter-American Bank for Growth and Development (IDB)
2.	Monetary Fund for River Plate Basin's Development (FONPLATA)
3.	Financial Institution for Rebuilding and Expansion in Europe (EBRD)
4.	Financial Institution for Infrastructural Venture in Asia (AIIB)

(Continued)

Table 12.7. *(Continued)*

S/No.	Relation of NDB With Various Institutions
5.	Financial Institution for Atlantic Development (CDB)
6.	Financial Institution for European Investment (EDB)
7.	Financial Institution for Worldwide Investment (IIB)
8.	A Latin American financial institution (CAF)
9.	Bank for Asian Development (ADB)
10.	Bank for Islamic Development (IsDB)
11.	Bank for European Investment (EIB)
III.	*The National Development Banks*
1.	Southern Asian Development Bank (DBSA)
2.	Chinese Agricultural Development Bank (ADBC)
3.	China Exim Bank
4.	Bank of China for Development (CDB)
5.	Financial Institution for Social and Economic Progress in Brazil (BNDES)

Source: The Authors' Own Compilation.

Table 12.7 states various development banks which are tied up with NDB for helping in various kinds of developments like infrastructural, social, etc. NDB's President, Mr K.V. Kamath, emphasized the financial institution views organizations like the IMF and World Bank as allies rather than competitors.

Bank for Asian Development

In July 2016, the NDB and the Asian Development Bank (ADB) signed a Memorandum of Understanding on Intentional Cooperation (Asian Development Bank, 2017). The two parties expressed a desire to work together on sustainable development initiatives that use sewage treatment, renewable energy, sustainable water management, and energy-efficient transportation ("New Development Bank. Asian Development Bank," 2019).

Bank for Investment in Asian Infrastructure

There is currently no evidence of competition between the Asian Infrastructural Investment Financial Institution (AIIB) and the NDB, despite some analysts' predictions to the contrary (Kasahara, 2020). When discussing the NDB's relationship with the AIIB, the differences between the memberships of the two organizations, as well as the potential for complementarity in their combined efforts to address development and infrastructure needs, representatives from the NDB's associated states highlight (Dollar, 2015).

An official from the Bank's administration claimed that the NDB and AIIB are very similar organizations (He, 2017). Both organizations have complementary objectives and focus on distinct geographic regions, with the NDB placing more of an emphasis on the BRICS nations (Pardo & Rana, 2018). As both organizations are focused on building infrastructure and give special attention to sustainable development, there is some overlap between their respective mandates. He did, however, add that there is "room for newcomers" as a result of the present monetary, and investing trends are insufficient to meet monetary demands. Concerns about overlapping interests between the NDB and the AIIB, which is supported by China, were disregarded by the NDB president in February 2016.

World Bank

According to media reports, the World Bank Group (WBG) and other multilateral development organizations have expressed a desire to collaborate with the NDB ("World Bank Group," 2016). In terms of wages and employment, financial support is needed for social and economic recovery. It was revealed after the signing of a cooperation agreement in September 2016 ("World Bank Lay Groundwork," 2016). See Table 12.8.

Table 12.8. Prospects of NDB in India.

S/No.	Various Future Prospects of NDB
1.	A focus on enhancing healthcare capabilities.
2.	National readiness in terms of health for its membership.
3.	The spread of COVID-19 is being slowed down with special assistance.
4.	Aiding the social and economic recovery financially in terms of wages and employment.
5.	Investments for reinforcing urban resilience.
6.	Megacities and densely populated areas are the focus for mitigating negative effects.
7.	It was important to concentrate on the effects of air pollution and climate change adaptation.
8.	Supporting the development of technologies for renewable energy.
9.	Utilizing biomass, solar, and wind as renewable energy sources.
10.	For long-term financial success, develop public–private partnership-supporting policies.

Source: The Authors' Own Compilation.

Increased healthcare capabilities and national level health readiness for its associated countries and other countries that are at risk should be prioritized soon, with a focus on halting the escalation of COVID-19 and fostering economic and social recovery in terms of incomes and employment (Mehra & Mehra, 2020).

The focus should be on medium-term investments that will increase urban adaptability in megacities and areas with a high population in order to lessen the air pollution effects and prepare for global warming ("New Development Bank," 2021).

To increase the adoption of renewable energy technologies (solar, wind, and biomass) in the global energy mix of BRICS member countries and elsewhere, financial support for these technologies should be a medium- to long-term priority (Modak, 2021). In all these endeavors, the Bank could try to create mechanisms to promote public–private partnerships for long-term financial sustainability ("India wants BRICS NDB's Resources," 2021).

Conclusions

NDB has a very strong futuristic approach in India. The current financial year and future years predicted to be strong in terms of economic growth and development of India. According to Nirmala Sitharaman, Finance Minister, Indian subcontinent's financial progress is projected to be strong in the current fiscal year at 8.9%, reflecting the nation's strong resilience and quick recovery (PTI, 2022). According to a statement from the finance ministry, Sitharaman exhibited assurance that India will maintain a rapid rate of growth in the upcoming financial year (AIR News, 2022).

The finance minister emphasized the significance of international relations and the spirit of international collaboration in her speech, which she delivered via video conference to the 7th Yearly Meet of the Board of Governors of NDB (Business Line New Delhi Bureau, 2022).

NDB has been successful in establishing its own self as a dependable development partner for developing nations, and opening of the India Regional Office in Gujarat's GIFT City was praised as a step toward progress of the country (HT Correspondent, 2022).

Over the ensuing decades, NDB will have a significant and meaningful impact on the development of its member countries (BW Online Bureau, 2022).

It can be claimed that due to the recent pandemic, this year's Annual Meeting of NDB, which was hosted by India, was essentially held. The year's Annual Meeting had the following theme: NDB's Maximizing the Impact on Development, which is especially pertinently given the current state of the global economy. It also mentioned that the year's Annual Meeting was taking place in London (Shares Bazaar, 2022).

In highlighting the fact that India is commemorating its 75th anniversary of independence, the country's economic growth in the most recent fiscal year was strong and is anticipated to be 8.9%, the highest among developed countries.

Brazil, China, Russia, South Africa, Bangladesh, and the United Arab Emirates, two new members, sent governors and alternate governors to the meeting (UAE). The BRICS nations established the NDB in July 2014, and it began operations a year later with an initial subscribed capital of USD 50 billion and a combined paid-in capital of USD 10 billion (HT Correspondent, 2022). These are signs of economic development of the nations.

To supplement the current efforts of multilateral and regional financial institutions for global growth and development, the bank's mission is to mobilize resources for infrastructure and sustainable development projects in the BRICS and other emerging market economies and developing countries (Masamba, 2022). Henceforth, conclusion can be drawn that the economic status of the countries will be progressive in the forthcoming years.

In 2015, the bank began operations, with Shanghai, China, serving as its administrative center. Four new nations joined the NDB last year: Bangladesh, the UAE, Egypt, and Uruguay (BW Online Bureau, 2022). NDB has already approved 21 Indian projects totaling USD 7.1 billion (New Development Bank Press Release, May 20, 2022). These projects will help in bringing health and financial prosperity to the nations.

Mission and Vision of NDB

NDB is a multidimensional progressive bank for the 21st century that builds on lessons learned from other organizations to create practices and policies that can handle the challenges posed by global trends (NDB Mission Vision, 2022). The establishment of the Bank reflects the Emerging Market and Developing Countries (EMDCs) expanding economic influence and increased willingness to act independently on issues pertaining to global economic development and governance (Byjus, 2020).

The NDB is required by its Articles of Agreement to raise money for projects aimed at sustainable and infrastructure development in the BRICS nations and EMDCs (Byjus, 2021). In order to assist with meeting, the investment requirements of the founding members and other EMDCs, the Bank will use the multilateral progressive banks (MDBs), monetary organizations established by administrations to boost capital for developmental purposes (Business Line Bureau, 2021).

In three crucial areas – relationships, initiatives and tools, and methodologies – NDB aims to be "new" (NDB, Investor Relationship, 2022).

New Connections. All facets of the Bank's policies and procedures are based on equality, respect, and trusting relationship between NDB and member nations (Byjus, 2020). The priority is national sovereignty. Considering each country's specific needs and development priorities and strategies, NDB supports projects (Byjus, 2021).

The Bank implements projects in accordance with national laws and regulations whenever possible without sacrificing quality (Drishtiias, 2021). Even though the NDB is open to members from advanced countries, EMDCs will continue to run the Bank, and that will be reflected in policies, project selection, and interactions with lenders (NDB, 2020). No NDB member has the power to veto any matter, and most decisions are made with a simple majority (NDB, 2021a, 2021b). These agreements strengthen NDB by ensuring that each member has a stake in the organization's success (Khandelwal, 2021).

New strategies. By developing an improved project review and implementation oversight process without redundancy, NDB aims to be quick, adaptable, and effective (Business Line Bureau, 2021). The Bank oversees and approves projects using a risk-based methodology, requiring more thorough ex ante reviews for complex projects, risky projects, and an easier, ex post review process for low-risk projects (Ganguly & Roy, 2021). Instead of just focusing on approvals, risk assessment, disbursement, and results will be highlighted in staff performance indicators and incentives (Kasahara, 2020). Lower administrative costs and more effective decision-making will result from a lean and flat organizational structure that can change as NDB expands (Journals of India, 2021). As of right now, a nonresident Board of Directors oversees NDB, which also lowers administrative costs and concentrates Board discussions on important policy issues, particularly complex projects, rather than routine day-to-day operations (Aspireias, 2021).

Portfolios of Loan and Prime Areas of Operation. According to the NDB's overall strategy for 2017–2021, most of the projects funded by the Bank were either overseen or guaranteed by sovereign entities. As the Bank's operational capacity increases, nonsovereign operations, particularly those involving the private sector, were expected to expand (BRICS India, 2021). Clean energy, transportation infrastructure, irrigation, water resource management, sanitation, sustainable urban development, and economic integration between member countries are NDB's primary operational areas.

Increase in Membership. NDB is currently developing criteria and a plan to admit new countries as members with the intention of conducting business on a large scale (Morozkina, 2015). NDB plans to gradually expand membership in order to prevent straining its operational capacity and decision-making procedures (Byjus, 2020). To guarantee geographic diversity and an equitable distribution of high-, middle-, and low-income nations, membership expansion will be implemented (Byjus, 2021).

District Offices. The regional offices' primary task will be to locate and prepare bankable projects in BRICS and other participating nations (NDB, Investor Relations, 2022). The headquarters will oversee their operations in close coordination with the institutional strategy (CFI Team, 2022). In Johannesburg, the first regional office was established ("Goals for Sustainable Development Awarded RMB 5 billion by NDB," 2021).

Partnerships. With national development banks, commercial banks, and international organizations for development, the Bank has already signed several partnership agreements and will continue to do so in the future (NDB's Approach, 2022). Depending on what is necessary to achieve the NDB's objectives, this group will include significant international and regional relations, less significant subregional organizations, organizations working on bilateral development, national development organizations in borrower nations, and individual investors (He, 2017). As a result of these collaborations, NDB will be better able to assess and implement projects, strengthen its capacity for doing so, and create financial packages that will enable projects to be scaled up meaningfully (NDB, Investor Relations, 2022). The Bank is attempting to establish collaborative connections with universities, think tanks, and nongovernmental organizations, especially those that are directly related to infrastructure and sustainable development issues ("NDB Board of Governors Approved," 2022).

Resource People. The Bank is dedicated to fostering a diverse workplace based on the principles of efficiency and meritocracy (Dissanayaka, 2021). Although the guiding principle is still merit. By considering diversity, NDB aims to achieve widespread representation of member nations at all levels of employment (New Development Bank, 2022). Young, qualified professionals working together will bring fresh perspectives and novel ideas that will upend the status quo (NBD Bank, 2017). Additionally, the Bank is hiring qualified and experienced personnel to develop younger professionals who will make up the Bank's future core (Kumar, 2022).

Independent Review. To encourage an organizational learning culture at the Bank, an evaluation framework was created (Kusek & Rist, 2004). Evaluations of the Bank's plans, initiatives, and investment choices were assisting in identifying necessary course corrections and disseminating learned lessons (World Bank Group, 2021). The Bank's operations were being evaluated independently, considering the risks involved and the effects on the environment and society (Banks for International Settlements, 2015).

Approaches of NDB

- A lean governance framework speeds up the decision-making procedure.
- NDB strives for speed and efficiency without compromising quality by cutting out pointless red tape during the project approval and implementation phases.
- Lower administrative costs will be attained by having a flat and lean organizational structure that can change as NDB expands.
- The work and culture of the Bank will be infused with innovation and adaptability.
- The use of laws, rules, and oversight procedures from borrowing countries is a priority for NDB.
- The Bank will develop a diversified and balanced portfolio based on maturity, the projects' public–private structure, sectors, locations, and the financing methods used.
- The operational program of NDB will assist BRICS and other member nations in pursuing their development goals.
- Preserving shareholder capital is NDB's top financial priority.
- A strong repayment history and preferred creditor status are crucial indicators of shareholders' support for the Bank and are crucial to its financial stability.
- NDB will try to make money so that it can accumulate cash reserves.
- The Bank will look for creative ways to improve its balance sheet.
- NDB wants to be known as a trustworthy and sound financial intermediary.

- Goal of NDB's funding strategy is to guarantee that there are sufficient funds to meet the Bank's liquidity requirements.
- A critical early task for NDB is to become known as a trustworthy borrower in both domestic and international financial markets by receiving favorable ratings from international credit rating agencies.
- NDB will select its funding currencies in accordance with the state of the market, investor demand, and funding costs to provide loans at competitive rates.
- NDB is actively investigating the possibility of investing in green bonds and other green finance products.
- Effective risk management is crucial for the Bank to succeed.
- The risk function is under the control of the Board of Directors, which is centralized and separate from the business lines.
- The NDB may only create or manage capitals which will assist the financial institution in raising capital for sustainable and infrastructural development ventures.
- In accordance with the Articles of Agreement, NDB may establish funds to finance special operations or may be entrusted with their management.
- The Bank will only accept investments that will aid in raising funds for infrastructure, and sustainable development plans may be created or managed by the NDB.
- Specifically, special funds will support project preparation.
- The Bank will establish unique guidelines and policies for the creation, management, and utilization of each special fund.
- The primary responsibilities of the offices at the regional level are to locate and prepare lucrative projects in BRICS countries and other associate members.
- Regional offices will conduct business in accordance with NDB's General Approach and as directed by the corporate office.
- NDB was established as a development organization focused on productivity, results, and efficiency.
- The Bank will review its staffing requirements annually and recruit human resources in accordance with its growth plan.

Recommendations

Recommendations are based on observations from the literature review of government reports, records, websites, research papers, and the rules and regulations of NDB and other development banks.

- Development banks provide support and assistance to people who are financially weak and need capital to start a small business, farmers, artisans, and self-employed people can get financial assistance from development banks.
- It has become necessary to inform people about the development banks, their functions, and the process of getting connected with the development banks.

- Educated volunteers among citizens should take the initiative of taking the detailed information of development banks. And then to inform those who need financial help and assistance.
- Farmers, artisans, small business owners, and other needy and financially downtrodden people in every nook and corner of the country should be informed about the development banks on regular and frequent intervals.
- Rules, regulations, bank formalities to get loan required to be explained to the needy people so that they feel free to go to these development banks and take its benefit fully.

References

AIR News. (2022, May 20). India's economic growth in current FY is estimated to be 8.9 percent, says Finance Minister Nirmala Sitharaman. https://newsonair.com/2022/05/20/indias-economic-growth-in-current-fy-is-estimated-to-be-8-9-percent-says-finance-minister-nirmala-sitharaman/

ANI. (2021, August 24). Ajit Doval chairs BRICS 2021 NSA meeting. https://www.aninews.in/news/world/asia/ajit-doval-chairs-brics-2021-nsa-meeting20210824175645/\

Aspireias. (2021, November 16). *New Development Bank (NDB) – BRICS*. https://www.aspireias.com/upsc-study-notes/New-Development-Bank-NDB-BRICS

Banks for International Settlements. (2015, July). *Guidelines for identifying and dealing with weak banks*. https://www.bis.org/bcbs/publ/d330.pdf

Bajaj Finserv Limited. (2022). *Difference between credit rating agencies and credit information bureau*. https://www.bajajfinserv.in/insights/credit-rating-agencies-india

BS Reporter. (2022, July 27). PM Modi to inaugurate regional center for New Development Bank on July 29. https://www.business-standard.com/article/economy-policy/pm-modi-to-inaugurate-regional-centre-of-new-development-bank-on-july-29-122072701630_1.html

Business Line Bureau. (2021, August 18). India wants BRICS NDB's resources used for strengthening social infrastructure too. *The Hindu, Business Line*. https://www.thehindubusinessline.com/news/national/india-wants-brics-ndbs-resources-used-for-strengthening-social-infrastructure-too/article35986127.ece

Business Line New Delhi Bureau. (2022, May 19). Indian economy likely to grow 8. 9% this fiscal, says FM Sitharaman. *The Hindu. Business Line*. https://www.thehindubusinessline.com/economy/indian-economy-likely-to-grow-89-this-fiscal-says-fm-sitharaman/article65431330.ece

BW Online Bureau. (2022, May 20). India will continue to achieve high growth rate in current and next FY: FM. https://www.businessworld.in/article/India-Will-Continue-To-Achieve-High-Growth-Rate-In-Current-And-Next-FY-FM/20-05-2022-429587/

Byjus. (2020). *Functions of commercial banks: Primary and secondary functions*. https://byjus.com/commerce/functions-of-commercial-banks/

Byjus. (2021). *New Development Bank*. https://byjus.com/free-ias-prep/new-development-bank-ndb/

CFI Team. (2022, May 7). *Commercial bank, bankers for small businesses to large corporates*. https://corporatefinanceinstitute.com/resources/knowledge/finance/commercial-bank/

Cofinanced Project. (2019, December). *New Development Bank*. https://www.adb.org/multimedia/partnership-report2019/partners/multilateral/new-development-
Department of Financial Services, Ministry of Finance, Government of India. (2022). *Public sector banks*. https://financialservices.gov.in/banking-divisions/public-sector-banks
Dissanayaka, N. (2021). *Strategic human resource management and the human resource planning of the nations development bank*. Available at SSRN 3870470.
Dollar, D. (2015). *The AIIB and the 'one belt, one road'*. https://www.brookings.edu/opinions/the-aiib-and-the-one-belt-one-road/
Drishtiias. (2021, August 19). *New Development Bank*. https://www.drishtiias.com/daily-updates/daily-news-analysis/new-development-bank
External Agency. (2022, September 10). What is 'commercial bank'. *Economic Times*. https://economictimes.indiatimes.com/definition/commercial-bank
Ganguly, S., & Roy, M. (2021, December 4). Development banks and the changing contour of industrial credit in India. *Economic and Political Weekly*, *6*(49). https://www.epw.in/journal/2021/49/special-articles/development-banks-and-changing-contour-industrial.html
Gutierrez, E., Rudolph, H. P., Homa, T., & Beneit, E. B. (2011). *Development banks: Role and mechanisms to increase their efficiency*. World Bank Policy Research Working Paper, (5729).
He, L. (2017, April 1). Asian Infrastructure Investment Bank and New Development Bank sign memorandum of understanding to promote cooperation. *Asian Infrastructure Investment Bank*. https://www.aiib.org/en/news-events/news/2017/Asian-Infrastructure-Investment-Bank-and-New-Development-Bank-Sign-Memorandum-of-Understanding-to-Promote-Cooperation.html
HT Correspondent. (2022, May 20). Economic growth at 8.9% this FY, estimated highest among major economies: FM. *Hindustan Times*. https://www.hindustantimes.com/business/indias-economic-growth-stands-at-8-9-this-fy-fm-sitharaman-at-ndb-annual-meet-101653035450949.html
Insights on India. (2021, March 31). *New Development Bank (NDB)*. https://www.insightsonindia.com/2021/03/31/new-development-bank-ndb/
Journals of India. (2021, August 20). *New Development Bank*. https://journalsofindia.com/new-development-bank/
Kasahara, S. (2020). The New Development Bank vs the Asian Infrastructure Investment Bank: A comparative perspective on their past, present and future. In *International development assistance and the BRICS* (pp. 91–118). Palgrave Macmillan.
Khandelwal, T. (2021, February 12). *Role of development banks*. https://swastika.co.in/blog/role-of-development-banks/
Kumar, S. (2022, January 28). The impending tech-onslaught on skilled human resources. https://www.peoplematters.in/article/hr-technology/the-impending-tech-onslaught-on-skilled-human-resources-28290
Kusek, J. Z., & Rist, R. C. (2004). *Ten steps to a results-based monitoring and evaluation system*. The World Bank. https://www.oecd.org/dac/peer-reviews/World%20bank%202004%2010_Steps_to_a_Results_Based_ME_System.pdf
Malik, D. S. (2017, March 31). Multi-lateral New Development Bank to aid India. *Press Information Bureau, Government of India*. Special Service and Features. https://pib.gov.in/newsite/printrelease.aspx?relid=160263

Masamba, M. (2022, July 13). *How BRICS' New Development Bank can improve transparency and accountability*. https://theconversation.com/how-brics-new-development-bank-can-improve-transparency-and-accountability-186265

Massdorp, L. (2019, September 20). *BRICS' New Development Bank turns four: What has it achieved?* World Economic Forum. https://www.weforum.org/agenda/2019/09/brics-new-development-bank-four-sustainability/

Mehra, A., & Mehra, M. K. (2020, November 16).BRICS New Development Bank: Last five years and looking ahead to the next five. https://www.financialexpress.com/economy/brics-new-development-bank-last-five-years-and-looking-ahead-to-the-next-five/2129502/

Modak, P. (2021, July 26). *The New Development Bank turns six: Evaluating success, failures and challenges*. Centre for Public Policy Research. http://www.brics.utoronto.ca/biblio/the-new-development-bank-turns-six.html

Morozkina, A. (2015). The New Development Bank in the global financial architecture. *Education, 3*(5.2), 4–5.

Musacchio, A., Lazzarini, S. G., Makhoul, P., & Simmons, E. (2017). *The role and impact of Development Banks*. World Bank working paper.

n. a. (2019). *New Development Bank*. Asian Development Bank. https://www.adb.org/multimedia/partnership-report2019/partners/multilateral/new-development-bank/

n. a. (2017, October 13). Asian Development Bank, New Development Bank meet to discuss new project co-financing. *News Release*. https://www.adb.org/news/asian-development-bank-new-development-bank-meet-discuss-new-project-cofinancing

n. a. (2021, September 22). *What are commercial banks? – Definitions, roles and functions*. https://study.com/academy/lesson/what-are-commercial-banks-definition-roles-functions.html

Nanda, V. (2022, July 11). *Difference between commercial banks and development banks*. https://www.tutorialspoint.com/difference-between-commercial-banks-and-development-banks#:~:text=Commercial%20banks%20are%20established%20as,Act%20passed%20by%20the%20government.&text=Commercial%20banks%20lend%20to%20both,banks%20lend%20to%20the%20government

NDB Bank. (2017). *Human capital. Annual report 2017*. https://www.ndbbank.com/annual-report/2017/management-discussion-and-analysis.humcap

NDB Official Website. (2017). *NDB's general strategy: 2017-21* (pp. 1–36). New Development Bank. https://www.ndb.int/wp-content/uploads/2017/08/NDB-Strategy.pdf

NDB Official Website. (2019). *New Development Bank. Asian Development Bank*. https://www.adb.org/multimedia/partnership-report2019/partners/multilateral/new-development-bank/

NDB Official Website. (2022a). *Investor relations*. New Development Bank. https://www.ndb.int/investor-relations/borrowings/

NDB Official Website. (2022b, May 20). *NDB Board of Governors approved the bank's general strategy for 2022-2026*. https://www.ndb.int/press_release/ndb-board-of-governors-approved-the-banks-general-strategy-for-2022-2026/

NDB Official Website. (2022c, July 22). *NDB at 7: New Development Bank celebrates seven years of accomplishments*. https://www.ndb.int/press_release/ndb-at-7-new-development-bank-celebrates-seven-years-of-accomplishments/

NDB Official Website. (2022d). *Overview. Our vision our mission.* https://www.ndbbank.com/about/overview#:~:text=Our%20Mission,dedicated%20team%20committed%20to%20excellence

NDB Official Website. (2022e). *List of all projects.* https://www.ndb.int/projects/list-of-all-projects/

NDB Official Website. (2022f). *Building sustainable future.* New Development Bank. https://www.ndb.int/about-us/essence/our-work/#:~:text=The%20New%20Development%20Bank%20(NDB,emerging%20economies%20and%20developing%20countries

NDB Official Website. (2022g). *Corporate culture.* New Development Bank. https://www.ndb.int/careers/corporate-culture/

NDB Official Website. (2022h). *NDB's approach.* New Development Banks. https://www.ndb.int/partnerships/partnership-approach/#:~:text=Partnerships%20support%20the%20achievement%20of,knowledge%2C%20human%20resources%20and%20information

NDB Official Website. (2015, July 15). *Agreement on the New Development Bank – Fortaleza.* https://www.ndb.int/wp-content/themes/ndb/pdf/Agreement-on-the-New-Development-Bank.pdf

NDB Official Website. (2021a, March 25). *NDB issues RMB 5 billion sustainable development goals bond.* https://www.ndb.int/press_release/ndb-issues-rmb-5-billion-sustainable-development-goals-bond/

NDB Official Website. (2021b). *Environment and social sustainability.* https://www.ndb.int/about-us/strategy/environmental-social-sustainability/

NDB Official Website. (2020, May 25). *New Development Bank Sustainable Financing Policy Framework governing the issuances of green/social/sustainability debt instruments.* Treasury and Portfolio Management Division. Version 2020, V1. https://www.ndb.int/wp-content/uploads/2020/05/2020_FC22_AI13_018_b-NDB-Sustainable-Financing-Policy-Framework.pdf

NDB Official Website. (2016, September 9). *NDB, World Bank lay groundwork for cooperation.* https://www.ndb.int/event/ndb-world-bank-group-lay-groundwork-cooperation/

NDB Website. *New Development Bank. Building sustainable future.* https://www.ndb.int/about-us/essence/our-work/

New Development Bank. (2021). *BRICS India.* https://brics2021.gov.in/ndb

New Development Bank. (2022). *Budget, human resources and compensation committee.* 2022-BRIC18-DOC-003. https://www.ndb.int/wp-content/uploads/2022/03/Minutes-of-the-17th-BHRC-Meeting.pdf

Njogu, T. (2019, July 5). *Difference between commercial bank and development bank.* http://www.differencebetween.net/business/difference-between-commercial-bank-and-development-bank/

Pardesi, M. S. (2022). India's China strategy under Modi continuity in the management of an asymmetric rivalry. *International Politics*, *59*(1), 44–66.

Pardo, R. P., & Rana, P. B. (2018, March). Co-operation not competition: The new multilateral development banks and the old. *Global Asia*, *13*(1). https://www.globalasia.org/v13no1/feature/co-operation-not-competition-the-new-multilateral-development-banks-and-the-old_ramon-pacheco-pardopradumna-b-rana

Prasad, K. N. (2020, September 22). *Difference between commercial bank and development bank.* https://www.dynamictutorialsandservices.org/2016/04/difference-between-commercial-bank-and.html

PTI. (2022). India's economic growth likely to be robust at 8.9% in current fiscal: FM at NDB. https://economictimes.indiatimes.com/news/economy/policy/indias-economic-growth-likely-to-be-robust-at-8-9-in-current-fiscal-fm-at-ndb/articleshow/91673100.cms?from=mdr

Romero, M. J. (2017). Public development banks: Towards a better model.

Shares Bazaar. (2022, May). India's economic growth likely to be robust at 8.9% in current financial year: Nirmala Sitharaman. *Shares Bazaar.* https://www.sharesbazaar.com/news/view/911493

Singh, J. *Commercial Bank: Definition, function, credit creation and significances.* https://www.economicsdiscussion.net/banks/commercial-bank-definition-function-credit-creation-and-significances/607

Singh, H. (2019, March 30). *Classification and operations of commercial banks in India.* https://www.jagranjosh.com/general-knowledge/operations-of-commercial-banks-1446804943-1

Singh, H., Varghese, M., & Damle, H. (2017, March 30). *New Development Bank through a peoples' lens.* https://sabrangindia.in/ann/new-development-bank-through-peoples-lens

Smirti. (2021, March 31). *Difference between commercial bank and development bank.* https://www.managementnote.com/difference-between-commercial-bank-and-development-bank-types-of-banks/

Srnivas, P. S., & Hofman, B. (2022, July 25). New Development Bank's role in the international financial architecture. *Global Policy.* https://www.globalpolicyjournal.com/blog/25/07/2022/new-development-banks-role-international-financial-architecture

Sudarvizhi, A. (2014, November). BRICS Bank [New Development Bank (NBS) or BRICS Development Bank (BDB)]. *Global Journal for Research Analysis, 3*(11), 69–71. Nov. Special Issue 2014. https://www.worldwidejournals.com/global-journal-for-research-analysis-GJRA/special_issues_pdf/November_2014_1476528069__44.pdf

Suneja, S. (2021, August 18). BRICS meet India for expanding New Development Bank's scope to strength social infra. *ET Bureau.* https://economictimes.indiatimes.com/news/india/brics-meet-india-for-expanding-new-development-banks-scope-to-strength-social-infra/articleshow/85434009.cms?from=mdr

Sunil, K. D. (2022, July 6). *New Development Bank – Indian economy notes.* https://prepp.in/news/e-492-new-development-bank-indian-economy-notes

Surbhi, S. (2020). *Difference between commercial bank and development bank.* https://keydifferences.com/difference-between-commercial-bank-and-development-bank.html

Tadas, G. A. (2020, August). *Need for setting up of a New Development Bank. Research and information system for developing countries.* https://www.ris.org.in/sites/default/files/Publication/DP%20254%20G%20A%20Tadas.pdf. https://keydifferences.com/wp-content/uploads/2020/04/commercial-bank-vs-development-bank.jpg

Vazquez, K. R., Roychoudhury, S., & Borge, C. (2017). *Building infrastructure for 21st century sustainable development: Lessons and opportunities for the BRICS-led*

New Development Bank. https://jgu-dev.s3.ap-south-1.amazonaws.com/building_infrastructure_for_21st_century.pdf

World Bank Group. (2021, March). *Realizing the World Bank Group's knowledge potential for effective development solutions: A strategic framework.* https://documents1.worldbank.org/curated/en/309981617140869469/pdf/Realizing-the-World-Bank-Group-s-Knowledge-Potential-for-Effective-Development-Solutions-A-Strategic-Framework.pdf

World Bank. (2016, September 9). *World Bank Group, New Development Bank lay groundwork for cooperation.* https://www.worldbank.org/en/news/press-release/2016/09/09/world-bank-group-new-development-bank-lay-groundwork-for-cooperation

Yadav, P. (2022, September 9). *Difference between commercial bank and development bank.* https://askanydifference.com/difference-between-commercial-bank-and-development-bank/

Conclusion

Irina Yarygina

BRICS Expert Council, Russia

There is no denying the fact that BRICS play an important role in global economy and finance, and it goes without saying that an exploration of BRICS nations in different spheres is extremely important and challenging. The publication of the book, dedicated to the role and the influence of the New Development Bank (NDB) on sustainable economic growth, is very timely. This book can become a milestone in the transfer of priorities of scientific diplomacy and financial instruments of cooperation of our member – countries.

Actually, we are facing geopolitical changes that pose complex challenges to partner countries, far from purely academic problems. One of them is ensuring the safe development of the BRICS.

In 2023, there was a historic turning point in the development of BRICS. Thanks to the summit in South Africa in August, the BRICS not only expanded but also began to be perceived as the main platform for representing the interests of the "world majority." Thanks to this, scientific and technical cooperation within the framework of BRICS acquires a new, truly global dimension. The accession of new members to the BRICS and the interest in establishing cooperation of dozens more countries opens up new horizons and opportunities where BRICS science can act from a strong position, including as a donor of ideas and a generator of new directions.

Proposals, which are presented in this book, are based on a professional and objective analysis of challenges and feasibility of a democratic global financial governance, finance, and sovereignty after COVID-19. Presentation of mechanisms, that contribute to BRICS financial development, climate diplomacy with its problems and challenges, de-dollarization of the global economy and strengthening the role of the NDB in supporting economic entities as well as other current issues contribute to finding the tools and help to establish secure environment for our people.

The BRICS countries are distinguished by their scientific potential, priorities, and thematic areas of application of efforts, geopolitical ambitions, and

The Multilateralism of the New Development Bank on the Sustainable Economic Growth in BRICS Nations and Beyond, 225–226

doi:10.1108/978-1-83662-292-520251017

orientation to "centers of power," features of the innovation policy, international strategy for science, and technology transfer. BRICS countries possess comparative advantages of their peculiarities that are to be studied and shared for improving the living standards and strengthening sustainable development of our nations. The book opens up important areas of research, which, I am sure, will need to be supplemented by a thorough consideration of the potential of new and promising BRICS members and partners.

www.ingramcontent.com/pod-product-compliance
Ingram Content Group UK Ltd.
Pitfield, Milton Keynes, MK11 3LW, UK
UKHW031128130425
457215UK00005B/120

9 781836 622932